EGYPTIAN BOOK OF THE DEAD HIEROGLYPH TRANSLATIONS

Volume 6 - Featuring:
THE OSIRIAN RESURRECTION

Translated Texts of: Stele of Amenmose, Metterniche Stele, Chester Beaty Papyrus, Temple of Osiris, Temple of Isis, Temple of Horus, and selected sections from the Ancient Egyptian Book of the Dead

Dr. Muata Ashby

EGYPTIAN BOOK OF THE DEAD HIEROGLYPH TRANSLATIONS Volume 6: Featuring The Osirian Resurrection

The Hieroglyph Translations Book Series

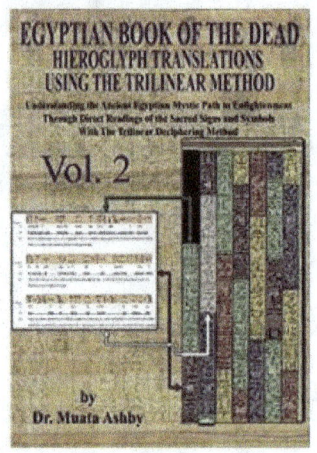

Egyptian Book of the Dead Hieroglyph Translations Using the Trilinear Method: Understanding th Mystic Path to Enlightenment...

Egyptian Book of the Dead Hieroglyph Translations Using The Trilinear Method Vol. 2: Understanding the Mystic Path to...
by Muata Ashby

EGYPTIAN BOOK OF THE DEAD HIEROGLYPH TRANSLATIONS USING THE TRILINEAR METHOD Volume 3: Understanding the Mystic Path to...
by Muata Ashby

EGYPTIAN BOOK OF THE DEAD HIEROGLYPH TRANSLATIONS USING THE TRILINEAR METHOD Volume 4: Understanding the Mystic Path to...

EGYPTIAN BOOK OF THE DEAD HIEROGLYPH TRANSLATIONS USING THE TRILINEAR METHOD Volume 5: Featuring Temple of Amun-Ra at Ab...
by Muata Ashby

EGYPTIAN BOOK OF THE DEAD HIEROGLYPH TRANSLATIONS Volume 6: Featuring The Osirian Resurrection

Sema Institute
Kemet University

Copyright © 2021 Muata Ashby, Sema Institute of Yoga

All rights reserved. ISBN: **9781937016647**

https://aerbook.com/store/Egyptian_Yoga_Books

www.Egyptianyoga.com

www.Egyptianmysteryschool.org

To see the full presentation that this book is based on GO HERE:
https://www.asarucollege.org/2020conference

Cruzian Mystic Books
Sema Yoga
P.O.Box 570459
Miami, Florida, 33257
(305) 378-6253 Fax: (305) 378-6253
First U.S. edition 2016
All rights reserved. No part of this book may be used or reproduced in any manner whatsoever without written permission (address above) except in the case of brief quotations embodied in critical articles and reviews. All inquiries may be addressed to the address above.
The author is available for group lectures and individual counseling. For further information contact the publisher.
Ashby, Muata EGYPTIAN BOOK OF THE DEAD HIEROGLYPH TRANSLATIONS USING THE TRILINEAR METHOD: Understanding the Mystic Path to Enlightenment Through Direct Readings of the Sacred Signs and Symbols of Ancient Egyptian Language With Trilinear Deciphering Method Vol. 1

Library of Congress Cataloging in Publication Data
1 Egyptian Book of the Dead, 2 Egyptian Philosophy 3 Hieroglyphs 4 Meditation, 5 Self Help.
www.Egyptianyoga.com www.Kemetuniversity.com

FOREWORD
By
Dr. Karen Dja Ashby (editor)

Udja! Even though I know the myth, having the opportunity and privilege of reading and editing this translated hieroglyph texts of the epic Myth of Asar (Osiris), Aset (Isis) and Heru (Horus), from various Ancient Kemetic (Egyptian) steles and texts that Dr Muata Ashby (Sebai Maa) has translated is an epic mystic delight! It's one thing to know the story of this epic myth....and as I read it, totally another to read it word for word, looking at the glyphs, their images for the words, and their direct transliterations and translations and then the applied meaning or contextual translation that gives it context. The feeling, the suspense, the breath holding anticipation as to what happens next, what does the next verse reveal, the insights, the connection to the characters as the saga unfolds, the mental imagery, in addition to the images Dr Muata Ashby is presenting to further give a visual sight and feel for the unfolding saga, as it unfolds, verse by verse...as it unfolds before one's inner vision as a movie unfolds on the screen...from Heru's (Horus') birth to his death, and his resurrection, to his war with Set (Seth), to his father's resurrection, to the ultimate victory...of Maakheru, Spiritual Victory! It feels as though the wisdom and intent of the Ancient Sages are flowing through a lotus fountain of blessings and spiritual wisdom and mysticism that never run dry, and is overflowing with every glyph and translated word.

If you are on a Spiritual Path based on Ancient Kemetic (Egyptian) spirituality, or you just Enjoy Kemetic/Ancient Egyptian Mysticism, or just mysticism, or Even if you just enjoy African-Kemetic story telling, or Ancient African Egyptian myths,you will enjoy this shower of Divine Blessings that will support and no doubt en-lighten your spiritual path.

HTP
Seba Dja

Table of Contents

- FOREWORD 4
- INTRODUCTION 10
  - Understanding Mythic Wisdom - What is Myth? 10
    - Process of Mythology: 10
    - Religion and Myth 10
    - Origin of the term "myth" 11
  - Ancient Egyptian term: *Matnu - legend, story, myth.* 11
    - Misconception about the term "Myth" 11
    - The Keys to Reading and Understanding a Myth 12
    - PURPOSE OF MYTH: Answers to the important questions of life: 12
    - How to Live a Mythic Life 12
    - Myth and Religion and the Purpose of Religion 13
    - • The Purpose of religion is to help a human being to discover their higher nature through a three-fold process: 13
    - • Myth –Heart or Religion 13
    - • Ritual 13
    - • Mysticism/metaphysics 13
  - TRANSLATION FORMATS USED FOR PRESENTING THE TRANSLATIONS WITH THE TRILINEAR METHOD 14
    - Conventional Interlinear Format 14
    - Trilinear Contextual Format 15
    - Reading the Philosophy Embedded in Ancient Egyptian Hieroglyphic Writings 20
  - ORGANIZATION OF THIS BOOK 22
- The Ancient Egyptian Book of Coming Forth By Day (Book-of-Enlightenment, Book of the Dead) Excerpts from Chapters 17 and 78 24
  - PERT EM HERU (Egyptian Book of the Dead) Chap 4/17 (Trans by Muata Ashby ©2021 25
  - PERT EM HERU (Egyptian Book of the Dead) Chap 4/17 (Trans by Muata Ashby ©2021 26

PERTEMHERU (Egyptian Book of the Dead) Chap 78 28
THE ASARIAN RESURRECTION MYTH AS TOLD IN Stele of Amenmose Part 1 30
    Adorations to Osiris 31
TEMPLE OF ASET(ISIS) IMAGE OF ASET(ISIS) RETURNING TO KEMET(ANCIENT EGYPT) WITH THE HELP OF THE GOD SEBEK(SOBEK) 40
Goddess Aset*(Isis)* Returning the body of Asar*(Osiris)* to Kemet (Egypt) 41
RESURRECTION OF OSIRIS 45
Stele of Amenmose Part 2 55
CONCEPTION OF HORUS 57
Stele of Amenmose Part 3 73
    BIRTH OF HORUS AT THE TEMPLE OF ASET(ISIS) 75
    TEMPLE OF ASET (ISIS) IMAGE OF GODDESS ASET GIVING BIRTH 76
THE ESCAPE INTO HIDING-METTERNICHE STELE 80
    ASET/ISIS IN PRISON-COMES OUT OF PRISON 81
    Episode with the Noble Woman, her child and the fire 88
    SECTION EXPLAINS HOW ASET(ISIS) OBTAINED KNOWLEDGE FROM GEB 94
    HORUS IS BITTEN BY A SCORPION AND DIES 99
    RUBRIC: ASET REFLECTS ON THE SITUATION AND HOW IT OCCURRED 109
    DEATH OF HORUS 115
    THE GODDESSES NEBEHET (NEPHTHYS) AND SELKET (SERQET) OFFER ASSISTANCE AND DIVINE INSPIRATION 119
    ASET (ISIS) MAKES AN INVOCATION TO STOP THE BOAT OF RA AND RESURRECT HERU (HORUS] 122
CONTENDINGS OF HERU(HORUS) AND SET(SETH) Version 1 128
    The Conflict Between Heru (Horus) and Set (Seth)-Fundamental Problem and Confusion Between the Higher Self and the Lower Self 130
    The High God Does Not Agree with The Other Gods and Goddesses that Heru (Horus) should be Given the Throne of His Father Asar (Osiris) 137
    Sending a Letter to Goddess Net(Neith) for Her Advice 141

EGYPTIAN BOOK OF THE DEAD HIEROGLYPH TRANSLATIONS Volume 6: Featuring The Osirian Resurrection

The God BABA Berates the God Ra 146

Goddess Hathor Comes in to Lift the Animus of Ra 147

The Oaths of Aset (Isis) and Set (Seth) 151

Aset (Isis) and the Boatman 155

Aset (Isis) Tricks Seth into Speaking Truth and Decreeing His Own Fate 156

Seth Complains to Ra about What Isis has done but Gets No Relief and Still Does Not Accept His Fate 163

Ra Decrees That The Crown Should Be Given to Heru (Horus) 165

Set (Seth) Does Not Agree with the Decree to Give the Throne to Heru (Horus) and Vows to Fight On by Taking an Oath 167

Horus and Seth Fight as Hippopotamuses 168

The image above has been provided to give the reader a visual impression of the events and meaning at this stage in the text. 169

Heru (Horus) Cuts Off the Head of Aset (Isis) and a Deep Truth is Revealed About Her Nature 172

Heru (Horus) Leaves the Battle and Goes to the Mountains to Find Rest from the Fight 175

Heru (Horus) is Found by Set (Seth) and he Injures Heru (Horus) 176

Goddess Hetheru (Hathor) Finds Heru (Horus) and Heals Him 179

The Gods Heru (Horus) and Set (Seth) are Sent Away and told to Stop fighting. They Go Away Together as Set (Seth) Makes Overtures of Friendship with Ulterior Motives 182

Set (Seth) Again Vows to Reject any Attempt to Give the Throne to Heru (Horus) and Challenges Him to Fight With Ships on the Water 197

HERE BEGIN THE FINAL INVOCATIONS OF THE SCRIPTURE (Chester Beaty) -UTTERED BY GODDESS ASET (ISIS) 231

WINGED DISK & CONTENDINGS OF 234

HERU (HORUS) AND SET (SETH) 234

Version of the Conflict between Heru and Set based on the text of the Temple of Horus at Edfu 234

Contextual wisdom in the translated text about the term "auf maat" 252

STELE OF AMEMNOSE Part 4 291

BACK TO AMENMOSE-Epilog for the End of the Contendings of Heru and Set and the Joy in every Heart that sees Heru and the Splendor of Heru's Spiritual Victory for and Spiritual Redemption of Every Soul 291

A Royal Offering of non-dualism for the Soul and Ritual of Communing with Pure-existence. {From the STELE OF AMEMNOSE} 301

INDEX 304

Other Books From C M Books 309

TABLE OF FIGURES

Figure 1: The Leonine bed (bier) of Asar 49
Figure 2: Image of Ptah-Zokar Hall panel #13B highlighting the "TWO" Kite goddesses: A and C are Aset, B is Nebethet. 51
Figure 3: Aset (at the foot of the leonine bed) and Nebethet (at the head of the leonine bed) adore-Asar-in-shrine- with serpents headdresses signaling that they are the same serpent goddesses Wadjit and Nekhebet, depicted under the leonine bed in #13B. 53
Figure 4: Front of the Asar Projection Room (Heru Conception Room) as exists today. 59
Figure 5: Asar Projection & Heru Conception Room South (S) wall-showing Panel #22A and Panel #22B on the west wall (W)..60
Figure 6: (Above) Dr. Muata Ashby pointing Out Key Section of the Iconography on *Asar(Osiris)/Heru(Horus)* Complex: Central (ASAR/OSIRIS) Projection Room panel #2-West Wall-clearly showing that Goddess *Aset(Isis)* "Sitting" and not hovering over the body of *Asar(Osiris)* as she was on Initiatic Stop #13 Panel B...62
Figure 7 (Below): Temple of *Asar(Osiris)* Projection Room West Wall (Panel #22B) detail......................................62
Figure 8 (Below): Dr. Muata Ashby pointing Out Key Section of the Iconography on *Asar(Osiris)/Heru(Horus)* Complex: Central (ASAR/OSIRIS) Projection Room #2-West Wall-showing Goddess *Aset(Isis)* "Sitting on and not "hovering" over the body of *Asar(Osiris)*, Conceiving *Heru(Horus)*. *Asar(Osiris)* is lying on a leonine bed. 63
Figure 9 (Below): Differences between Temple of Asar Ptah-Zokar Hall Panel #13B and Temple of Asar Projection Room/Heru Conception Room Panel #22A 63
Figure 10: Middle Kingdom era Ancient Egyptian black granite sculpture of the conception of *Heru(Horus)* found in the area close to the Temple of *Asar(Osiris)* corroborates the scene presented in the Temple of *Asar(Osiris)* Projection room west wall (P. #22B). It depicts *Asar(Osiris)* lying on the leonine bed with *Aset(Isis)* in the form of a Kite sitting on his penis. 64
Figure 11: Images of the Temple of Asar(Osiris) Projection Room West Wall and the Stone Sculpture Conception scenes of Heru(Horus) 65
Figure 12 (Below): Temple of Asar-Asar Projection Room (I.S. #22) View: South to North- Architrave Inscription..67
Figure 13: Below-Close-up view of East Architrave Inscription in Asar Projection Room Looking from South to North..68
Figure 14: The God Asar (Osiris) with the two Serpent Goddesses wearing the headdresses of Aset (Isis) and Nebethet (Nephthys) together composing a Caduceus 70
Figure 15: Ancient Egyptian Coffin Lid-The God Asar (Osiris) with the two the Goddesses Aset (Isis) and Nebethet (Nephthys) (all in an anthropomorphic form) together composing a Caduceus 71

INTRODUCTION

Understanding Mythic Wisdom - What is Myth?

The subject of this volume centers around the Ancient Kemetic (Ancient Egyptian) myth of the Asarian (Osirian) Resurrection. Myth is a language of the soul that relates to the folk expressions of religion, as told through ancient and legendary stories involving humans and divine entities, which leads to higher philosophical insights about life culminating in a mystic movement of self-discovery.

<u>Process of Mythology:</u>
- Study of Wisdom Philosophy or teaching of the myth through study of the mythic journey and practice of rituals of the myth as a way to identify with and understanding the meaning of life.
- Metaphor: Language involving exchange – understanding the nature of self as the nature of the myth.
- Protagonist: Identification of the practitioner of myth with the subject of the myth
- Ontology: The nature of being and existence
- Eschatology: What happens at the end of life and beyond

<u>Religion and Myth</u>

Religion provides a venue for the mythic process whereby answers to the basic human spiritual questions are discovered.

Origin of the term "myth"

Ancient Egyptian term: *Matnu - legend, story, myth.*

The word myth comes from Ancient Greek language:

"story-telling", μυθολογία, from muthos, "story, legend", and logos, λόγος, "account , speech". The word muthos, μῦθος, itself is of unknown origin.

The term mythology has been in use since the 15th century, and means "an exposition of myths". The current meaning of "body of myths" itself dates to 1781 (Oxford English Dictionary [OED]).28 The adjective mythical dates to 1678.

Myth in general use is often interchangeable with legend or allegory, but some scholars strictly distinguish the terms. The term has been used in English since the 19th century. The newest edition of the OED distinguishes the meanings.

Misconception about the term "Myth"

1a. "A traditional story, typically involving supernatural beings or forces, which embodies and provides an explanation, aetiology, or justification for something such as the early history of a society, a religious belief or ritual, or a natural phenomenon", citing the Westminster Review of 1830 as the first English attestation

1b. "As a mass noun: such stories collectively or as a genre." (1840)

2a. "A widespread but untrue or erroneous story or belief" (1849)

2b. "A person or thing held in awe or generally referred to with near reverential admiration on the basis of popularly repeated stories (whether real or fictitious)." (1853)

2c. "A popular conception of a person or thing which exaggerates or idealizes the truth." (1928)

The Keys to Reading and Understanding a Myth

- ✓ Key #1: Myths (Religious/Mystical) are relevant to our lives in the present and not necessarily historical.
- ✓ Key #2: Myth is a journey of spiritual transformation.
- ✓ Key #3: Myths are to be lived in order to understand their true meaning.
- ✓ Key #4: Myth points the way to victory in life.

PURPOSE OF MYTH: Answers to the important questions of life:

- Who Am I and Who are Gods and Goddesses?
- Why Am I Here?
- Where Did I and Creation Come From?
- What Do I need to Do To Fulfill the Meaning of My Life?

How to Live a Mythic Life

- Realize the meaning and purpose of myth
- Consciously *Choose* to be on a path of transformation, believe that you can learn, grow, and become the highest and best expression of your higher nature.
- Choose a myth to live by that resonates with your character and which leads its characters to victory in life and in death.
- Assume the characters of the myth and live their journey and allow them to live yours.
- Learn the morals of the myth and apply those in your mythic journey.

Myth and Religion and the Purpose of Religion

- <u>The Purpose of religion is to help a human being to discover their higher nature through a three-fold process:</u>
  - Myth –Heart or Religion
  - Ritual
  - Mysticism/metaphysics

Matnu -the Myth: - legend, story, myth.

Aru - ritual – ceremony.

Shetaut Neter - the Mystical.

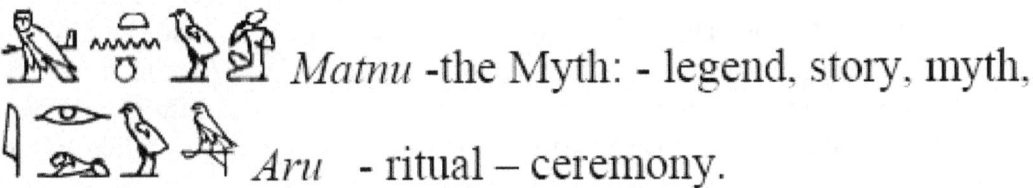

Human evolution from Myth to Mysticism

TRANSLATION FORMATS USED FOR PRESENTING THE TRANSLATIONS WITH THE TRILINEAR METHOD

Conventional Interlinear Format

The conventional or regular interlinear format of translating Ancient Egyptian hieroglyphic texts presents a phonetic transliteration of the Ancient Egyptian hieroglyphs and transposes the hieroglyphs into the characters of the language they are being translated into. The second line presents a word for word translation. This level of translation can sometimes result in a limited, choppy, and less intelligible presentation of the original intent of the script. When the translation is between languages of dissimilar structure and cultural references such as the difference between the Ancient Egyptian language, which is rich in metaphor and iconographical implied wisdom versus the European languages which are based on a stricter alphabetic matrix, the structural differences along with differences of culture mean that a strict word for word translation can be insufficient to convey a full understanding of the intended meaning. So, while the conventional interlinear format is useful to a certain extent, a more comprehensive translation matrix is needed to gain the deeper richness of the meaning and import of the original hieroglyphic text.

Example of the Regular Interlinear Format:

Verse 1.   ORIGINAL TEXT

    1.1.   Transliteration into the phonetic letters of the language of the reader

    1.2.   Translation into the words of the language of the reader

Ex:

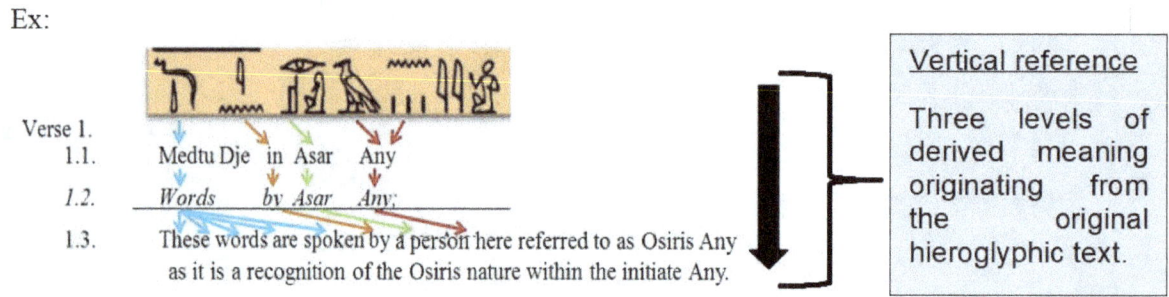

Trilinear Contextual Format

The Trilinear Format for translating the Ancient Egyptian writing is a method as well as, to some degree, also a decipherment protocol that allows a layout for viewing the meaning from its source through layers of meaning extraction to the final rendition. The term "decipherment" is used because to the modern mind, whose concerns are often far removed from the world and philosophy of the Ancient Egyptians, the contexts and philosophy of the ancients are akin to more than a mystery, but also as a scarcely fathomable idea that is like a code or formula to be discovered to unlock the secrets of life, death, and the afterlife. Over the years, Dr. Muata Ashby has developed a format of translating Ancient Egyptian hieroglyphs into the native language of the reader that incorporates three levels of translation instead of the two levels of the ordinary conventional interlinear format. In a few cases, the conventional interlinear format is used in this volume. However, in most other cases a Ternary System will be used. The Ternary System devised by Dr. Muata Ashby adds a third layer of translation to the work that includes a contextual translation beyond the word for word translation. This added layer of the translation may be termed "Contextual Translation" and all together constitutes the ***Trilinear Contextual format***.

The Trilinear Form (which is a ternary system) of translations is a format developed by Dr. Muata Ashby for translating the Ancient Egyptian Hieroglyphic texts. It contains a *tripartite* arrangement composed of three translation sections or layers/levels. The <u>first level</u> is a phonetic transliteration. The <u>second level</u> is a direct word for word translation from hieroglyphic to the native language of the reader. These two levels generally constitute the "Conventional Interlinear Format" of translation. The Trilinear Format adds a new level of translation. The <u>third level</u> of translation is a contextual translation bringing out the meaning in an informal colloquial context in prose style incorporating:

A- the Ancient Egyptian Sebait (philosophical) tenets along with

B- the Ancient Egyptian Matnu (mythic) references and Ancient Egyptian "Maut" (morals or takeaways of the myth to which the text appertains) contained in the text in order to better reveal the intended meaning for the reader's language and culture.

C- In this volume, a new feature has been added to the trilinear system; the last translated verse will also include, where possible, a summary making contextual sense of the wisdom presented throughout the text, with particular focus on the beginning verse so as to clarify the takeaway by recalling the status of the spiritual aspirant at the beginning, then the transformation experiences throughout the text in its key hieroglyphic expressions and concluding with the outcome expressed in the final verse.

EGYPTIAN BOOK OF THE DEAD HIEROGLYPH TRANSLATIONS Volume 6: Featuring The Osirian Resurrection

Example of the Trilinear Format:

Verse 1.   ORIGINAL HIEROGLYPHIC TEXT
    1.1.   ***Transliteration into the phonetic letters of the language of the reader***
    1.2.   Translation into the words of the language of the reader
    1.3.   Translation with contextual insights which may include philosophical and or mythological and/or historical background insights with colloquial references.

Ex:

Verse 1.
1.1.   Medtu Dje in Asar   Any
1.2.   Words   by Asar   Any;
1.3.   These words are spoken by a person here referred to as Osiris Any as it is a recognition of the Osiris nature within the initiate Any.

NOTE: Each level of translation is designed to be both a reference to the other levels (vertically) but also to the previous and next statement in each level; so, for example, Verse translation Level 2.1 relates to 2.2 and 2.3 (vertical) but 2.2 also relates to 1.2 and 3.2 (horizontal). Therefore, if all the Level 2 translations are read by themselves or Level 3 translations are read by themselves one after the other, there will be a continuous and coherent rendering of the text

Example

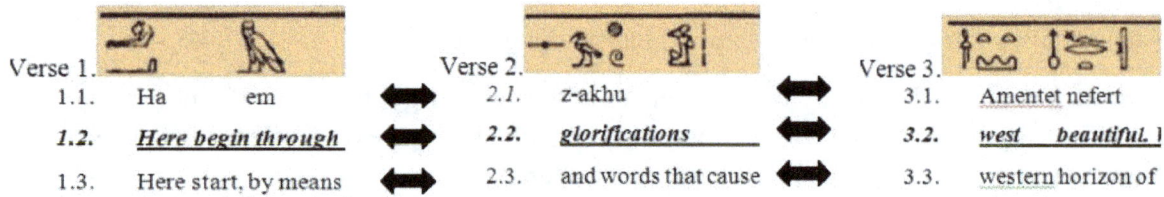

(Horizontal relationship)

In this way, the readings of Verse 1.2 followed by Verse 2.2, followed by Verse 3.2, translations, one after the other (ignoring .1 and .3 levels), horizontally, provide a continuous and coherent word for word narrative of the translation.

Also, the readings of Verse 1.3 followed by Verse 2.3, followed by Verse 3.3, translations, one after the other (ignoring .1 and .2 levels), horizontally, provide a continuous and coherent prose narrative of the translation.

Note: When some text appears in red it is because the original hieroglyphic text was written in the same way. This was done to highlight certain parts of the text or to highlight the chapter titles of the text. See the example below.

Verse 1.
- *1.1.* *Pu*   *tra*   *er –f su*   *Asar*   *pu*   *ky*   *djed*   *Ra*
- 1.2. That   what   as to-he? He   Osiris   that   otherwise said: Ra
- *1.3.* **What is that personality that is being talked about?** That personality is Osiris. Another way of thinking about it is that Osiris is also Ra…

EGYPTIAN BOOK OF THE DEAD HIEROGLYPH TRANSLATIONS Volume 6: Featuring The Osirian Resurrection

How is the translation format organized? Below: Sample papyrus sheet with hieroglyphic text

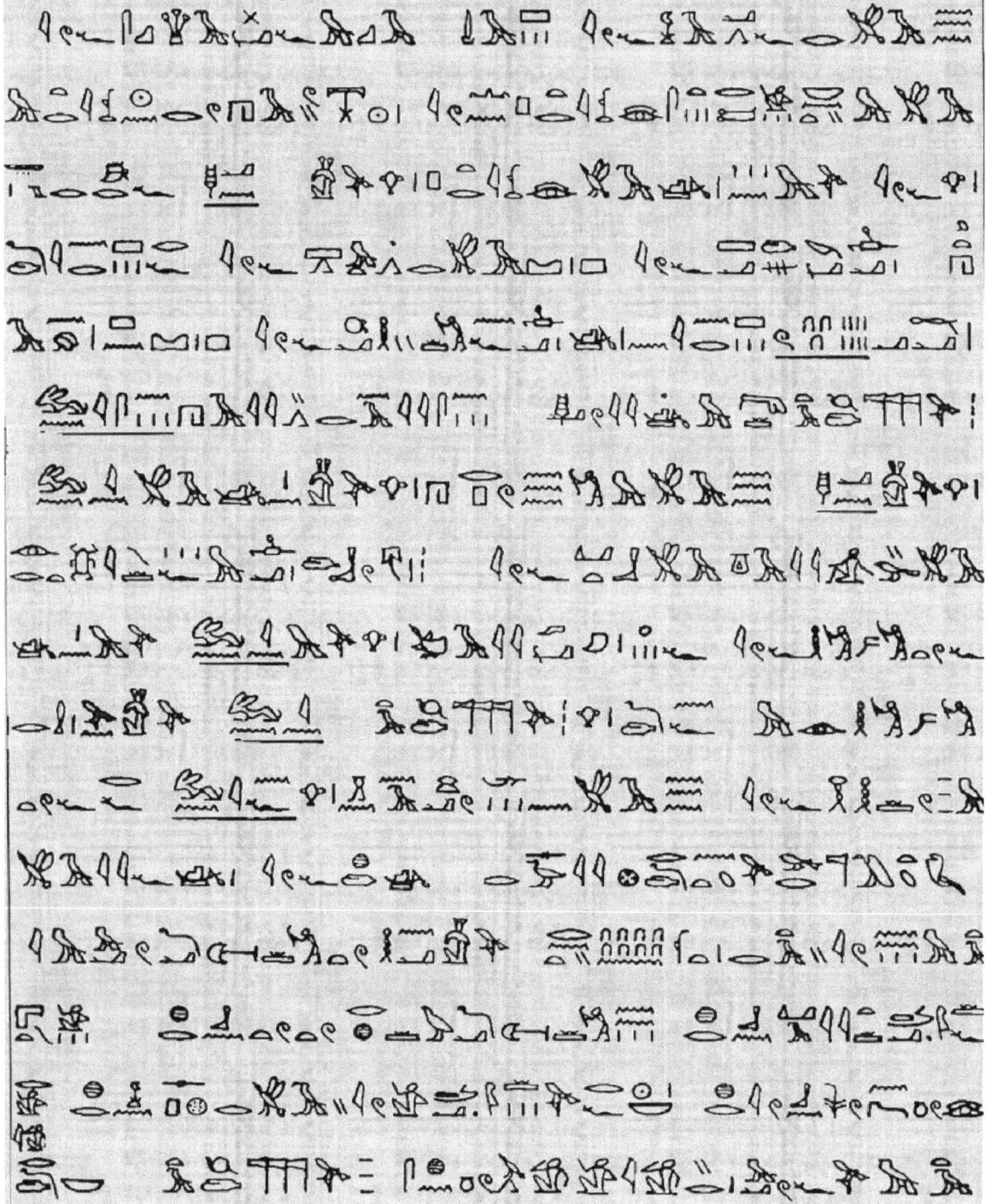

EGYPTIAN BOOK OF THE DEAD HIEROGLYPH TRANSLATIONS Volume 6: Featuring The Osirian Resurrection

A trilinear translation is created by photographing the sheet and dividing the lines of text into strips. Then the text is converted to a TRANSLITERATION followed by WORD FOR WORD TRANSLATION and finally a CONTEXTUAL TRANSLATION.

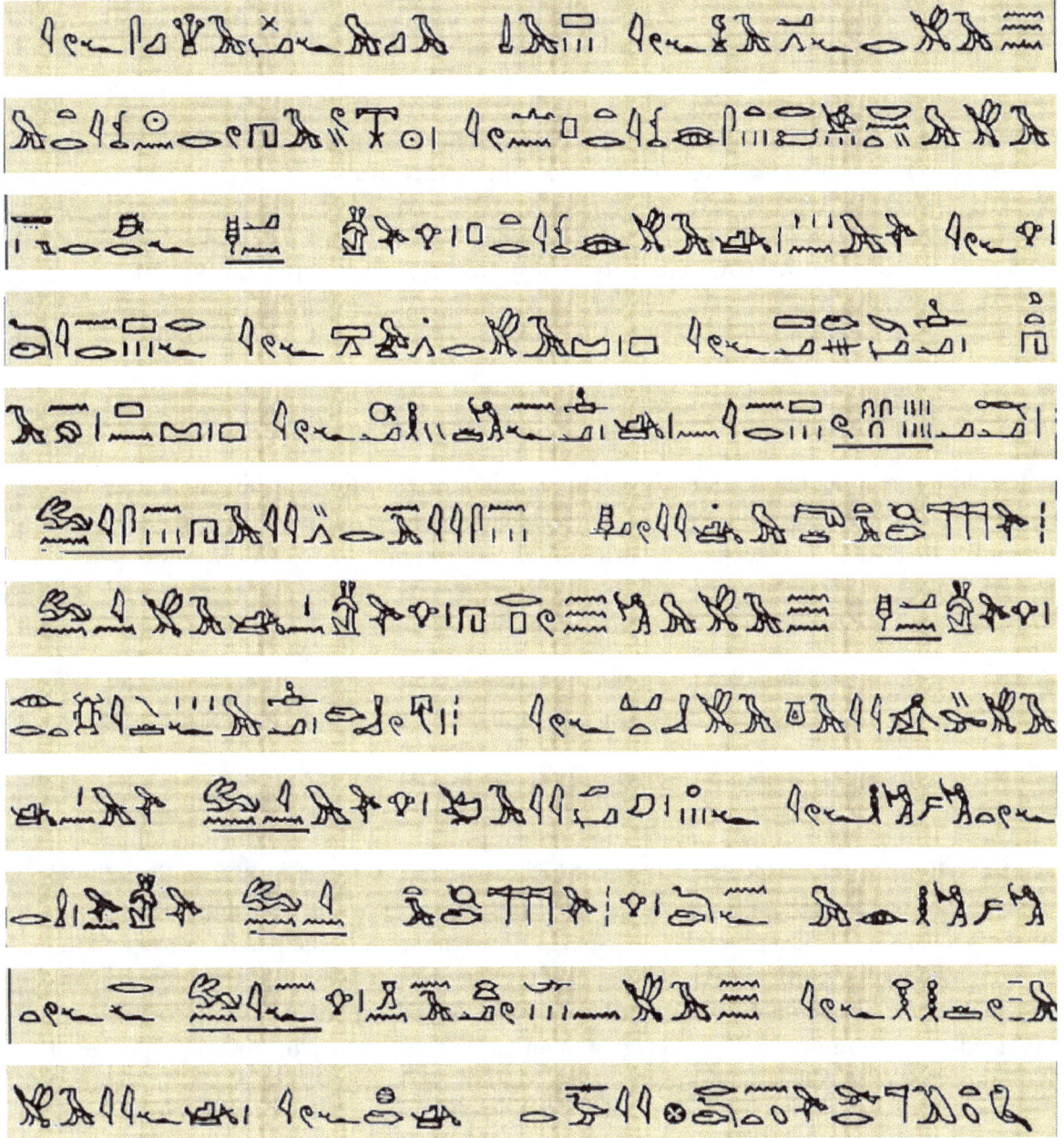

EGYPTIAN BOOK OF THE DEAD HIEROGLYPH TRANSLATIONS Volume 6: Featuring The Osirian Resurrection

EXAMPLE OF A VERSE OF TEXT TRANSLATED WITH THE TRILINEAR FORMAT:

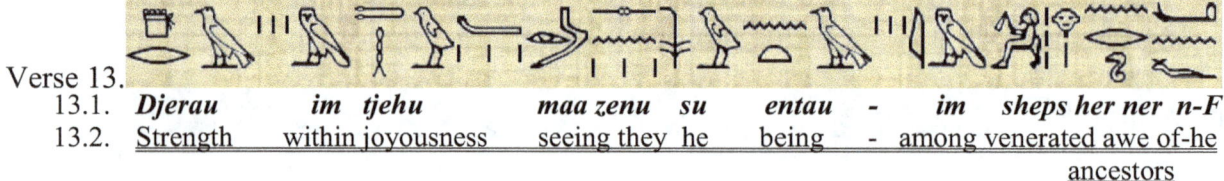

Verse 13.
    13.1.   *Djerau*   *im tjehu*   *maa zenu su*   *entau*   -   *im*   *sheps her ner n-F*
    13.2.   Strength   within joyousness   seeing they he   being   - among venerated awe of-he ancestors

    13.3.   There is a strong feeling of joyousness when they see Osiris, among those who are in the ranks of the venerable, noble ancestors; when they see him they are in awe of him.

Reading the Philosophy Embedded in Ancient Egyptian Hieroglyphic Writings

Here I will provide two examples, using two of the most important hieroglyphs to demonstrate why and how the philosophy of the Ancient Egyptian Mysteries is determined in the texts to be read. As stated earlier, reading the Ancient Egyptian texts in a literal way, ascribing meanings that relate to the culture of the reader is a disservice to the ancient culture and also it is a distortion of the meaning of the texts and the legacy of the original priests and priestesses who created them.

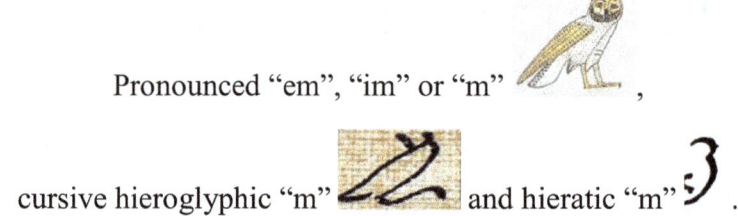

Pronounced "em", "im" or "m", cursive hieroglyphic "m" and hieratic "m".

The first glyph is the owl. Perhaps one of the most important glyphs, unlike determinatives, which do not convey phonetic aspects to the word, the owl has a phonetic and philosophical meaning. Whenever the owl appears the meaning can range from "in, within, inside, though, as, in the form of. This means that it is a pivotal term especially when it relates the person for whom the text has been created to any particular or general Divinity [god or goddess]. It, therefore, means that such a person is being identified with that divinity or with an aspect of divinity or they are being recognized as "becoming, or appearing or manifesting as". This, of course, signifies a movement of transformation either in progress or already attained. This glyph is seldom interpreted in such a manner and thus the overall outcomes of such neglectful translations will render a mundane and or erroneous insight into the Ancient Egyptian hieroglyphic writings.

Another important glyph is the scroll.

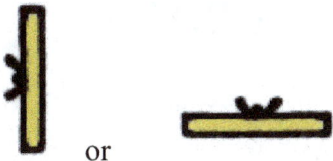

Generally, the Ancient Egyptian language is composed of phonetic, ideographic, and determinative glyphs. The determinative glyphs do not contribute a phonetic aspect to the word but rather contribute a reference and or philosophical implication to be inferred by the reader. The scroll is a determinative glyph that, when appears, forces the application of a perspective abstractness that allows a vision of a meaning that transcends a strictly mundane or specific application. This is a reading that incorporates a philosophical and or conceptual basis to the meaning of the particular word. An example of how to apply the scroll in reading a word or sentence or passage is that its conceptual abstractness is to be applied to the regular meaning of the world, and the abstractness relates to the Ancient Egyptian philosophy of the spiritual mysteries that affirms a transcendental nature of life that goes beyond physical reality.

As a group, determinatives provide a similar function and constitute an integral and essential means of understanding the deeper wisdom and intent of the Ancient Egyptian written language. Below are some of the most important determinatives.

For more on the Ancient Egyptian Hieroglyphic Writing see the book *Ancient Egyptian Hieroglyphs for Beginners* by Muata Ashby

ORGANIZATION OF THIS BOOK

This book is a compilation of the parts of the Ancient Egyptian Myth of *Asar(Osiris)*, *Aset (Isis)* and *Heru (Horus)* that appear in Ancient Egyptian Hieroglyphic texts. These texts include:

- Stele of Amenmose
- Metterniche Stele
- Chester Beaty Papyrus
- Temple of Asar(Osiris)
- Temple of Aset(Isis)
- Temple of Heru (Horus)
- Sections from the Ancient Egyptian Book of the Dead (Book of Enlightenment)

The aim of this book has been to render the main texts, associated with the Ancient Egyptian Osirian Resurrection, in the chronological order of the events of the myth and to present a translation that is grounded in the ancient texts, showing where the translated descriptions, wisdom and feelings expressed are coming from in the texts. Myth is a language of the soul by which the Ancient Kemetic (Egyptian) sages created a pathway for a human being to understand the nature of Creation, the powers (Neteru {gods and goddesses}) operating in it, and the manner in which to live a life that leads to happiness, fulfilment and spiritual enlightenment. The text of "Stele of Amenmose" contains references to the main scenes of the myth of the Asarian Resurrection, from the beginning of the myth to the end, but does not go into details related to some of those scenes. So, the text of "Stele of Amenmose" has been used as the foundational text, the trunk, as it were, of a tree. It begins the myth and describes the events of the myth, and as the tree (mythic rendition) grows, the branches extend the scenes not fully covered in the Amenmose scripture. So the contributing texts form expansions of the story which is taken up by another related scripture that goes into those details of hat section. Then, when that branch reaches a conclusion, we will return to the trunk of the tree again, the Stele of Amenmose, to again grow the tree, the mythic journey, until we reach another branch and so on to the end of the myth.

As the text is presented, the characters in the myth, which represent aspects of the Divine as well as expressions of the human heart and soul, will be introduced. Then, as the saga unfolds, the reader will be able to identify with the characters and experience their passions, sorrows, victories and spiritual exaltations leading to the final victory of exhilaration and contentment over despondency, depression and frustration, and wisdom over delusion, and eternal mystic life over physical death.

THE TREE OF MYTHIC SCRIPTURES OF THE ASARIAN RESURRECTION MYTH RENDERED IN ANCIENT EGYPTIAN HIEROGLYPHIC TEXT:

EGYPTIAN BOOK OF THE DEAD HIEROGLYPH TRANSLATIONS Volume 6: Featuring The Osirian Resurrection

The Ancient Egyptian Book of Coming Forth By Day (Book-of-Enlightenment, Book of the Dead) Excerpts from Chapters 17 and 78

INTRODUCTION

The Ancient Kemetic (Egyptian) text, the PERT EM HERU, or Book-of-Coming into Light (Enlightenment), more commonly referred to as the Book of the Dead, is a text related to the Ancient Egyptian mysteries and philosophy for coming into the understanding of and attaining awareness of the nature of one's own transcendental consciousness (Enlightenment) beyond the mortal aspects of the personality. Below are presented sections from two chapters of the Ancient Egyptian Book of Enlightenment. It contains references to the Ancient Kemetic (Egyptian) myth of Asar (Osiris), Aset (Isis) and Heru (Horus). The mythic teaching related to Asar (Osiris), Aset (Isis) and Heru (Horus) is about the nature of the human personality, its fall into the delusion of mortality and the means for its redemption and spiritual emancipation. The references in the Ancient Kemetic (Egyptian) Book-of-Enlightenment are written in such a way that a person would need to already know the myth in order to understand the context of the message in the writing. The subsequent sections of this book (Egyptian Book of the Dead Hieroglyph Translations Vol. 6.) will provide details into the main events of the Asarian (Osirian) myth that are rendered in hieroglyphic text form. However, the Ancient Kemetic (Egyptian) Book-of-Enlightenment section is being presented first, before the mythic text is presented from the various sources listed above. Then after reading the subsequent portions of this volume, the reader may refer back to this section of the Pert Em Heru, and noticehow the deeper meaning of the Ancient Egyptian Book-of-Enlightenment is augmented through the reading of the mythic hieroglyphic texts.

EGYPTIAN BOOK OF THE DEAD HIEROGLYPH TRANSLATIONS Volume 6: Featuring The Osirian Resurrection

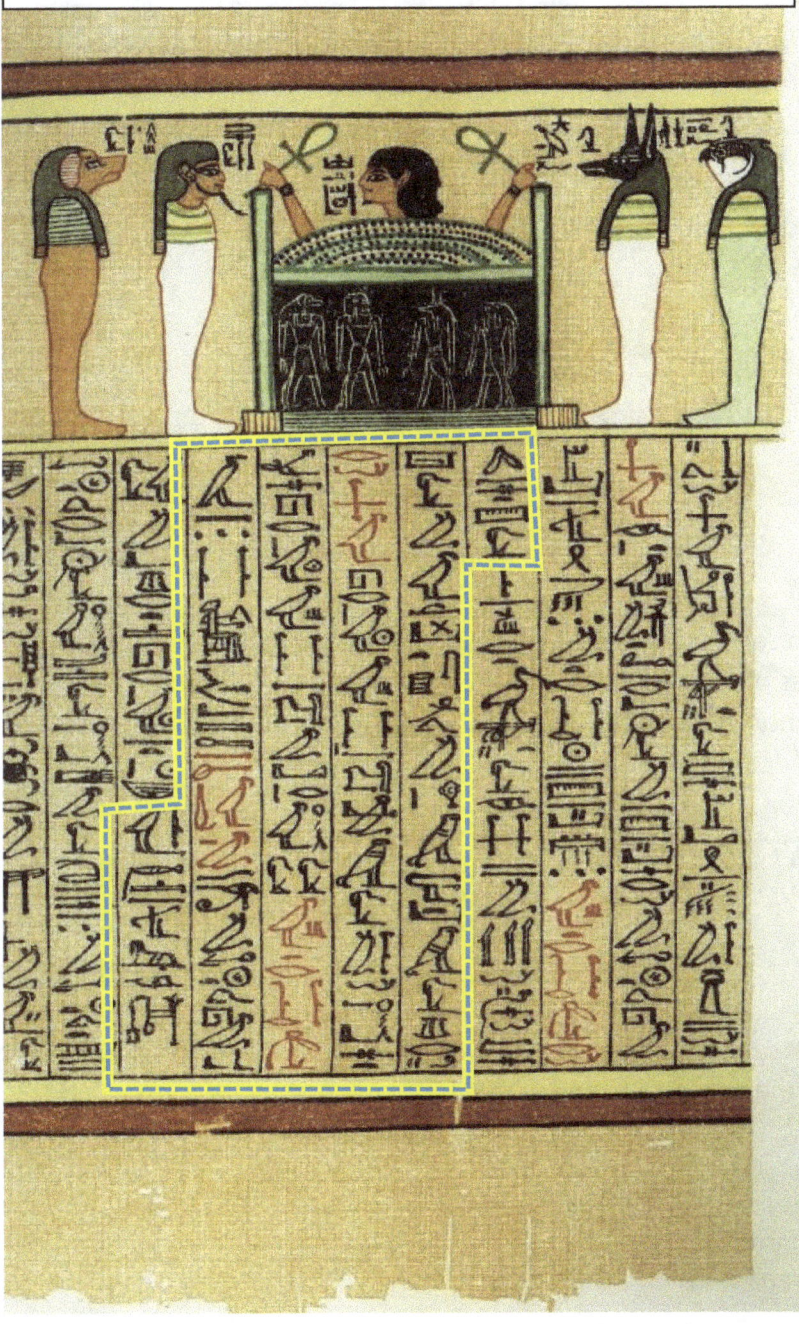

PERT EM HERU (Egyptian Book of the Dead) Chap 4/17 (Trans by Muata Ashby ©2021

Verse 64.

64.1. iu   meh n-A   Asar   sesh   Any   {shp}   maa-kheru

64.2. it is   fill to-I   Osiris   scribe   Any   {venerable}   true-speech

64.3. It is I who satisfy myself, the scribe Any, the holy and spiritually–victorious…

Verse 65.

65.1. n-K   udjat   emchet

65.2. for-thee   divine-eye   after

65.3. …for you, oh, my spiritual-eye, this, after…

Verse 66.

66.1. hab   z   heru   puy   en   aba   rehuy

66.2. failed   it   day   that   of   clash   two-contenders

66.3. …it failed to see the truth of the oneness of Creation and the transcendental essence and oneness of my existence with the Divine which occurred on the day when there was distraction and ignorance due to a clash between the truth, *Heru/Horus,* and the delusion of egoism, *Set/Seth.*

Verse 67.

67.1. pu   tra   ref   su   heru   puy   en   aba   Heru   im   F

67.2. that   then   thus he?   Day   that   of   clash   Horus   in   he

67.3. So, what then was that all about which disturbed his vision of spiritual reality? It was the time when there was a clash between, *Heru/Horus*, the spiritual vision aspect of the soul of the personality and within his own personality…

Verse 68.

68.1. hena   Zetep   im   ud   setau   im   hera   Heru   tjet
68.2. with   Seth   in   flinging excrement in   face   Horus   seizes
68.3. mixed up with *Set/Seth*, the ego-vision of reality that separates, obfuscates and agitates the personality, thereby distorting the vision of spiritual reality by producing and casting ignorance, distortions of reality, thoughts, feelings and desires in front of the mind to distract and deflect the interest in truth, thereby contaminating the visage of reality of self and the reality of what the personality perceives as real and true or nonexistent and false. This leads to ignorance and delusion with doubts, and weak-will in *Heru/Horus*, the spiritual vision aspect of the soul of the personality. That was Set/Seth trying to emasculate *Heru/Horus*; yet it was *Heru/Horus* who instead seized…

Verse 69.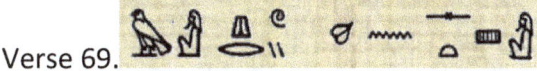

69.1. Heru   kheruy   en   Zetep
69.2. Horus   testicles   of   Seth
69.3. …it was *Heru/Horus* who seized the generative power (testicles) of Set/Seth, the ego aspect of the personality, and instead controlled and subjugated that agitating and distorting aspect of the personality, and thereby *Heru/Horus,* attained spiritual victory.

PERTEMHERU (Egyptian Book of the Dead) Chap 78

(Trans by Muata Ashby ©2021)[1]

Verse 97.
- **97.1.** qa   ta   her   aset-per K   Asar   sedjem K   nefertu{mdj} Asar   wadj {mdj}
- 97.2. exalted   upon throne thine Osiris   listen thee good-things{fig} Osiris green-vitality{fig}
- 97.3. Oh, *Asar/Osiris*, you are exalted on your throne. You are listening to good things, good news. Oh, *Asar/Osiris*, green-vitality{fig}...

Verse 98.
- **98.1.** peh K   Asar   [tjezu]   tu n-K tep Asar   zemen tu n-K   usert K
- 98.2. arrive thee Osiris [tied]   you for-thy head Osiris established to for-thee neck thine
- 98.3. ...has arrived to you. You are healthy and vital and your body parts have been [reattached and bound up] reintegrated, reattached to your body, as your head, which was disintegrated by the god *Set/Seth*, is now attached and restored to your body; your self-awareness and cognitive ability have been restored. Also, your neck, your cervical vertebrae, your capacity to control your body and experience integral nervous perceptions has also been restored.

Verse 99.
- **99.1.** Asar nedjem{mdj} ab K
- 99.2. Osiris sweetness   heart thine
- 99.3. Oh, *Asar/Osiris*, sweetness is in the experience of your mind and feelings because of this turn of events from.

---

[1] Verses 19-101 chapter ending from Paris papyrus text of Chapter 78.

EGYPTIAN BOOK OF THE DEAD HIEROGLYPH TRANSLATIONS Volume 6: Featuring The Osirian Resurrection

Verse 100.
- **100.1.** Sa   K   Heru   cha {mdj} her   nest   K   ankh   neb   chery   F
- 100.2. Son thine Horus crowned{fig} person throne thine living all presence his
- 100.3. Oh, *Asar/Osiris*, your son, *Heru/Horus* has been crowned{fig} and he is the person on your throne. All life, the true existence beyond the mortality of life on earth, is with him.

Verse 101.
- **101.1.** Sa   K   di   F   hehu
- 101.2. Son thine gives he   millions
- 101.3. Oh, *Asar/Osiris*, with that abundance of life existence, your son gives millions of years to his followers, those who follow the path of ethics and vanquishing the unrighteousness that seeks to remove you from your throne and disintegrate your conscious awareness of Spirit Being, which is the desecration of your throne, the placing of the iniquitous personality (*Set/Seth*) on your throne.

EGYPTIAN BOOK OF THE DEAD HIEROGLYPH TRANSLATIONS Volume 6: Featuring The Osirian Resurrection

THE ASARIAN RESURRECTION MYTH AS TOLD IN
Stele of Amenmose Part 1

Stele of Amenmose – Louvre C 286 – Offerings of Amenmose and spouse Nefertari

EGYPTIAN BOOK OF THE DEAD HIEROGLYPH TRANSLATIONS Volume 6: Featuring The Osirian Resurrection

Adorations to Osiris

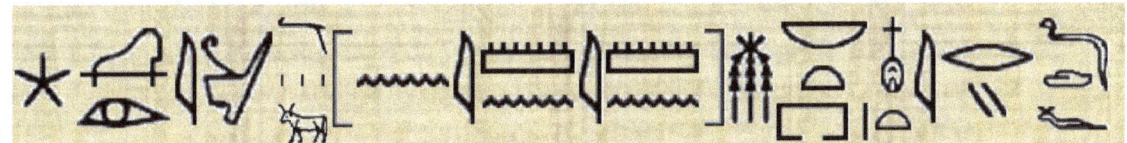

Verse 1.
- 1.1. ***Dua Asar   in   nes-ka en   Amun   Amun-mes nebt-per Nefertary   djed-F***
- 1.2. Adore Osiris   by   overseer of cattle Amun   Amun-mes   mistress house Nefertary. Says he

- 1.3. Here begin the adorations of the God *Asar(Osiris)* being proffered by the official overseer of the cattle belonging to the God Amun (Hidden Conscious One), whose name is Amun-mes (Child of the God Amun [Hidden Conscious One]), and the lady Nefertary(beautiful/good friend). He says the following:

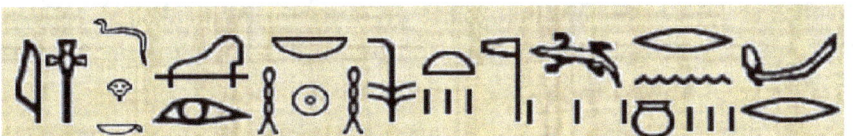

Verse 2.
- **2.1. *Anetedj her k Asar neb heh sutu neter ashau renu   djezer***
- 2.2. homage personality thine Osiris lord eternity lordship divinity many name sacred

- 2.3. Acclamations, praises to you *Asar(Osiris)*, lord of eternity and monarch over the multitude of gods and goddesses. Acclamations, praises to you *Asar(Osiris)*, whose sacred names are the foundation and glory behind the…

- 2.4.
- 2.5. ***Kheperu sheta aryu im   ra   peru***
- 2.6. creations secret actions mouths temples

- 2.7. … creations manifesting in the mouths of the temples.

31

Verse 4.

4.1.   Neb sekhau im Maaty ba   sheta neb-qerrt   djezer im aneb-hedj ba Ra djet F djezef

4.2.   Lord remembrance in Maaty Hall soul secret lord cataract cave/cavern sacred in Memphis, soul Ra, body his, his own

4.3.   He (Asar/Osiris) is the Lord of recollection, who recalls all deeds when they are judged in the Hall of double truth (Maaty), that of below and that of above. Asar is the secret soul at the bottom of the first cataract (so Asar/Osiris is being equated with the Hapi, the god of the Nile, who mythically lives within a cavern associated with the first cataract) which is the source of the Nile that is life giver to all. He is also considered sacred in Memphis, the city of the god Ptah and additionally this Asar is the soul of Ra, the Creator Spirit, and even more, Asar is the body of Ra himself!

Above: Image presented to convey the idea of *Asar(Osiris)* as King of Egypt enjoying a festivity.

EGYPTIAN BOOK OF THE DEAD HIEROGLYPH TRANSLATIONS Volume 6: Featuring The Osirian Resurrection

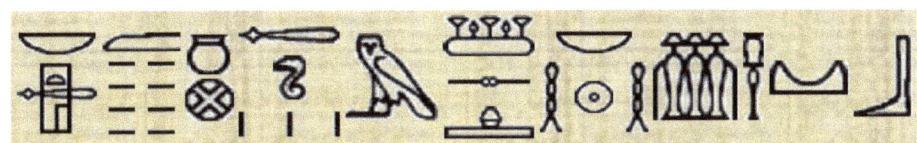

Verse 6.
- **6.1.** ***Neb het-aah im Khemenu aneru im shaz Hetep neb-heh Khenty abdu***
- 6.2. <u>Lord of the great house in Hermopolis; awe-inspiring in travelers peace lord eternity; foremost in Abydos</u>

6.3. *Asar(Osiris)* is the Lord of temple of Hermopolis (the city of Thoth-Hermes / Egyptian: Djehuty), God of Cosmic Mind and Purified Intellect), presided over by the god Djehuty (Thoth/Hermes). So great is *Asar(Osiris)* that he inspires awe in people who are nomadic and brings peace to them. *Asar(Osiris)* is the Lord of Eternity; he is the foremost being in the city of Abydos, the spiritual heart of Ancient Egypt…

- 6.4.
- **6.5.** ***her   aset-per F   im   ta-djeser***
- 6.6. <u>therefore abode his in   land-sacred</u>

6.7. …thus, his presence, in his abode, at the heart of the country, this is what makes Ancient Kemet(Egypt) a sacred land indeed.

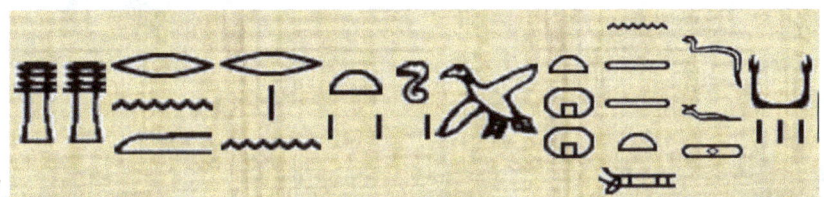

Verse 7.
- **7.1.** ***Djeddu ren im   ra en   tenu   pauty   en tawy tem djefa kau***
- 7.2. <u>Dual stability name in mouth of them company of two 2-lands complete provisions minds Gods/Goddesses</u>

7.3. Asar's name is dually stable in the mouths of those in the Company of Gods and Goddesses who came into existence at the inception of the Creation of the two lands of Ancient Kemet/Egypt (symbolic of the higher and lower self, duality). Thus, what the gods and goddesses speak, that is, what they project through their mouths as they express their cosmic forces throughout Creation, is infused with the power and essence of *Asar(Osiris)*. Asar also is the complete provisioner of people's minds, that is, Asar is the sustainer and provider of full consciousness that allows minds to exist and function.

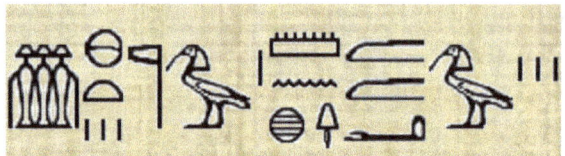

7.4.
7.5. ***khenty paut Neter akh mench imim akhu***
7.6. <u>foremost Company shining spirit perfect shining spirits</u>
　　　　　Gods/
　　　　　Goddesses
7.7. *Asar(Osiris)* is the foremost being among the primeval Company of Gods and Goddesses as well as the THE SHINING SPIRIT (AKH) among the Shining Spirits (Akhu).

Verse 13.

13.1. ***Djerau　　im tjehu　　maa zenu su　　entau　-　im　sheps her ner n-F***
13.2. <u>Strength　within joyousness　seeing they he　being　-　among venerated awe of-he ancestors</u>

13.3. There is a strong feeling of joyousness when they see *Asar(Osiris)*, among those who are in the ranks of the venerable, noble ancestors; when they see him they are in awe of him.

Verse 14.
14.1. ***Tawi demjet her erta n-F　aa　　　im　chesefu　　hem　F***
14.2. <u>Two-lands together faces give to-he adorations as approaches　majesty he</u>

14.3. The faces of the people of the two lands of Upper and Lower Egypt are joining together as one, looking at, paying homage, adoring this majestic personality as he approaches them.

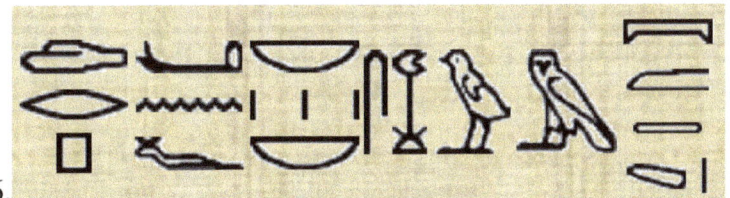

Verse 16.
  16.1. derp   n-F   nebu neb se-khau   im   pet im ta
  16.2. offering to-he   lords all recollection in   heaven in earth

  16.3. All the royalty make offerings to him. He is remembrance personified, in the heaven and on the earth, of the spiritual essence of life which transcends both.

Verse 18.
  18.1. ur   sems   tep senu   F   semsu   en pautu Neter semen Maat
  18.2. great   elder chief brothers   his eldest of company Divine establish Righteousness

  18.3. *Asar(Osiris)* is the eldest and therefore the chief of his brothers and sisters who are his Company of Gods and Goddesses that establish righteousness. ..

  18.4.
  18.5. *chet idbu   ra   sa   her- nest -F*
  18.6. object   act   son   person -throne-his
         two-banks
  18.7. …throughout the two lands of upper and lower Egypt (duality) assert, act by setting his son, as the personality on his throne when he leaves the earth plane.

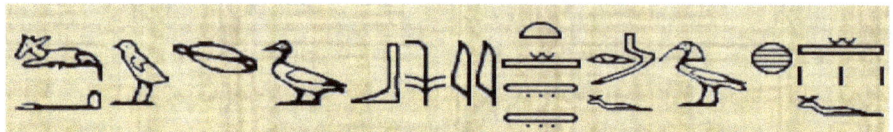

Verse 21.
21.1. *au   geb   suty {mdj}tawy ma F akhu   {mdj} F*
21.2. <u>heir   God-earth royalty{fig}two lands see glories{fig} his</u>

21.3. *Asar(Osiris)* is the heir of Geb, the god of the earth and of physical reality. He represents the royalty of the two lands of Upper and Lower Egypt and he recognizes the glories of his son *Asar(Osiris)*.

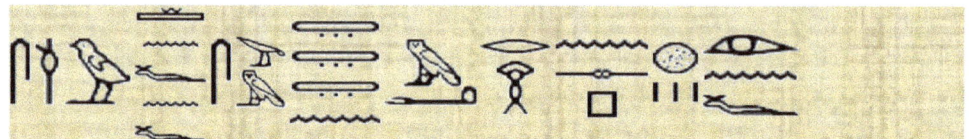

21.4.
21.5. *seudj   {mdj} nefnef seshem tawiu en mar en zepu   ari en F*
21.6. <u>bequeath {fig} that leadership lands to flourish of medicine actions of he</u>

21.7. Having recognized the glories of *Asar(Osiris)*, Geb bequeathed to *Asar(Osiris)* the position of leadership and entrusted to him the guidance of the lands, realizing that his actions would be like medicine for them to heal the wounds of mortal experience and thereby allow them to have a life that flourishes in spiritual health and achievement of the goal of life.

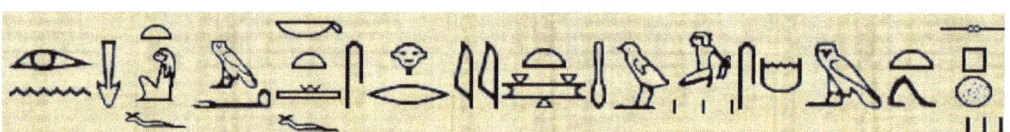

Verse 26.
26.1. *ari en sent F makt{mdj} F se-heryt   kheru   se-hemt   zepu*
26.2. <u>action of sister his protection{fig} he cause-defeat   speech   cause-warding off   medicine</u>

26.3. *Asar's (Osiris')* sister, *Aset(Isis)* acted as his protector, with her speech, causing the defeat of inimical forces and driving away (warding off) of unrighteous personalities that might try to harm him; she is his healer, providing that which bolsters the soul and also heals it from sorrowful eventualities in life when they occur,…

Above: Image presented to convey the legendary situation being alluded to of *Asar(Osiris)* as King of Kemet (Ancient Egypt) enjoying a festivity and the god Set presents a coffin to him to trick him into getting in and then Set and his minions dispose of the coffin thereby killing *Asar(Osiris)* so that *Set(Seth)* can take over the throne.

EGYPTIAN BOOK OF THE DEAD HIEROGLYPH TRANSLATIONS Volume 6: Featuring The Osirian Resurrection

Above: Image presented to convey the idea of Set dumping the coffin, with *Asar (Osiris)* inside, into the Nile

26.4. *shed   kheru   im   achu{mdj}   ra   se*

26.5. <u>**trained words form Shining Spirit{fig} mouth hers**</u>

26.6. …she having been trained, being studied in the knowledge and disciplines of wisdom, her words of power, Hekau, come through her mouth, and are derived from the Enlightening Spirit within.

EGYPTIAN BOOK OF THE DEAD HIEROGLYPH TRANSLATIONS Volume 6: Featuring The Osirian Resurrection

Verse 27.
27.1. ***aqert   nj an   uh   en medu   se-menchtu   udj {mdj} medu***
27.2. <u>excellent tongue not deficient speech causing-perfection   commanding{fig} speech</u>

27.3. The Goddess *Aset's (Isis')* mastery of the speech power is most excellent; it is not deficient or in any way ineffective; her speech causes perfection and it is commanding, authoritative, strong and forceful. Hence, she is mistress of Hekau, words of power.

Verse 28.
28.1. Aset   akhut   netedjnu   sen   se-hehet   su   antet   begag   se
28.2. <u>Isis   Shining-Spirit   protector   brother   cause-bird   he   not   relenting she</u>

28.3. *Aset(Isis)*, the lady who achieved Shining-Spirit-Consciousness (Intuitional Spirit awareness) by discovering the sacred hidden Divine name of the *All*, acted as a protector to her brother. When he was in his time of injury, having been assaulted by the god *Set(Seth)*, left for dead and his body dumped in the Nile River to be lost, she took the form of a kite (bird) and with relentless perseverance she…

28.4.
28.5. ***pekhart[2] ta pen   im   hayt   an   chen   ne-z   an gemtu   se   su***
28.6. <u>turn   earth this in   lamentation   not alighting of-she not finding   she he</u>

28.7. …turned around, searching this earth planet, making utterances of divine words of caring and searching for the lost one, *Asar(Osiris)*, to be found and returned to his previously glorious state. She did not even stop to take rest as long as she had not yet found where he was.

---

[2] Alternatively *kabert*

EGYPTIAN BOOK OF THE DEAD HIEROGLYPH TRANSLATIONS Volume 6: Featuring The Osirian Resurrection

TEMPLE OF ASET(ISIS) IMAGE OF ASET(ISIS) RETURNING TO KEMET(ANCIENT EGYPT) WITH THE HELP OF THE GOD SEBEK(SOBEK)

The following images depict the Temple of Aset *(Isis)* and a temple panel depicting the returning of the body of *Asar(Osiris)* to Kemet (Ancient Egypt).

Dock at the Temple of *Aset(Isis)* depicting images of the *Asarian(Osirian)* Resurrection- including the return of the body of *Asar(Osiris)* back to Kemet(Ancient Egypt) -see below:

Goddess Aset*(Isis)* Returning the body of Asar*(Osiris)* to Kemet (Egypt)

This image below is found at the Temple of Aset*(Isis)* in current day Aswan, Egypt (Kemet). It depicts a scene from the *Asarian(Osirian)* Resurrection myth showing goddess Aset*(Isis)* returning the body of Asar*(Osiris)* to Kemet (Ancient Egypt) with the help of the crocodile god Sebek who is carrying the coffin of *Asar(Osiris)* on his back. At this stage of the myth, they are in the papyrus swamps of northern Kemet (Ancient Egypt). The hieroglyphs at the top of the image depict the symbol *sba* or star (illumination) which also represents time or days. The items include: a full moon, 18 stars and one crescent moon. These relate to the lunar nature of *Asar(Osiris)*, the time traversing between his death and return to Kemet (Ancient Egypt) and the pieces or parts which *Set(Seth)* tore the body of *Asar(Osiris)* into, which number 14 or 16, depending on the particular tradition cited. Within the central circular image are two male figures, one an adult, seated, and the other a child. These are expressions of *Asar(Osiris)* as the King and as his own heir, *Heru(Horus)*, that are contained within himself (on the back of Sebek), and which span the time of the movement from crescent to fullness, just as a parent contains the child within and the child is an expression, an incarnation of the parent that will grow to fullness in time.

EGYPTIAN BOOK OF THE DEAD HIEROGLYPH TRANSLATIONS Volume 6: Featuring The Osirian Resurrection

EGYPTIAN BOOK OF THE DEAD HIEROGLYPH TRANSLATIONS Volume 6: Featuring The Osirian Resurrection

Above: Image presented to convey the idea of *Aset(Isis)* returning with the coffin of *Asar(Osiris)* to Kemet (Ancient Egypt)

Verse 29.

29.1. *arit   shutu   {rau}   im   shutu   Ze   se-khepert {naf} im denhuy Ze*
29.2. deed feathers {solar} form wings   hers causing-creation {breath} through two wings hers

29.3. Upon finding where he was, she used her feathers, which possessed solar life-force which took form as her plumage; she then used her plumage to blow the life force on to *Asar's (Osiris')* body creating breathing (breath of life/conscious awareness) in him by using her two wings as she hovered over him and blew the life containing energy of the north-wind from *Ra-Tem*.

Image from the Temple of *Hetheru(Hathor)* at Dendera-Goddess *Aset(Isis)* using her wings to protect and resurrect *Asar(Osiris)*

Image from the Temple of *Asar(Osiris)* at Abydos

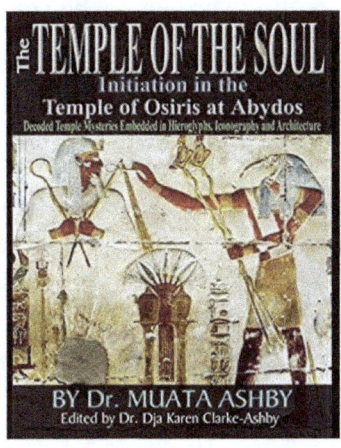

We will temporarily leave the Stele of Amenmose to go to one of the Ancient Egyptian temples that contains texts related to the resurrection of *Asar(Osiris)* and the role of goddess *Aset(Isis)* and other divinities in that process. Also, this temple contains a panel relating to the conception of the god Horus. After exploring the visual and text contributions to the Ancient Egyptian myth of the *Asarian(Osirian)* Resurrection, then we will return to the Stele of Amenmose.

Revival and Reconstitution of the Body of *Asar(Osiris)* from Initiatic Stop 13 from Temple of *Asar(Osiris)* at Abydos

RESURRECTION OF OSIRIS

THE FOLLOWING SECTION IS PART OF A CHAPTER FROM THE BOOK "**Temple of the Soul Initiation Philosophy in the Temple of Osiris at Abydos: Decoded Temple Mysteries Translations of Temple Inscriptions... Iconography and Architecture in color** –by Dr. Muata Ashby.

In the Ptah Zokar panel #13B (see image below), we see how the salamander energy (from the Salamander Panel, #13A) is brought down and used to regenerate and restore the body of *Asar(Osiris)*. In this panel, Asar is depicted as an inanimate mummy with the crown of the south. So he is of the south and this is the south wall and the south section of the Temple. Also, notice that he does not have any arms and his body is wrapped and immobile.

In the reintegration panel, the image below, from the Temple of Asar (Osiris), Ptah-Zokar Hall, Asar, the Royal Personality is labeled #1. *Aset(Isis)* is labeled #2. The God *Heru(Horus)*, at the foot of the bed, is labeled #3. The God *Djehuty(Thoth)* is labeled #4. The two Serpent Goddesses are labeled #5. *Aset(Isis)* has two depictions in the scene. She is the personality at the head of the bed. She is also in the form of a kite, that is hovering over the body of Asar and helping to make his penis erect.

EGYPTIAN BOOK OF THE DEAD HIEROGLYPH TRANSLATIONS Volume 6: Featuring The Osirian Resurrection

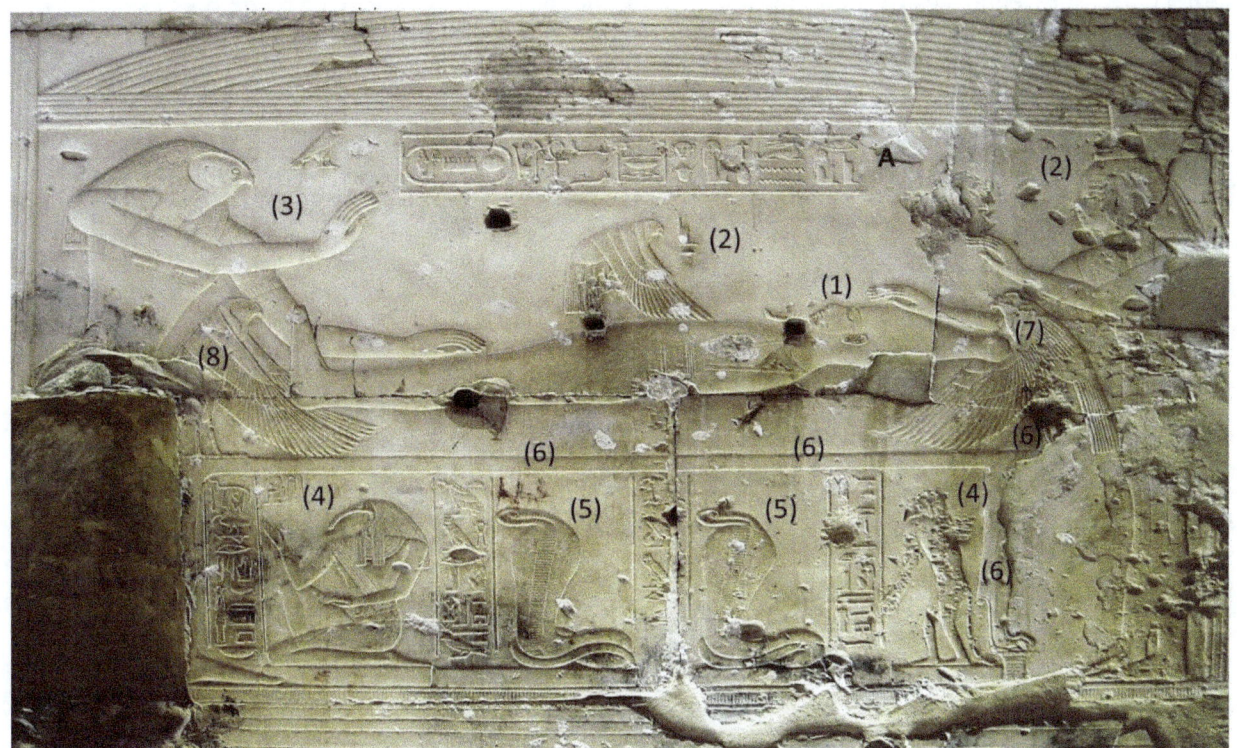

In the image above: Lord Djehuty, the god of intellect, appears in two forms under the leonine bed. On the left, he appears in his form as a man with an Ibis head and on the other side, as a baboon. The divinities under the bed are all, according to the texts, protective divinities; they are protecting the Divinity who is in the shrine, who is on the leonine resurrection bed, being worked on by

Aset(Isis) and *Heru(Horus)*. The two Serpent Goddesses, Wadjit and Nekhebet (forms of Aset and Nebethet) are representatives of the dual positive and negative Serpent Power principles assisting the regeneration process.

Thus, the iconographical message is that the regeneration occurs on a bedding or environment of Sekhem (raw life-Force) energy within which the intellect and the serpent power are active and in a creative mode. Later we will learn more about the creative roles of Aset, Nebethet, and Heru.

The main text of Temple of *Asar(Osiris)* Ptah-Zokar Hall Panel #13B text A is translated below:

Transliteration: *Asar   Un   Nefer   her ab het Zokar di f ankh was n Men Maat Ra*

Translation: "Osiris the beautiful/good existence the innermost reality of the Royal Person in the house of the Zokar (King of the Netherworld) he gives the flow of life force to the Royal One who goes by the name "One established in the righteousness of the Creator Spirit""

Contextual Meaning: First of all we are told that this personality who is lying on the bed in this shrine is "*Asar(Osiris)* Un Nefer", "*Asar(Osiris)* the Beautiful Existence". "Un" means "existence", "Nefer" means "beautiful" or "good" or "beneficent" or "righteous", etc. He is the innermost heart of the "Het Zokar", the "House of Zokar". Zokar means King in the Netherworld, thus, *Asar(Osiris)* as King in the Netherworld. Then we are told that this King in the Netherworld gives life flow. Therefore, Zokar (our soul residing as ruler in the Netherworld) is not just the life principle, but he is the source from which life arises for the personality. Therefore, we are to know that this "*Asar(Osiris)* Zokar Being" is the giver of life to the Royal Personality, who is currently being restored and regenerated. That is the ultimate and essential nature of the Royal Person to be this King in the Netherworld. The Netherworld may be thought of as the unconscious and subconscious mind where the deeper aspect of the person, where their soul, their self-concept of individuated being, resides. What is trying to be engendered here is the regeneration of that Higher Self so that it can give birth to one's own redemption and one's own spiritual aspiration to become a King effectively in time and space also. A fully realized personality is a King in their inner self, in their unconscious (the soul level) and also a King of their own life, in the outer world (the physical world [time and space]). That is a fully realized and well-adjusted personality and that is the goal of life.

Putting the Mythic Wisdom of the Asarian (Osirian) Resurrection legend together with the wisdom of the Ancient Egyptian Pyramid Text of Teta, and the Ancient Egyptian Book of the Dead, and applying them to what we see in Ptah-Zokar Hall panel, #13B we get the following synthesis:

> The Myth and the Pyramid Text instruct about the nature and function of *Heru(Horus)*. In a mythic context, *Aset(Isis)* finds the body parts of *Asar(Osiris)*, after Set tore his body into 14 pieces. Heru makes sure the pieces are gathered and accounted for and puts the pieces of *Asar(Osiris)* back together. Goddess Aset blows life force on them and then *Heru(Horus)* opens the mouth of *Asar(Osiris)*. Opening the mouth means opening conscious awareness, which is accomplished by *Heru(Horus)* sharing his eye of intuitional vision with Asar.* This process, in turn, allows Asar and Aset to copulate in a mystic union, between Soul and Transcendent Wisdom, that gives birth to *Heru-sa-Aset-sa-Asar*, "*Heru(Horus)* son of *Aset(Isis)* son of *Asar(Osiris)*", or *Heru(Horus)* the younger, who represents the new birth with emergent aspirational and redemptive conscience.

Figure 1: The Leonine bed (bier) of Asar

A divinity that has an important presence in this scene of the Ptah-Zokar hall, but is not specifically mentioned, is Goddess Sekhemit (Sekhmet), the aspect of the lion power (gross life force or Sekhem), represented here as the leonine bed upon which the regeneration, of Asar, occurs. Usually, the lion power is presided over by Goddess Sekhemit, a lioness goddess, is an aspect of Goddess Hetheru,. The symbolism of the leonine bed is alluding to the process of manipulating Sekhem, life force energy. So this process of resurrection, reconstitution, and redemption is occurring in a bed of life force; a platform, a support of raw life force. An analogy of this idea is: making a pot of rice. The rice can be put in a pot and if heat is applied the rice will burn unless there is water. The bed is the water in which the grains of rice (parts of the body of Asar), are "cooking" with the application of the "fire of wisdom" (of goddess *Aset(Isis)*) and divine intent (called "khu") that manipulate the life force into a creative form (the penis) as well as the vitality that allows the body to reanimate. Thus, a regenerative capacity has been put together in panel #13B. Now, *Asar(Osiris)* lies as if sleeping on the bed of the life force.

There are some additional divinities under the bed, within the bed, enclosed by the legs of the bed. Those divinities include Lord Djehuty, who represents intellect, as well as the two Serpent Goddesses that allow duality to come into being. So, from above and below, we have an evolutionary process ensuing, working on the body of Asar, our soul. This process, being described iconographically, occurs as a Royal Personality that reflects, through the auspices of *Aset(Isis)*, and with the support and grace derived from spiritual strength and valor, along with the impetuses of the gathered divinities and lies down to meditate, on the capacity of being this Asar (individual ignorant soul) who is really Zokar (Universal Soul and sovereign of Spirit Being). Thus, the meditative, metaphysical process of transformation, described in panels #13A-B, occurs in an environment surrounded by the life force that is the substratum with which the reconstitution of the astral body, the higher mind, and feelings, Asar, are reconstructed and reconstituted. The process is directed with mind controlling the serpent power conversion to regenerative power in order to reconfigure the ignorant ego personality (Asar) into its own Higher Self (Zokar-Asar). Therefore, Zokar is the Higher Self of the Royal Personality. This is the Self that needs to be regenerated and revived before the higher form of Heru can be given birth to.

In other words, a person has to work on their inner self, reconstituting their fragmented soul (due to Setian corruption {egoism}), in order to bring forth their Higher Self in the time and space physical realm of existence.

SAHU – "Causal Body"

The image of panel #13B is also a reference to the hieroglyph and name of the Ancient Egyptian "causal body." *SAHU*. Sahu may be thought of as a causal body. It therefore is the subtlest body of the human personality (Causal body, Astral body and Physical body) and it contains the higher elements of the personality *Akh* (Shining Spirit), and *Ba* (Soul). So *Asar(Osiris)* is on the leonine bed, which is where the soul rests. The Sahu sustains the soul and the shining spirit, allowing them to maintain integration of the Higher Self and a time and space foundation from where the soul and shining spirit may project into the lower elements of the personality. Thus, in this hall, as well as the Nefertem Hall, we are witnessing the higher aspects of the personality as opposed to the lower. We are seeing starkly depicted, their interactions, relationships and how they relate to the spiritual journey and the process of their integration, reconstitution and revival.

Figure 2: Image of Ptah-Zokar Hall panel #13B highlighting the "TWO" Kite goddesses: A and C are Aset, B is Nebethet.

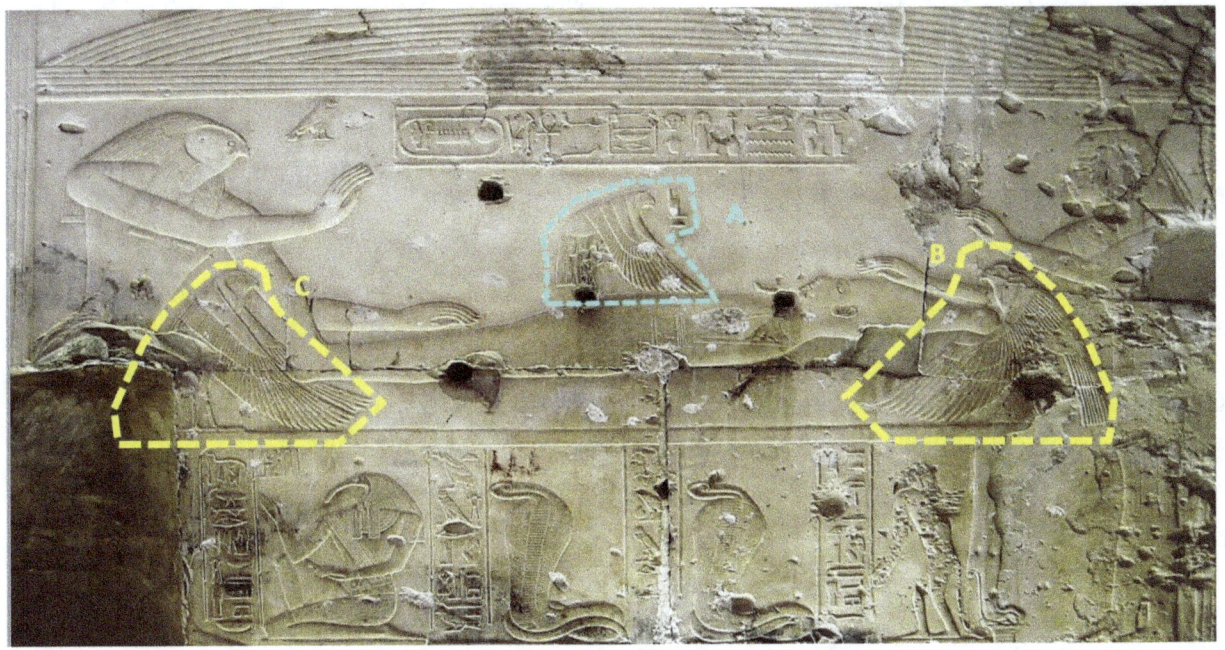

Asar ➡ Zokar = Rakoz

Zokar is the name of *Asar(Osiris)* after he has been resurrected. At that point he resides in a heavenly abode as the King of the netherworld. ***Zokar*** is also ***Rakoz.***

When the name ***Zokar*** is reversed it reads ***Rakoz*** which means the god who defeats ***Apep*** or Apophis, the divinity that opposed and tries to tear down Creation by stopping the movement of the boat of Ra. Therefore, the attainment of ***Zokar*** means that the soul has attained a state of mastery over the negative forces of Creation (Apep) and exists in a state of mastery over nature instead of being a victim or being susceptible to the changes of nature. ***Zokar*** is beyond the forces of Creation and presides over the spiritual existence of the personality instead of the lower forces being the masters over the personality, as exemplified by the character of the god ***Set(Seht).*** The raising of *Asar(Osiris)* to the status of ***Zokar*** is afforded by the acts of the goddess ***Aset(Isis);*** in other words the activity of attaining intuitional wisdom in life, wisdom about the spiritual nature of one's essential being; this is what raises one's soul to **Zokar** status. The final redemption of the soul occurs when *Heru(Horus)* is victorious over Set. Then a status of the soul being in its rightful conscious state in heaven as well as on earth, occurs and this is consciousness on the physical and astral planes being aligned with each other in awareness and non-dual peace which is spiritual enlightenment.

Conclusion

Finally, the goddesses *Aset(Isis)* and *Nebethet(Nephthys)*, in the form of kites or female hawks, are at the foot and the head of the leonine bed, helping to regenerate *Asar(Osiris)*. We have already gained insight into goddess Aset but we have not gone into much detail about Goddess *Nebethet(Nephthys)*. In the Asarian (Osirian) Resurrection myth, *Nebethet(Nephthys)* ("mistress of the house") is recognized as the twin sister of *Aset(Isis)* and also the sister of *Asar(Osiris)* and she is the goddess that presides over physicality, and thus over the mortality of the physical body as well as the composition and arrangement of the physical body.

In the image below, which is another ancient depiction of the same process as #13B, the use of the goddess serpent designation, makes clear that goddesses *Nebethet(Nephthys)* and *Aset(Isis)* are actually aspects of the serpent Goddesses Nekhebet and Wadjit, respectively, depicted under the leonine bed in #13B. In the Asarian (Osirian) Resurrection Myth[3], *Nebethet(Nephthys)* copulated with Asar (physical nature and soul interaction) and they produced the god *Anpu Wepwat (Anubis)* who is known as the *Opener of Ways*, as the divinity who helps *Asar(Osiris)*, the soul, incarnated as a human being, to find its way on the spiritual path. When human beings shift from thinking of themselves solely as physical mortal personalities and seek to understand, discover their immortal soul-essence (Zokar *Asar(Osiris)*), then the spiritual path of self-discovery opens up and there is inner discerning guidance that leads the way (Anpu Wepwat/). Anpu's older half-brother, Heru-Ur (Horus the elder), also helps *Asar(Osiris)* find his way. Anpu is a jackal divinity, four-legged and earthbound, while *Heru(Horus)* is a hawk divinity and capable of flight.

---

[3] See the book *AFRICAN RELIGION V4: ASARIAN THEOLOGY* by Dr. Muata Ashby

Figure 3: Aset (at the foot of the leonine bed) and Nebethet (at the head of the leonine bed) adore-Asar-in-shrine-with serpents headdresses signaling that they are the same serpent goddesses Wadjit and Nekhebet, depicted under the leonine bed in #13B.

Thus, mating with *Nebethet(Nephthys)* produces an offspring, Anpu/Wepwat, that is a positive spiritual divinity that helps the spiritual aspirant in all of the spiritual journey, but with focus on navigating the lower (earthly and heavenly) aspects of the spiritual journey, from its beginning to an advancing stage. The mating of the Soul (Asar/Royal Person) with Aset (Intuitional Wisdom) produces Heru (Intuitional Capacity) as the offspring, the redeeming, enlightening victorious divinity epitomizing the highest achievement of the spiritual journey beyond heaven and earth. Consequently, *Nebethet(Nephthys)* is also the goddess of mortality from the standpoint of her presiding over the ephemeral nature of time and space and limited human existence.

In the writings of Plutarch, he states that Nebethet, translated in the Greek mythology, which was transferred from Ancient Kemet (Egypt) to Greece, as "Nephthys, to whom they give the name of *Finality* and the name of *Aphroditê*, and some also the name of *Victory*." Thus, as a goddess who supervises the body, its vitality and procreative impulses and the disposition of its destiny, *Nebethet(Nephthys)* has an integral role to play in the reconstruction and reconstitution of the body of the Asar initiate which is why she appears in a standard iconographical format with *Aset(Isis)* at the foot of the leonine bed and *Nebethet(Nephthys)* at the head of the leonine bed.

In order to understand more details about the process that *Asar(Osiris)* is undergoing on panel #13B, we can draw on other Ancient Kemetic (Egyptian) texts for deeper insights. In support of the Asarian Resurrection myth and the writings of Plutarch, the earlier Ancient Kemet (Egyptian) Pyramid Text of Teta states:

EGYPTIAN BOOK OF THE DEAD HIEROGLYPH TRANSLATIONS Volume 6: Featuring The Osirian Resurrection

Verse:
Transliteration: *se udja   en – tju   Aset   hena   Nebethet*
Translation: cause vitality   to - thee   Isis   and   Nephthys

Cont. Translation: The goddesses, *Aset(Isis)* and *Nebehet(Nephthys)*, together have caused the body of *Asar(Osiris)* to have vitality.

Verse:
Transliteration: *Nebethet atu   k   nebet em   ren sepu en Seshat   {Heru}*
Translation: Nephthys body parts thine goddess in name   Sesheta {Horus standard}

Cont. Translation: The goddess *Nebehet(Nephthys)* arranges the body parts in her name Sesheta {who upholds *Heru(Horus)*}…

Verse:
Transliteration: *Nebet adu   se udja   en-en k*
Translation: Mistress planted construct cause vitality for to thee

Cont. Translation: …the goddess, mistress of the house/building arranges a construction that is firmly integrated and which causes there to be vitality in your (Asar's {Osiris'}) body.

Conclusion: Goddess *Nebethet(Nephthys)* is vital to the process being expressed iconographically on panel #13B. She organizes and oversees the construction process, in her name *Sesheta*, who is the Ancient Egyptian goddess of reckoning and organization.

Image of Goddess *Sesheta*

EGYPTIAN BOOK OF THE DEAD HIEROGLYPH TRANSLATIONS Volume 6: Featuring The Osirian Resurrection

Stele of Amenmose Part 2

BACK TO STELE OF AMENMOSE

===

THE TREE OF MYTHIC SCRIPTURES OF THE ASARIAN RESURRECTION MYTH RENDERED IN ANCIENT EGYPTIAN HIEROGLYPHIC TEXT:

29.4.
29.5. *Arit henu   menat   sen {Net} Ze*
29.6. **Deed jubilation   mooring post brother{Div} hers**

29.7. This great deed by *Aset(Isis)* was a cause for jubilation to she, who acted as his nurse (***menat***), and likewise to all; she had succeeded in creating a firm anchor for his soul to hold on to life as an integral (body reintegrated) focal point of conscious awareness.

Verse 30.
30.1. *se tjezt   nenu   en urd-hat chenpet[4] moo[5] F arit au   au*
30.2. **she raised inertness   of still-heart drawing water[6] his making child heir**

30.3. *Aset(Isis)*, the goddess of Shining Spirit Being, accomplished a magnanimous thing; she relieved *Asar(Osiris)*, the god of the Soul, from his state of inertness due to the injuries suffered by him at the hands of his brother *Set(Seth)*, who tried to kill *Asar(Osiris)*. *Aset*(Isis) raised *Asar(Osiris)* out of that inertness of death wherein his heart had been stilled. Then she was able to draw from him, through breath, some of the essence of his Soul-Spirit Being. Combining that essence of the soul (*Asar/Osiris*) with her own Shining Spirit Being, they produced a child who would be *Asar's(Osiris')* heir to the throne, the throne that *Set(Seth)*, overtaken by jealousy and greed and at this point acting as the god of egoism, had usurped from *Asar(Osiris)*.

[U]sing determinative of nose indicating through the nostrils

[5] *Negayt (semen/essence)*
[6] ibid

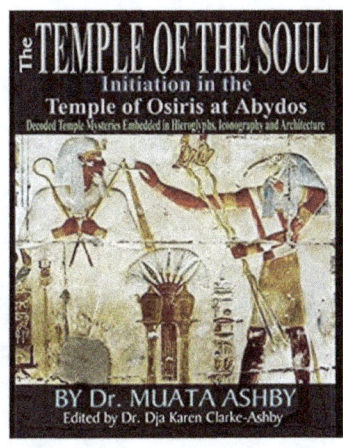

Now we will go to one of the Ancient Egyptian temples that contains texts related to the conception of the god Horus. After exploring the visual and text contributions to the Ancient Egyptian myth of the Osirian Resurrection, then we will return to the Stele of Amenmose.

CONCEPTION OF HORUS

THE FOLLOWING SECTION IS PART OF A CHAPTER FROM THE BOOK **"Temple of the Soul Initiation Philosophy in the Temple of Osiris at Abydos: Decoded Temple Mysteries Translations of Temple Inscriptions... Iconography and Architecture in color** –by Dr. Muata Ashby.

LOCATION: This section of the book "TEMPLE OF THE SOUL" by Dr. Muata Ashby is from the chapter (#25) containing the Initiatic Stop #22: The *Asar(Osiris)* Conception Room (Projection Room) situated next to the four columned hall of the temple in the Holy of Holies complex

4 Columned Hall in Asar/Heru complex looking north to south at 3 projection rooms (Of Asar, Aset, Heru [Osiris, Isis, Horus])
*Image taken from spot at center of the 4 Columned Hall

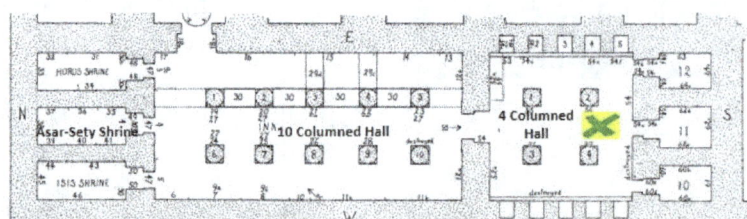

Contextual summary and overview of Temple of Asar Initiatic Stop #22

There are three main shrines in the 4 Columned Hall (image above-north to south view) that are referred to in a metaphysical sense, as "Projection Rooms." They are, from left to right: Projection Room of Heru (Horus), Projection Room of Asar, Projection Room of Aset (Isis). They are central to the operations of the Temple. The main study for Initiatic Stop #22 is the Asar Room and especially the west and south walls. Due to the extensive damage in the south wall, we will use a similar scene from another Ancient Egyptian Temple to reconstruct the image that is only partially seen in the Temple of Asar. We will begin with general descriptions of the projection room belonging to *Asar (Osiris)* [Initiatic Stop #22], its location, its condition and the scenes that should be visible in it:

EGYPTIAN BOOK OF THE DEAD HIEROGLYPH TRANSLATIONS Volume 6: Featuring The Osirian Resurrection

- The images below are from the interior of the Asar Projection Room South and West walls showing what is left of the panels and their iconography.
- The (S) South wall depicts the awakening and continued reanimation of Asar (Osiris) by Heru (Horus) who is putting a spear to the nose and mouth of Asar.
- Behind the south wall is the north wall of the Ptah-Zokar Hall (Initiatic Stop #13) where the reconstitution and reanimation of the body of Asar took place as he lay on his back. In this south wall (Stop #22), as we will see, Asar goes on his stomach and raises himself up on the bed.
- The (W) West wall depicts the conception of Heru (Horus) as Asar is lying on his back as Aset, in the form of a kite, sits on his penis.

Figure 4: Front of the Asar Projection Room (Heru Conception Room) as exists today.

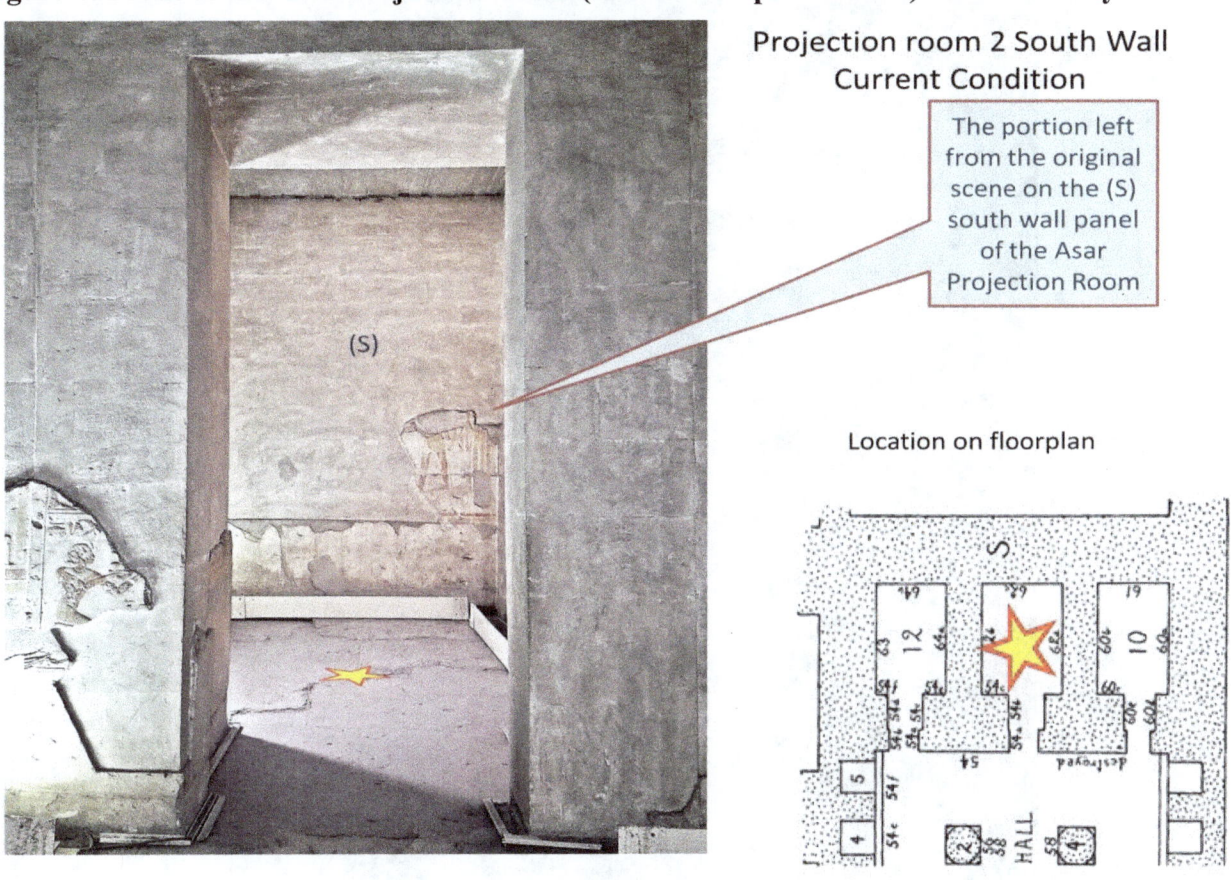

Figure 5: Asar Projection & Heru Conception Room South (S) wall-showing Panel #22A and Panel #22B on the west wall (W).

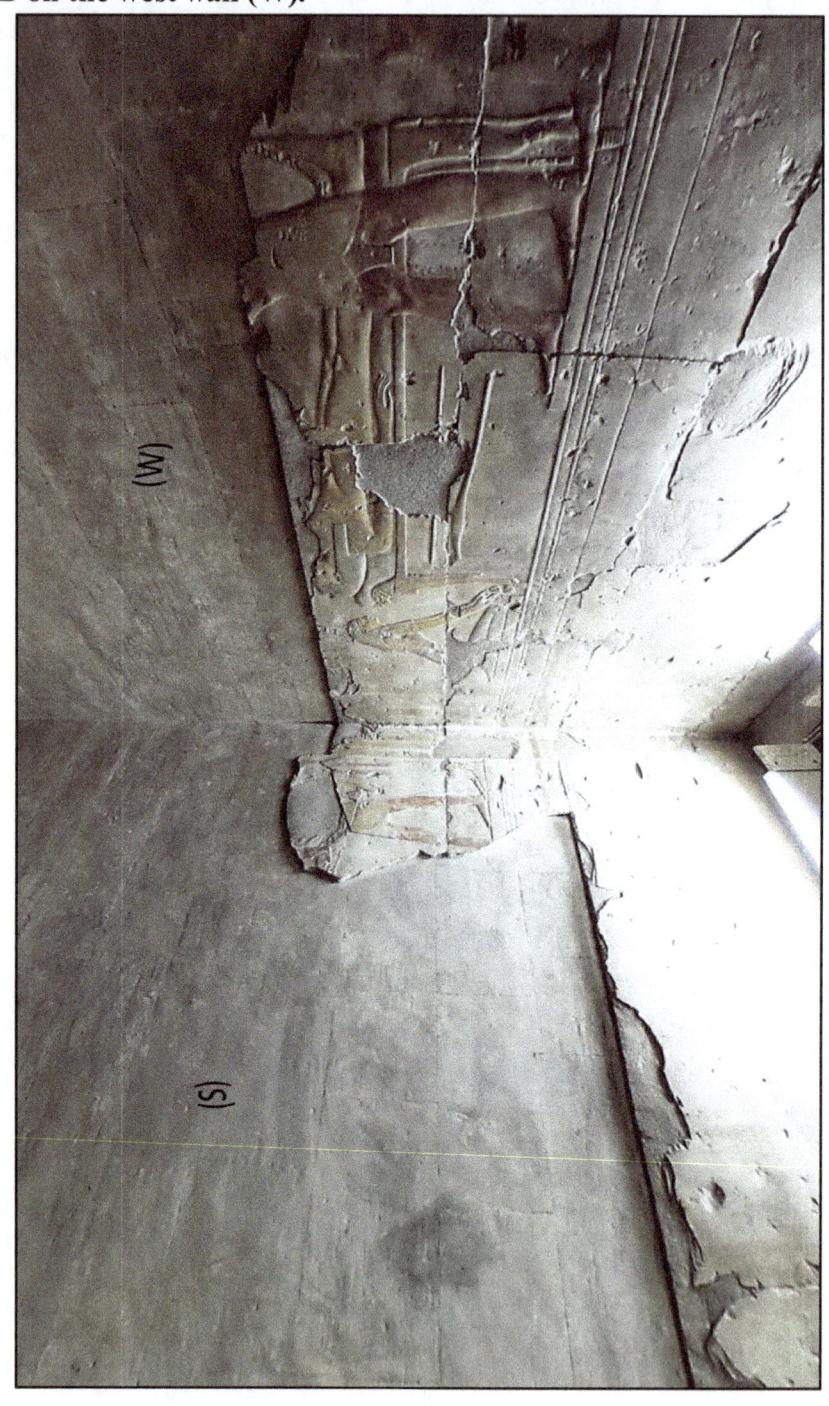

The following is a study of the West wall of the *Asar(Osiris)* Projection Room Panel #22B

Dr. Muata Ashby pointing Out Key Section of the Iconography on Asar/Heru Complex: Central (ASAR) Projection Room #2-West Wall-showing Goddess Aset "Sitting and not hovering over the body of Asar

EGYPTIAN BOOK OF THE DEAD HIEROGLYPH TRANSLATIONS Volume 6: Featuring The Osirian Resurrection

Figure 6: (Above) Dr. Muata Ashby pointing Out Key Section of the Iconography on *Asar(Osiris)/Heru(Horus)* **Complex: Central (ASAR/OSIRIS) Projection Room panel #2-West Wall- clearly showing that Goddess** *Aset(Isis)* **"Sitting" and not hovering over the body of** *Asar(Osiris)* **as she was on Initiatic Stop #13 Panel B.**

Figure 7 (Below): Temple of *Asar(Osiris)* **Projection Room West Wall (Panel #22B) detail**

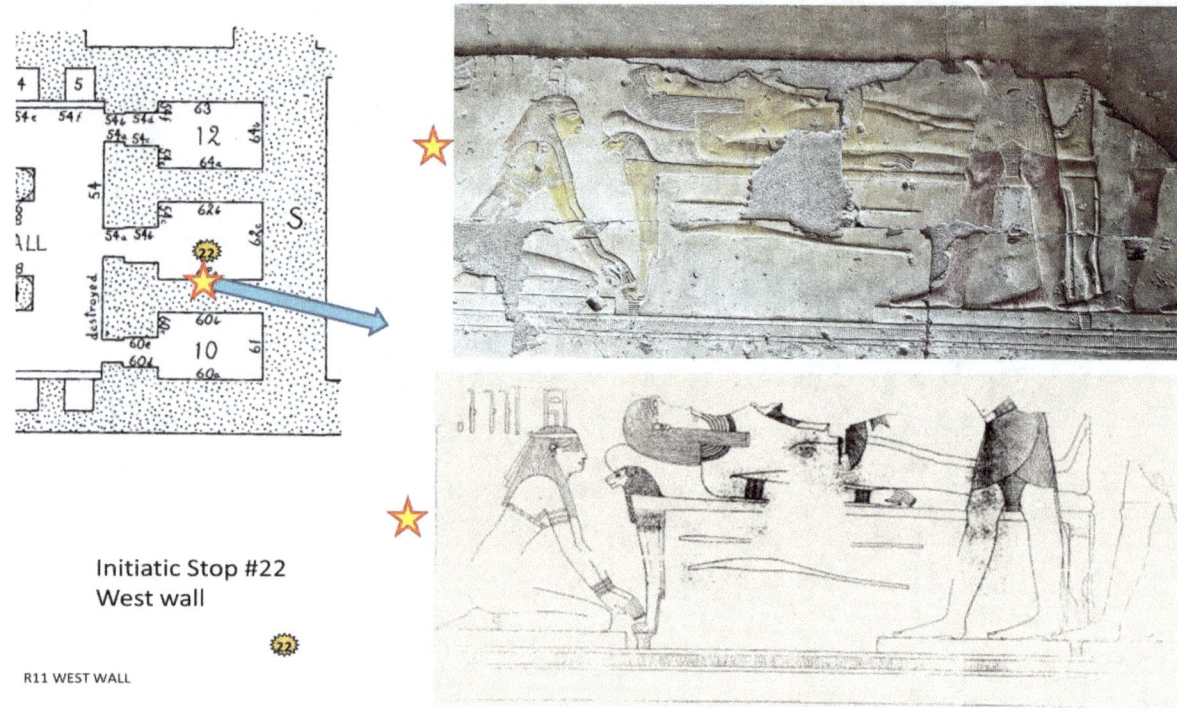

EGYPTIAN BOOK OF THE DEAD HIEROGLYPH TRANSLATIONS Volume 6: Featuring The Osirian Resurrection

Figure 8 (Below): Dr. Muata Ashby pointing Out Key Section of the Iconography on *Asar(Osiris)/Heru(Horus)* Complex: Central (ASAR/OSIRIS) Projection Room #2-West Wall-showing Goddess *Aset(Isis)* "Sitting on and not "hovering" over the body of *Asar(Osiris)*, Conceiving *Heru(Horus)*. *Asar(Osiris)* is lying on a leonine bed.

Figure 9 (Below): Differences between Temple of Asar Ptah-Zokar Hall Panel #13B and Temple of Asar Projection Room/Heru Conception Room Panel #22A

Figure 10: Middle Kingdom era Ancient Egyptian black granite sculpture of the conception of *Heru(Horus)* found in the area close to the Temple of *Asar(Osiris)* corroborates the scene presented in the Temple of *Asar(Osiris)* Projection room west wall (P. #22B). It depicts *Asar(Osiris)* lying on the leonine bed with *Aset(Isis)* in the form of a Kite sitting on his penis.

42 The late Middle Kingdom representation of Osiris placed in his supposed tomb at Umm el Qa'ab, the royal cemetery of the 1st and 2nd Dynasties. This statue was found in the tomb, and presumably was used for cult purposes well into the Late Period at least. The statue represents the inert Osiris impregnating his consort Isis, who has taken on the form of a kite.

Comparison of the Stone Sculpture to the Temple of *Asar(Osiris)* Projection Room Panel #22B (West Wall) The *Asar(Osiris)* Projection room panels are part of a sequence. *Asar(Osiris)* Projection Room South wall panel is #22A. *Asar(Osiris)* Projection Room West wall is #22B.

EGYPTIAN BOOK OF THE DEAD HIEROGLYPH TRANSLATIONS Volume 6: Featuring The Osirian Resurrection

Figure 11: Images of the Temple of Asar(Osiris) Projection Room West Wall and the Stone Sculpture Conception scenes of Heru(Horus)

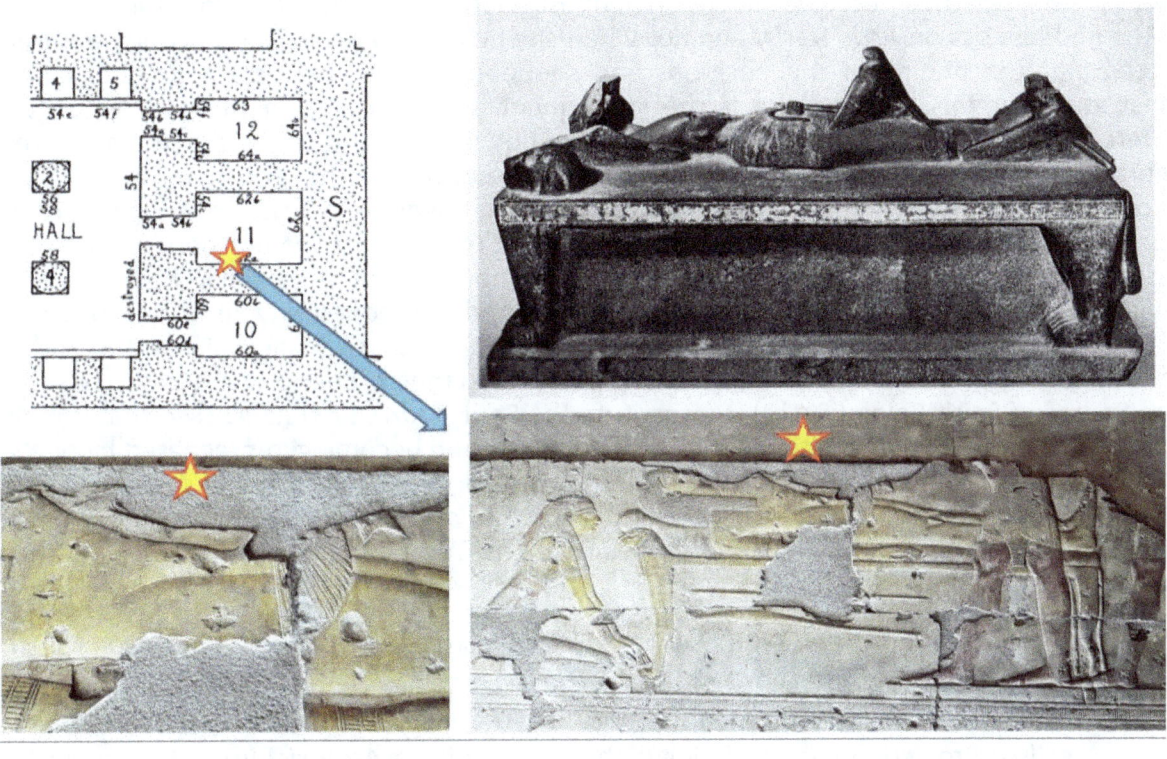

R11 WEST WALL

Conclusion: The images above, from the Temple of *Asar(Osiris)*, along with the previous images from the Temple of *Hetheru(Hathor)*, demonstrate that the conception scene of the god *Heru(Horus)* through the intercourse between goddess *Aset(Isis)* and the god *Asar(Osiris)* occurs when the goddess sits on *Asar(Osiris)* and not when she hovers over him. Those iconographical evidences plus the finding of the positions and sequence between panels #22A and #22B demonstrates that this sitting scene is the subsequent and final step in the conception of *Heru(Horus)*. Another supporting factor for this contention is the architectural directional matrix configuration of the Temple in which the hovering scene occurs further south and the sitting scene occurs further north in the Temple architecture, which signifies that the hovering is part of a preparatory theme while the sitting (conception) is part of a progressive northern movement of spiritual transformation towards enlightenment in the north. At the same time, the panels are informing the Temple initiate about the role of *Aset(Isis)* and the sequence of spiritual processes that must ensue in order to bring forth the desired *Heru(Horus)* consciousness. This informs the reflections and meditations that the aspirant is to pursue and their proper order, namely, to seek out the Source of Spirit Being (IS #12), reconstitute the Soul *Asar(Osiris)* (IS #13) so that it may commune with one's higher intuitional capacity, *Aset(Isis)*, and becoming impregnated by one's reconstituted and animated Soul, (IS #22) and thereby give birth to a fully conscious reality of life, *Heru(Horus)*(IS #23). What is the energy impetus for this process? Though we have already experienced that force, the next section will explore the Temple teaching that answers this question more fully.

Conclusion: Notice that the West (#22B) is where Goddess *Aset(Isis)* copulates with *Asar(Osiris)* and conceives (becomes pregnant with) *Heru(Horus)*, and it is on the other side of that wall where the Aset projection room/chapel is located. Therefore, the adjacent wall connection the *Aset(Isis)* Projection east wall allows the energy of the *Aset(Isis)* Projection room to transfer into the *Asar(Osiris)* Projection room though the Asar Projection west wall.

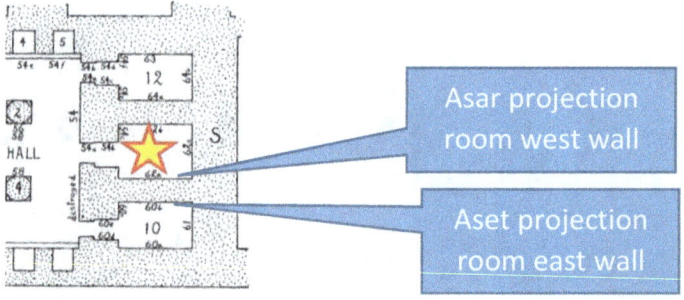

Figure 12 (Below): Temple of Asar-Asar Projection Room (I.S. #22) View: South to North- Architrave Inscription

- Thus, a similar scene from the nearby Temple of Rameses II helps clarify the impression and spiritual intent seen here in the Temple of Asar.

Dr. Ashby Examining the coiled Serpents in the Temple of Asar four columned hall Asar Projection Room

Figure 13: Below-Close-up view of East Architrave Inscription in Asar Projection Room Looking from South to North

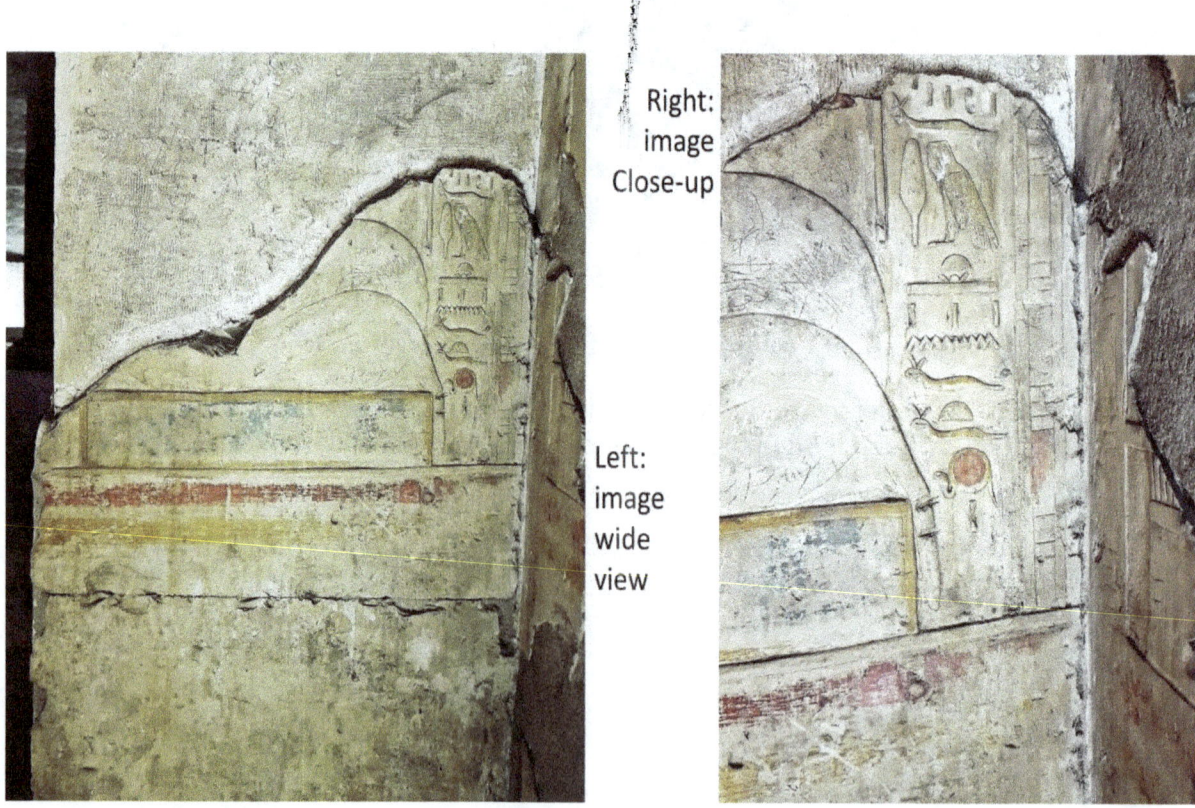

Right: image Close-up

Left: image wide view

EGYPTIAN BOOK OF THE DEAD HIEROGLYPH TRANSLATIONS Volume 6: Featuring The Osirian Resurrection

Temple of Sety 1 / Osiris Projection Room chamber door right side (east) architrave displaying coiled sitting **Cobra** Hieroglyphic text	Transliteration	Word Translation	Contextual Translation
	[damaged] [damaged]	[damaged] [damaged]	[damaged] [damaged]
	F	His	His spiritual grace, of his father, Ra, the Creator Spirit.
	Amtu	Grace	
	{mdj}	{abstract}	[i.e. the serpent power that enlightens a human being (gives birth to Heru consciousness in a human being) is provided by the grace of the Creator Spirit]
	en	of	
	F	his	
	tef	father	
	Ra	Creator Spirit	
			{The successful propitiation that draws the divine grace was performed by Goddess Aset in the episode of the Death of Heru.}

GLOSS:

The inner door architraves are visible from the inside of the room and therefore apply to a person already in the room and looking towards the north and the exit of the room. Based on the remaining text from the Temple of *Asar(Osiris)* Projection room south side architrave, we may intimate that the emergence out of the room, having communed with *Aset(Isis)* and having engendered *Heru(Horus)* and thus under the power of the activated Serpent Power goddesses, that ascendancy or "coming forth" process is under the auspices of the source of life force and the serpent power; that source is Ra, the Creator Spirit.

Figure 14: The God Asar (Osiris) with the two Serpent Goddesses wearing the headdresses of Aset (Isis) and Nebethet (Nephthys) together composing a Caduceus

In view of the evidences so far, we can further understand the following. The two serpents, who are Wadjit and Nekhebet {also Aset and Nebethet}, the goddesses of Upper and Lower Egypt, and of the south and north, respectively, represent the dual nature of the life force that allows manifest time and space to exist cognitively, as one cannot have cognition of time and space {Creation} without duality. Further, passing through the holographic convergence of the two serpents means that the person passing through the doorway is in the center of two facing cobras and as such becomes part of a caduceus that is one of the primary iconographical references to Asar, Aset, and Nebethet. The two Serpent goddesses assist the resurrection of Asar and birth of Heru which is the dynamic movement of the caduceus. This teaching is explained further in other Ancient Egyptian Texts and funerary papyri. The central shaft of the caduceus is at the same time the central axis between the two Asar Rooms of the Asar/Aset/Heru inner shrine complex which the Royal Person traverses and is also the central spine of the caduceus as well as the Djed of Asar. When the Serpent Power is activated, the two serpent goddesses, as if, work in unison to usher the conscience of the Royal Person along the path of higher consciousness-towards the north.

Figure 15: Ancient Egyptian Coffin Lid-The God Asar (Osiris) with the two the Goddesses Aset (Isis) and Nebethet (Nephthys) (all in an anthropomorphic form) together composing a Caduceus

So the birth of *Heru(Horus)* in the *Asar(Osiris)* Projection Room is concomitant with the movement of the Serpent goddesses that allow that birth of higher consciousness to be raised (towards the north) and towards higher realization and seating in the Higher Self.

According to the Temple mystery, the activation of the Serpent Power occurs when the personality of the Royal Person has purified and integrated their feelings about their nature and relation to the Divine, their intellectual understanding of the teachings has been honed, and their perspective of life has focused on the path of the Temple, which is the reconnection with the Divine and the discovery of the higher identity, which is Zokar Asar, manifesting as Heru, above all worldly paths or desires. Anything other than this amounts to living a life of delusion on the basis of identifying with the alternate illusory personality, *Set(Seth)* (the illusory ego).

Image from the 2017 Tour to Kemet/Egypt where the Conception Room was visited.

Stele of Amenmose Part 3

BACK TO STELE OF AMENMOSE-

==

THE TREE OF MYTHIC SCRIPTURES OF THE ASARIAN RESURRECTION MYTH RENDERED IN ANCIENT EGYPTIAN HIEROGLYPHIC TEXT:

30.4.
30.5. shedet nechen im uaau   an rech{mdj} bu F im bastu   su   a F nekhtu   im   khenu
30.6. suckling youth in   solitude not known{fig} place he form initiated him   arm his strength manner interior

30.7. *Aset(Isis)* suckled the child in solitude and in secret, in a place where no one knew that they were. *Aset(Isis)* nurtured him and when sufficient strength developed in his body, then she took him to the interior of…

30.8.
30.9. *ushchet geb*
30.10. hall   Geb

30.11. …the hall of his grandfather, the god Geb.

EGYPTIAN BOOK OF THE DEAD HIEROGLYPH TRANSLATIONS Volume 6: Featuring The Osirian Resurrection

BIRTH OF HORUS AT THE TEMPLE OF ASET(ISIS)

==

THE TREE OF MYTHIC SCRIPTURES OF THE ASARIAN RESURRECTION MYTH RENDERED IN ANCIENT EGYPTIAN HIEROGLYPHIC TEXT:

EGYPTIAN BOOK OF THE DEAD HIEROGLYPH TRANSLATIONS Volume 6: Featuring The Osirian Resurrection

TEMPLE OF ASET (ISIS) IMAGE OF GODDESS ASET GIVING BIRTH

Image above of the Temple of Aset(Isis), Philae, Birth House

Image above of the Birth of *Heru(Horus)* from inside the Temple of Aset(Isis) Birth House
Gods and Goddesses from left to right: Hu, Wadjt, Djehuty, Aset and Heru, Amun, Nekhebet and Saa

Image below: Close-up section of the Birth of Horus from the Temple of Isis

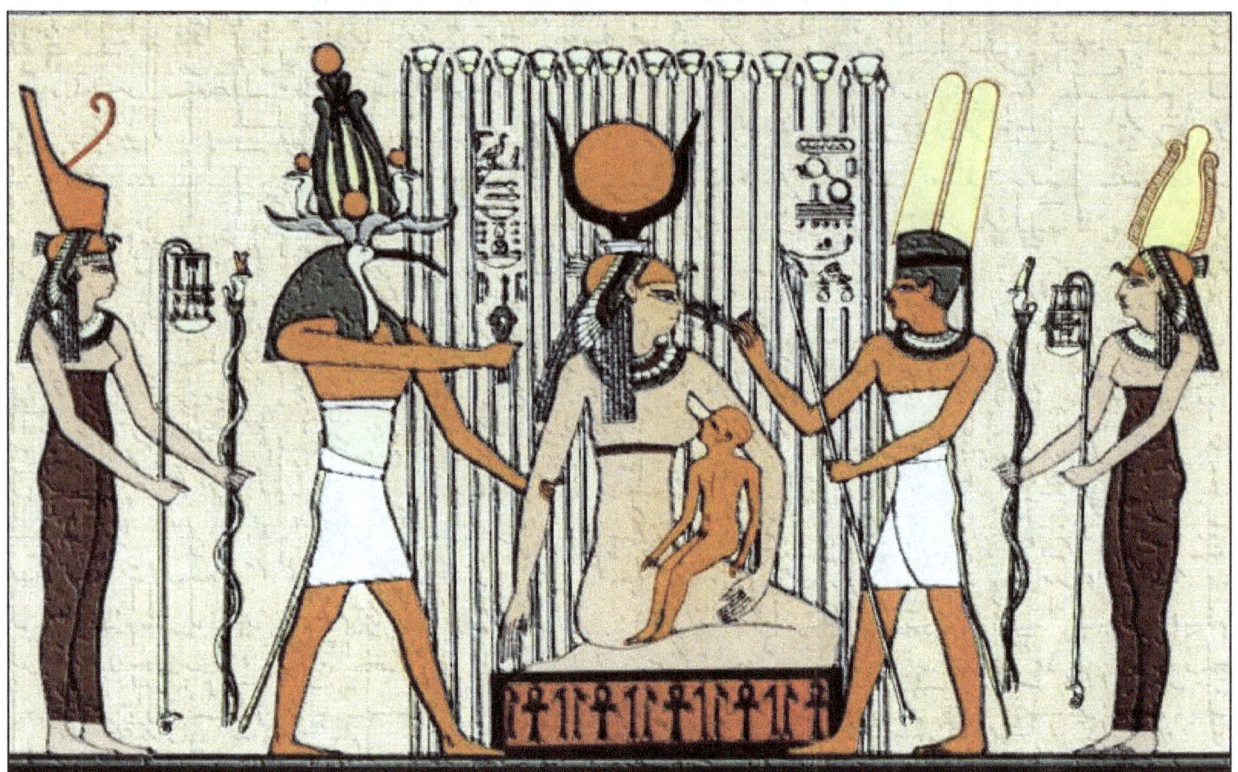

Description of image above:

Goddess *Aset(Isis)* sits in the center of the axis of the room, holding baby *Heru(Horus)* on her lap, who is suckling at her breast. The hieroglyphs in front of each standing divinity identify them. The gods *Djehuty(Thoth)*[left] and Amun (Hidden Witnessing Consciousness) [right] are attending on her, providing life essence. In harmony with the image from the temple of *Asar(Osiris)* Holy of Holies Conception room that presented the two Serpent power goddesses on either side of the room entrance (and exit), the image above from the Temple of *Aset(Isis)* we see, on the left of Djehuty, stands goddess Wadjit, the serpent power of the north. And on the right, behind Amun, stands the goddess Nekhebet, the serpent power goddess of the south. This signifies that the birth of *Heru(Horus)* entails the process of awakening and dynamically evolving the latent energy consciousness that arises from the union of *Aset(Isis)* (intuitional wisdom) with the awareness of Soul nature *Asar(Osiris)*. Djehuty is High Intellect that transcends mind and he holds an artifact called *"Sa"* which he is applying to the goddess and child.

The *Sa* artifact that Djehuty is holding is a special instrument that channels *protective life force energy consciousness* which is necessary for being able to "discover" and "understand" the nature of the Creator Spirit and attain spiritual victory in life, the discovery of Spirit Consciousness, spiritual Enlightenment, or Nehast in Kemetic (Ancient Egyptian). In other words, it is a kind of *Divine Grace* that is extended from the Divine reaching out to humans who are qualified to make the approach to the Divine so as to have their consciousness opened. The Sa often appears with the hieroglyph ANKH or Eternal Life Essence.

Amun brings life, empowered by the *Was scepter* or power-flow, that comes from conscious awareness of Spirit {Life comes from Spirit and not from Matter}. The gods Hu and Saa bring sense perception and understanding to the birthing process. The hieroglyphs below the siting goddess *Aset(Isis)* are:

"Was-Ankh-Was" – "Flow-Life-Flow" – Life process, from Spirit Consciousness, has become dynamic, moving up into the birthing process that gives rise to *Heru(Horus)*, the spiritual aspiration and spiritual redemption of the Soul that has retaken birth as the child. In the same way all human beings have emerged from the same process of Spirit manifesting as each person on earth. However, the "Divine Birth" occurs when the elements (principles represented by each god and goddess) are pure in conscious awareness. This means understanding theirs and one's own nature as proceeding from Spirit, and not from mortal, material existence.

EGYPTIAN BOOK OF THE DEAD HIEROGLYPH TRANSLATIONS Volume 6: Featuring The Osirian Resurrection

THE ESCAPE INTO HIDING-METTERNICHE STELE

===

THE TREE OF MYTHIC SCRIPTURES OF THE ASARIAN RESURRECTION MYTH RENDERED IN ANCIENT EGYPTIAN HIEROGLYPHIC TEXT:

Excerpts from Metternich Stele – Passion of Isis (Sorrows of Isis)

ASET/ISIS IN PRISON-COMES OUT OF PRISON

Verse 1.

1.1.	Nuk	Aset	perku	im	na	ahtper	erta	nu	A
1.2.	I am	Isis	come-forth-for-thee	through	my	prison	given	to	I

1.3. I am the goddess *Aset(Isis),* the goddess of intuitional wisdom that resides at the point between the eyebrows, and I want to let you know that I have come forth for you from the prison given/imposed on to me, by my brother *Set(Seth)*, egoism. This prison was a chamber in the Netherworld (*Pet*), the deep recesses of the mind, where the egoistic aryu (residue of mental imressions in the unconscious mind from actions performed) restricts your capacity to engage in mystical spirituality to benefit from my wisdom. There was so much egoism in the personality, that I was imprisoned, restricted. But now, due to your spiritual efforts to sublimate *Set(Seth)*, your ego, I have been freed, and thus, I will now come to help you further overcome *Set(Seth)*, egoism of…

THE IMPRISONMENT OF ASET

The image above has been provided to give the reader a visual impression of the events and meaning at this stage in the text.

EGYPTIAN BOOK OF THE DEAD HIEROGLYPH TRANSLATIONS Volume 6: Featuring The Osirian Resurrection

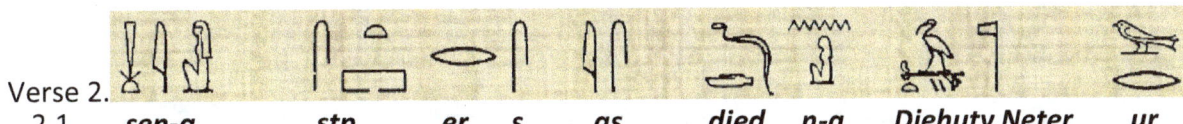

Verse 2.
2.1. **sen-a**   **stp**   **er**   **s**   **as**   **djed**   **n-a**   **Djehuty Neter**   **ur**
2.2. brother mine   Setep (Seth)   about it   Behold   words spoken to-I   Thoth Divinity   Great

2.3. …my brother *Set(Seth)*. Now look here! The following words are being spoken by my uncle, Lord Djehuty, who is a Great God…

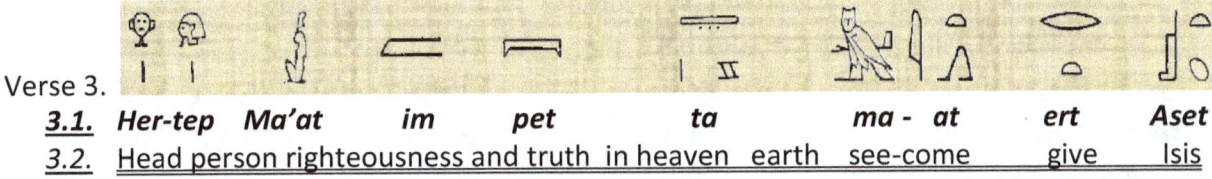

Verse 3.
3.1. **Her-tep**   **Ma'at**   **im**   **pet**   **ta**   **ma - at**   **ert**   **Aset**
3.2. Head person   righteousness and truth   in heaven   earth   see-come   give   Isis

3.3. …the Chief of righteousness and truth, both in heaven and on the earth, the wisdom of the cosmic law of Creation; He said unto me, "Come now, see what I am giving to you *Aset(Isis)*…

Verse 4.
4.1. **netert**   **nefer**   **cher**   **pu**   **sedjm**   **ankh**   **ua**   **seshms**
4.2. goddess   beneficent   under   the   hearkening   living   one   led

4.3. …"It is beneficial to allow oneself to be under the guidance of another, to be humble to the authority of one who is a chief of righteousness and truth and engage in the process of listening to and obeying what they say. There is life, and not death and suffering, for one who allows her/him-self to be led by, guided…

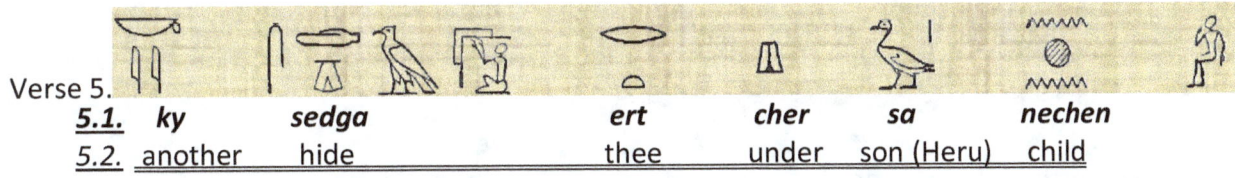

Verse 5.
5.1. **ky**   **sedga**   **ert**   **cher**   **sa**   **nechen**
5.2. another   hide   thee   under   son (Heru)   child

5.3. …by another. Therefore, listen to my instructions; Hide yourself under cover, keep a low profile, along with your son, the child of yours and of *Asar(Osiris)* …

Verse 6.

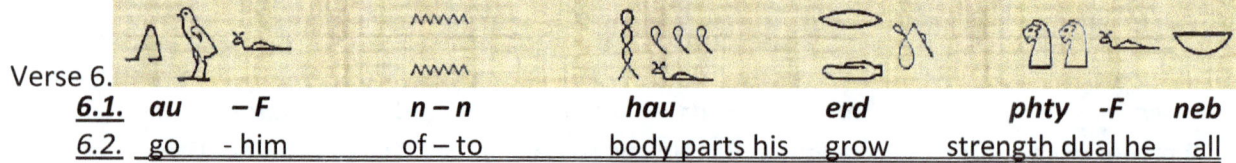

6.1.	au – F	n – n	hau	erd	phty -F neb
6.2.	go - him	of – to	body parts his	grow	strength dual he all

6.3. ...and go with him to live in secret. To his body will happen the following; his arms and legs and organs will grow with two fold strength and his limbs will be sound and healthy.

Verse 7.

7.1.	chep dit Hetep F	her	nest	tef F	netedjnu n-F
7.2.	Creator give peace he	person	throne	father his	redeemer of-he

7.3. Khepera, the Creator god, will give peace to him, *Heru(Horus)*, as he will attain the throne of his father, *Asar(Osiris)*, and thereby he will become the redeemer of his father.

Verse 8.

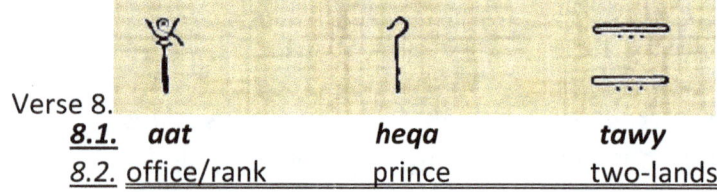

8.1.	aat	heqa	tawy
8.2.	office/rank	prince	two-lands

8.3. This redemption will occur by *Heru's(Horus')* obtaining the office, that is, the throne of his father. He will eventually defeat *Set(Seth)*, and when he does, *Heru(Horus)* will have his father's office and rank that *Set(Seth)* usurped; *Heru(Horus)* will be the sovereign and prince of the two lands of *Kemet(Egypt)*.

Verse 9.

9.1.	perku	her	tert	en
9.2.	came-forth	on	season	of

9.3. The coming forth of *Heru(Horus)*, in victory, will be in the season of ...

Verse 10.
- **10.1.** *mesher*   *pert*   *uhat {sefech}*   *chert*   *hat*   *a*   *maa*   *zen*
- **10.2.** night   coming-forth   scorpions {7}   below   front me   forging they

    10.3. …the nighttime." *Aset(Isis)* says, Seven scorpions are with me now. They are walking down by my feet, in front of me as they are spiritual cosmic forces, divinities that help forge a path for me…

The image above has been provided to give the reader a visual impression of the events and meaning at this stage in the text.

Verse 11.
- **11.1.** *n-a*   *a*   *tefen {uhat}*   *befen {uhat}*   *ha*   *a*   *zep-zen*   *mestet*
- **11.2.** for-I   side   Tefen{scorpion}   Befen {scorpion}   behind me   twofold   Mestet {scorpion}

    11.3. … for me at my side. *Tefen* helps me to discern my path. *Befen* helps me see my path, and they are behind me. In twofold manner, *Mestet* provides me youthful vigor for the journey together with…

EGYPTIAN BOOK OF THE DEAD HIEROGLYPH TRANSLATIONS Volume 6: Featuring The Osirian Resurrection

Verse 12.

12.1. mestetf {uhat} kher henket {per} a petet   tjetet   maatet
12.2. Mestetef.   Under given abode mine Petet breaks open, Tjetet speaks, Maatet vision

12.3. ...Mestetef. Under my abode, which is wherever I reside, also there is *Petet*, who breaks obstacles on my path. *Tjetet* helps with my capacity of speech and *Maatet* affords insight vision for my journey...

Verse 13.

13.1. her djezer n-a   wat   hen   A   en   zen   ur   zep-zen
13.2. upon exalted to-me   path   called   I   to   them   greatly   twice

13.3. ...on the path that I am on so that I may stay on an exalted, noble, elevated and dignified course. I called out to them commandingly, twice...

Verse 14.

14.1. Medu A   sechep   im   ankhui zenu   im   rech   sedjm
14.2. Words mine entered   into   living-ears theirs form wisdom   listen-obey

14.3. ...and my words entered into their ears in the form of living, eternal wisdom that was being imparted to them that is to be listened to and obeyed...

Verse 15.

15.1. ushed   desher   im   saa   sa
15.2. entreaty   wickedness   form of   understanding   son

15.3. ...as a serious entreaty. Otherwise, it is like listening to the entreaty but in the way understood by a son...

EGYPTIAN BOOK OF THE DEAD HIEROGLYPH TRANSLATIONS Volume 6: Featuring The Osirian Resurrection

Verse 16.
16.1.	s-a	er nedjez	her(u) tjenu	im	kher	hera	wat
16.2.	caused-person	related degraded.	Faces theirs	manner	down	face	path/road

16.3. ...of a person, a relation, that is degraded, that is, a child who was reared by a person with degraded morals and culture; a child who did not know about respect for wisdom and not having capacity to pay attention to wisdom and then be able to act on that wisdom. When on the path of life a person should hold their head low, that is, being humble, and also paying attention to the path they are on instead of being boisterous, insolent and disrespecting the wise, being distracted, paying attention to the sights and sounds all around instead of on the path they are on.

Verse 17.
17.1.	Ary	zshem	heh nua	er	peh	nu	persuy
17.2.	Leader theirs	guided-walking me	to	swamps	those	Persuy

17.3. The leader of the scorpion divinities that were around me, protecting and guiding me, led me to the swamp area of our country, an area called *Persuy*, near the beginning of the area containing papyruses.

Episode with the Noble Woman, her child and the fire

Verse 19.

19.1.	pehy-u	deb	sper	n-a	hem-u	ketetu
19.2.	arrive –at	Deb city	went	of-I	women houses	with children

19.3. I arrived at the settlement of *Deb* and there I went to the area where the houses of the women who take care of children are located. I figured that I, a fugitive woman with her child, could hide out in a place with many women and children...

Verse 20.

20.1.	Hai	iu	dega	nua	sheps-S	em	wa
20.2.	impregnated	It is	noticing	of me	exalted-lady	in	path{walking}

20.3. ...and pregnant women. It so happened that a noble woman walking along the road noticed me...

Verse 21.

21.1.	an	nez	unu-s	her-a	men - z	her-ab	n
21.2.	carrying she		doors hers	on – me	anguished - she	person heart	of

21.3. ...with what I was carrying, a young child. She slammed her doors on me, who am the Lady of Intutional Wisdom, when I looked at her and asked her for shelter when I was in a fugitive state, hiding from my brother *Set(Seth)*, egoism, who was now King. She had the mental disease of egoism, from fear of what *Set(Seth)* would do to her, which expressed in her innermost personality, her heart, as anguish and fear, loathing, pride, about my presence and...

Verse 22.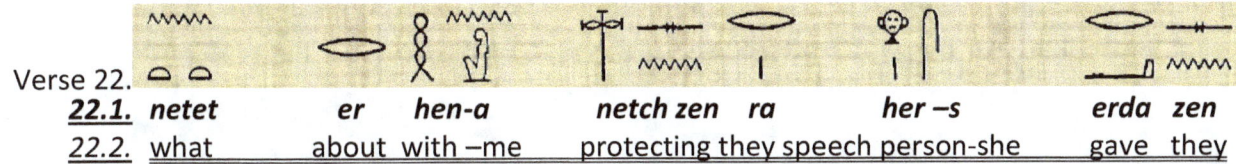
22.1. netet   er   hen-a   netch zen   ra   her –s   erda   zen
22.2. what   about with –me   protecting they speech person-she   gave   they

22.3. …over who was with me, my child, *Heru(Horus)*, he who is the Spiritual Aspiration and Redemption of his father, the true heir, and my seven protective scorpion divinities. Outraged at what had been done to me by this lady of high standing, my scorpion protectors talked about it amongst themselves, concerning this person and her disrespect. They decided to give…

Verse 23.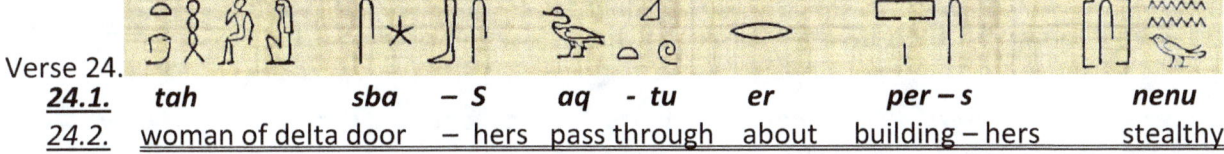
23.1. metut   zenu   en   zep   her dep   sed   n   Tefen   un   na
23.2. poison   theirs   to   time   captain   tail   of   Tefen scorpion open to I

23.3. …their poisons, from each of their seven stingers, all at one time, to their leader and placed it on the tail of *Tefen*. In the meantime, another door was opened to me.

Verse 24.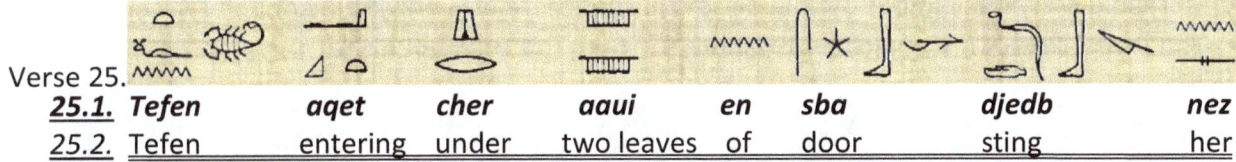
24.1. tah   sba   – S   aq - tu   er   per – s   nenu
24.2. woman of delta door   – hers   pass through   about   building – hers   stealthy

24.3. A common woman, of the Delta region, opened her doors to me and I walked into her home… Stealthily, though…

Verse 25.
25.1. Tefen   aqet   cher   aaui   en   sba   djedb   nez
25.2. Tefen   entering   under   two leaves   of   door   sting   her

25.3. The scorpion captain, *Tefen*, entered the house of the high class lady by crawling under the leaves of the door of her house and then he stung her…

The image above has been provided to give the reader a visual impression of the events and meaning at this stage in the text.

Verse 26.
26.1. sa　　　usert　　　chet　　　pertu　　　zchent　　　per　　　Usert
26.2. child　　　Usert　　　fire　　　came forth　　in　　　house　　Usert

26.3. ...child, the child of lady *Usert, the noble lady that closed her doors to me*. A ruckus developed and a fire started which spread in the house of the lady *Usert*. The fire spread quickly throughout the house so fast that there was only time enough for her to get out of the burning house but she had to leave the child behind.

Verse 27.
27.1. an　un　mu　im　er　achem mu-s　an　　pet　　hy
27.2. not　exist　water　in　to　lack　water-she　not　heaven　fall

27.3. There was no water available in her house; neither was there any help from the heavens in the form of rain...

EGYPTIAN BOOK OF THE DEAD HIEROGLYPH TRANSLATIONS Volume 6: Featuring The Osirian Resurrection

Verse 28.

28.1. mu –Z   im   per   usert   an   tert   aru
28.2. water – she in building Usert not season activity

28.3. …water to fall on her building, the house of lady Usert. At the time that this happened it was not the season of rain activity in that part of the country of *Kemet(Egypt)*.

Verse 29.
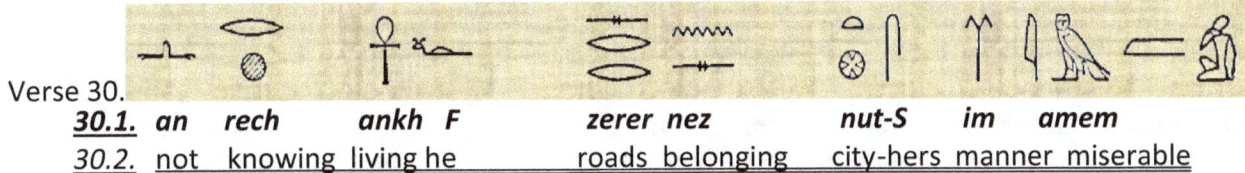
29.1. as   pu   tem -S   un   n-a   ab – s   and   er
29.2. behold that ended-she opening to-me heart-hers misery about

29.3. Look at this circumstance; she brought to a close the possibility of opening her heart to me. Then, as fate had it, she ended up in misery because of…

Verse 30.
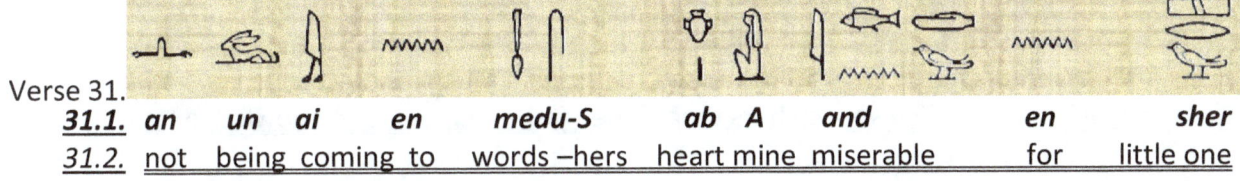
30.1. an   rech   ankh F   zerer nez   nut-S   im   amem
30.2. not knowing living he roads belonging city-hers manner miserable

30.3. …not knowing whether or not her child was still alive! She went throughout the streets of her city in a miserable state, distraught and even hysterical, as you can imagine…

Verse 31.
31.1. an   un   ai   en   medu-S   ab A   and   en   sher
31.2. not being coming to words –hers heart mine miserable for little one

31.3. …as she was not getting help from anyone; nobody came to her aid in answer to her calls for help! Despite her disrespect that she showed towards me, *Aset(Isis)*, the goddess of Intuitional Wisdom, and her unwillingness to open her home and open her heart to me when I called on her for help, I felt compassion, a heartrending feeling over her plight, about what had happened to the little, helpless child…

EGYPTIAN BOOK OF THE DEAD HIEROGLYPH TRANSLATIONS Volume 6: Featuring The Osirian Resurrection

Verse 32.

32.1. Her – S   er   s-ankh   sher   im   bet   - F   nas - A
32.2. of hers   about cause life innocent child in horrendous – he   call   - I

32.3. …of hers. So, I reflected that I would like to restore life to the child, he being innocent and not at fault for the horrendous deed his mother did by rejecting me. I called out…

Verse 33.
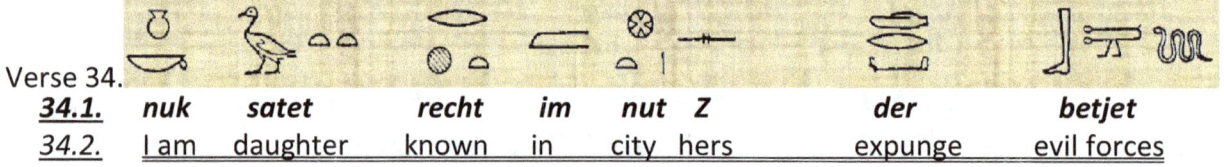
33.1. nez   her   mai   n - a   zep zen   mak   repat A   kher   ankh
33.2. to   her   come   to – me   twice!   Protection   speech mine under   life

33.3. …to her. I said "come to me, come to me! There is protection in coming to me, in opening your heart to me. Underneath my words, below the surface of what is heard audibly, there is life; my words contain a capacity to bring forth life.

Verse 34.

34.1. nuk   satet   recht   im   nut   Z   der   betjet
34.2. I am   daughter   known   in   city   hers   expunge   evil forces

34.3. I, Aset(Isis), am a daughter who is known in her city of origin; one who is known for having the capacity to ward off and expel evil earthly forces…

Verse 35.
35.1. im   tep-ra-s   seba   nua   atef   A   er   rech   nuk
35.2. through commanding speech hers taught me father mine about knowledge I-am

35.3. …by the power of my commanding speech that comes from my sovereign volition. My father, Lord Geb, the sovereign of the earth plane, taught me about such things.

Verse 36.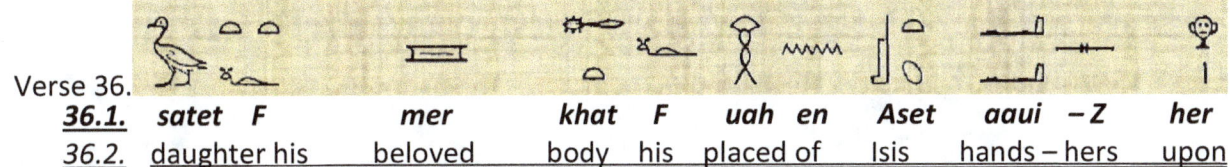

36.1.	satet	F	mer	khat	F	uah en	Aset	aaui – Z	her
36.2.	daughter	his	beloved	body	his	placed of	Isis	hands – hers	upon

36.3. I, *Aset(Isis)*, am his beloved daughter, who originated from his very body." *Aset(Isis)* then positioned her hands upon…

Verse 37.

37.1.	nekhen	er	s-ankh	netet	im	ga	ahet
37.2.	child	so as to	cause-life	what	in	constriction	throat

37.3. …the child for the purpose of causing life to return and cure the constriction on his throat, from the sting, that was preventing him from breathing, that was suffocating him to death. The throat relates to the trachea, which along with the two lungs, is the symbol of *Sema,* which represents the union of the two lands, and metaphorically, the union of the higher and lower self, and Enlightenment. If the throat is constricted, not only can the child not breathe, but metaphysically, the child (spiritual aspirant human) can't redeem its own Higher Self, the Soul essence, *Asar(Osiris)*.

Verse 38.

38.1.	mit	tefent	maat	per	her	ta
38.2.	poison	Tefen	come	forth	on	earth

38.3. "Oh, poison of scorpion *Tefen,* come forth out of the body of the child and fall on the ground.

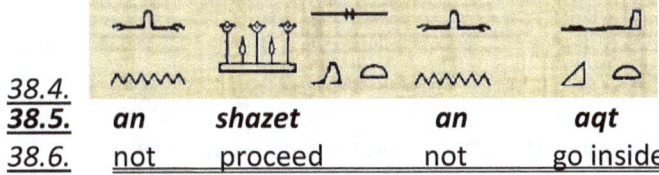

38.4.				
38.5.	an	shazet	an	aqt
38.6.	not	proceed	not	go inside

38.7. Do not proceed to cause damage, disease and death; do not go deeper into the body of the child any further."

SECTION EXPLAINS HOW ASET(ISIS) OBTAINED KNOWLEDGE FROM GEB

RUBRIC BEGINS

Verse 45.
- **45.1.** Aset   netert   urt   hekau   khent   neteru
- 45.2. Isis   goddess   great   words-power   foremost   gods/goddesses
- 45.3. *Aset(Isis)*, the Great Goddess, mistress of Words of Power, is the foremost of the gods and goddesses.

Verse 46.
- **46.1.** erta   n-Z   geb   khu   F   er   khesef   mit   im
- 46.2. given   to-her   Geb   powers   his   regarding   repulsing   poison   through
- 46.3. Geb, the earth god and presiding divinity over all earthly objects and creatures and people, who is the father of *Aset(Isis)*, gave her the powers regarding the repulsing of poisons, the power over that which is physical, which restricts the spiritual human being by promoting egoism and ignorance of True, Higher-Self. He gave her the powers which are in …

Verse 47.
- **47.1.** sekhem   S   khesef   chet   hem   hat   mit
- 47.2. Vital body   hers   repulsing   get-behind   retreat   go back   poison
- 47.3. …her vital body, her life-force astral-energy body. That power has the capacity to repulse and cause the poisons of toxic association with earth, time and space, such as egoism, the source of anger, hatred, greed, envy, etc. to get back instead of being foremost, to take a back seat, that is, be reduced in potency and reduced capacity to cause harm, and thus sublimated.

EGYPTIAN BOOK OF THE DEAD HIEROGLYPH TRANSLATIONS Volume 6: Featuring The Osirian Resurrection

ASET(ISIS) OBTAINS KNOWLEDGE FROM GEB
The image above has been provided to give the reader a visual impression of the events and meaning at this stage in the text.

Verse 49.

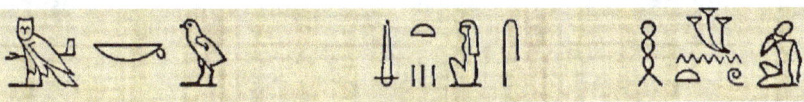

49.1.   *maku*   *medtu {hem} S*   *hentu*
<u>49.2.</u>   protections   words/speech {woman} she   commanding/equipped

<u>49.3.</u>   We must understand clearly that *Aset's(Isis')* speech capacity has special protective qualities against ignorance of one's True Self, and egoism. Her speech has commanding power as it is provisioned with the knowledge afforded by her father Geb. That power is the knowledge about earthly matters including about earthly-based poisons of ignorance and egoism and how to cure them. This power afforded by her knowledge and wisdom manifests and projects through her speech-capacity, which is the final act in the process of understanding, right thinking, right feeling and right intention. Thus, her wisdom power manifests in the world through wisdom speaking and those who speak wisdom, such as authentic Sages, are manifesting the *Aset(Isis)* speech-capacity. Now let us listen to her wisdom reflections:

RUBRIC ENDS

THE GODDESS' REFLECTIONS WITH YOU, THE SPIRITUAL ASPIRANT

Verse 50.
50.1. Medtu   A   en   tenu   tua   im   ua
50.2. Speech mine (Isis) to you   I am   form   alone

50.3. "I *Aset(Isis)* say this to you: Consider my situation; I am all alone, being that my dear lord, Asar (Osiris), has been taken from me.

Verse 51.
51.1. im   zeshen   ur   en   nu   em-chet   septu
51.2. in   grieving   great   of   you-all   dwellers   nomes

51.3. I am in a state of mourning that is greater than all the people of all the districts of *Kemet(Egypt)*, put together!

Verse 52.
52.1. im   nek   kamu   shed   gem   nen
52.2. in   sexuality   finished   seeking   find   observe

52.3. I am in a state as a person who is finished with sexual interests and the seeking to find, and watching…

Verse 53.
53.1. er   shepsetu   im   peru   zen   her   ten   im   kher
53.2. as to   admirable women   in   houses   theirs   her person   yours   in form   downwards

53.3. … and being concerned about noble good-looking women in their houses. My experiences in life have developed in me a state in which I am beyond passions of the flesh, unmoved by worldly desires. One's personality should rather be in the disposition of downward facing;…

EGYPTIAN BOOK OF THE DEAD HIEROGLYPH TRANSLATIONS Volume 6: Featuring The Osirian Resurrection

Verse 54.
54.1. her   a   wat   er   pehenu   er   amunu   im   chebt
54.2. faces facing path as to swamps   as to   hidden   in   chebet-region

54.3. …in other words, instead of looking all around your face should be humble, looking downwards, focusing on the path you are treading so that you may be able to discern the hidden paths in the swampy land of Chebet, that is to say, life on earth."

Verse 55.
55.1. A   ankh   nekhen   mit   metut   ankh   Ra   mit
55.2. Hey!   life   child   death   poison   live   Ra   death

55.3. I say: "life will return to the child and the poison will die! Just as, in an earlier time I performed the same utterance for Ra and life returned to Ra and there was death to…

Verse 56.
56.1. mit   ka   senab   Heru   en   mut   Aset
56.2. poison concomitantly healthy   Horus   of   mother   Isis

56.3. …the poison: in the same way, may there be health for *Heru(Horus)* the son of his mother, *Aset(Isis)*.

Verse 57.
57.1. ka   senab   enty   kher   medes   mit
57.2. concomitantly health   anyone   under   knife   likewise

57.3. Again, concomitantly, may there be health for whosoever is under the knife or the heat that burns the house of the body (fevers, physical or mental illness) or the house of the soul (spiritual illness, egoism, ignorance of True Self). In this case, it is awareness of a realized truth that she had previously achieved in her past relations with Ra [[arrangement with *Ra* in the scripture of *Isis* and *Ra*]][7]

REFLECTIONS END

---

[7] See book Mysteries of Isis and Ra by Dr. Muata Ashby

NEW RUBRIC BEGINS

Verse 58.

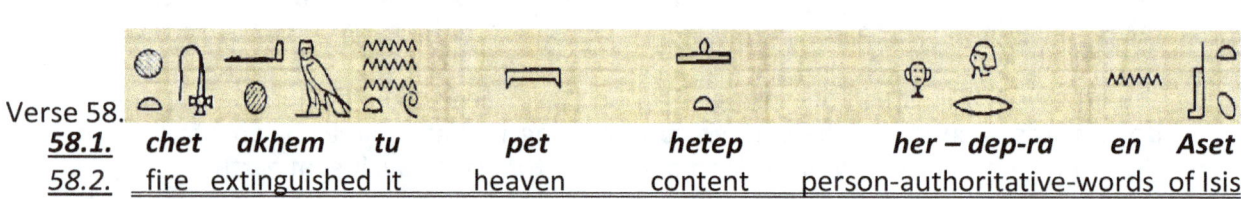

58.1. chet   akhem   tu   pet   hetep   her – dep-ra   en   Aset
58.2. fire extinguished it   heaven   content   person-authoritative-words of Isis

58.3. The fire that has engulfed the house of the privileged and anguished woman and the fire of the poison in the body of her child was put out with water provided from the heavens. Heaven, the abode of the higher gods and goddesses, the cosmic forces of Creation invoked by *Aset(Isis)*, is thus content with the outcome and thus afforded their grace on the mother and her child; it was pleased with the compassion and commanding words that were spoken by *Aset(Isis)*…

Verse 59.

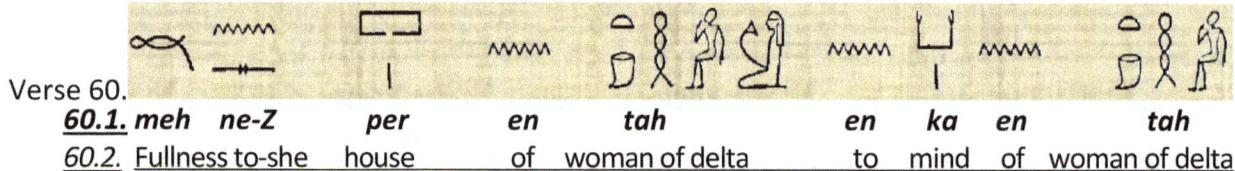

59.1. Netert   Usert   it   an   Z   n-A   chet - Z
59.2. Goddess   Usert   came carrying she to-me fire - she

59.3. … the Goddess. About lady Usert, the privileged and haughty but anguished conflicted woman who rejected me and whose house was on fire and burnt down, she came to me with her fire of her burdens, sorrows and pain.

Verse 60.

60.1. meh ne-Z   per   en   tah   en   ka   en   tah
60.2. Fullness to-she house of woman of delta to mind of woman of delta

60.3. Fullness was in the house of the common woman of the delta region. She had fullness from want in her mind, and freedom from agitation, from worries and anxieties were hers as well; hers was the fullness like that of a bowl of water that is full of water to the very top…

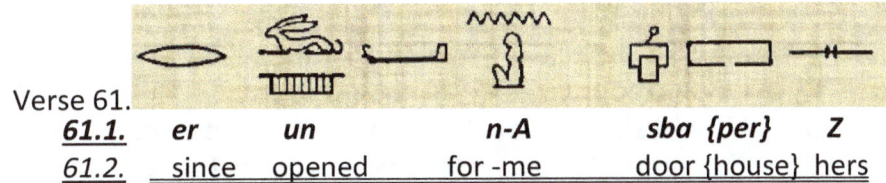

Verse 61.
61.1. er un n-A sba {per} Z
61.2. since opened for -me door {house} hers

61.3. … because she opened the doors to her house to me and thereby received all my blessings and also peace of mind which afforded her capacity to partake in my Divine Consciousness.

RUBRIC ENDS

HORUS IS BITTEN BY A SCORPION AND DIES

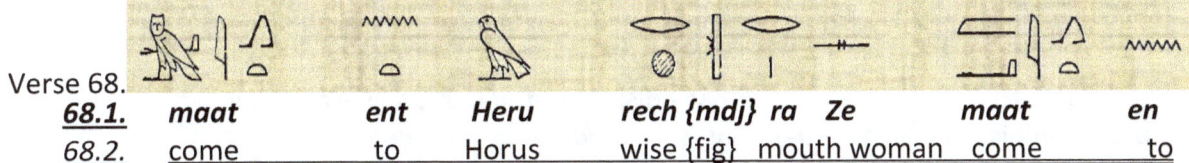

Verse 68.
68.1. maat ent Heru rech {mdj} ra Ze maat en
68.2. come to Horus wise {fig} mouth woman come to

68.3. Come here to *Heru(Horus)*, quickly, quickly, you who are the woman who is wise in words of power; come to…

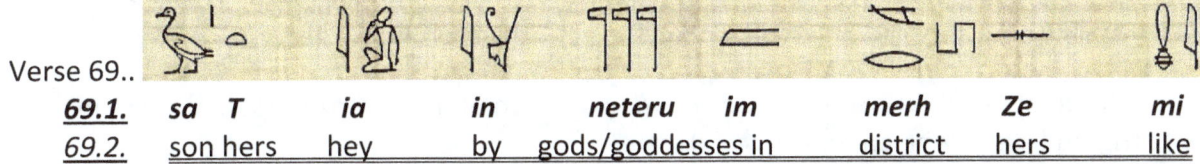

Verse 69..
69.1. sa T ia in neteru im merh Ze mi
69.2. son hers hey by gods/goddesses in district hers like

69.3. …the son of that woman. This call goes out from the local gods and goddesses of the locality. He is in a condition as…

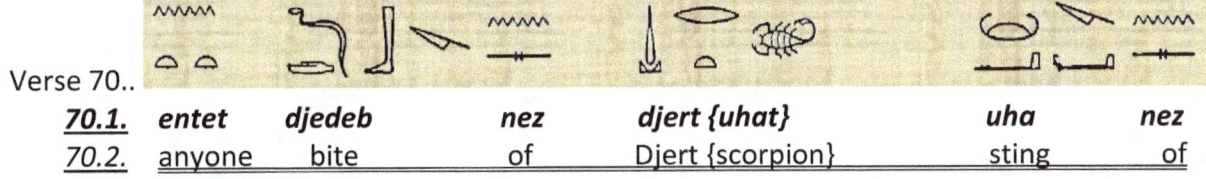

Verse 70..
70.1. entet djedeb nez djert {uhat} uha nez
70.2. anyone bite of Djert {scorpion} sting of

70.3. …any person who has been bitten by a scorpion. This is a sting of a…

Verse 71.

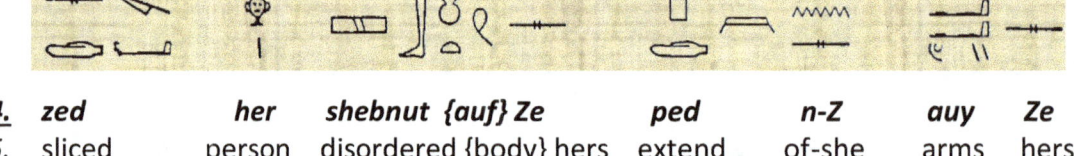

71.1. Uhat   zan   nez   antesh   per   Aset   im
71.2. scorpion cause-repulse of   creature-fetters comes-forth   Isis   as

71.3. ...scorpion. Cause it to be repulsed; cause the sting of that scorpion, which has the effect of fettering the body, binding the body's processes of life by separating the physiological functions of the body from each other and thereby causing death. Hearing those calls, *Aset(Isis)* came forward to the scene and she was in a condition as...

71.4. zed   her   shebnut {auf} Ze   ped   n-Z   auy   Ze
71.5. sliced   person   disordered {body} hers   extend   of-she   arms   hers

71.6. ...cut up into pieces, as an emotionally disintegrated person, like a person whose body is in disarray (in disorder). She extended her arms wide...

Verse 72.

72.1. mak   A   zep-zen   sa   A   Heru   im   zend   zep-zen
72.2. protect   I   twice   son   mine   Horus   in   fear   twice

72.3. ...to protect her child. "Son of mine *Heru(Horus)*, Son of mine *Heru(Horus)*, who are in a frightful state, who are in a frightful state.

EGYPTIAN BOOK OF THE DEAD HIEROGLYPH TRANSLATIONS Volume 6: Featuring The Osirian Resurrection

The image above has been provided to give the reader a visual impression of the events and meaning at this stage in the text.

Verse 73.
- **73.1.** sa   akhut   A   an   kheper   chet   neb   du   er-k
- **73.2.** son   spirit   mine   not   create   thing   any   untoward   about-thee

73.3. You *Heru(Horus)* are my son of my very Shining Spirit. No, absolutely there cannot be any untoward thing that can be allowed to happen to you! There can be no created thing that can harm you.

Verse 74.
- **74.1.** may   im   k   en   ary   unentu   ennt-k   sa
- **74.2.** water   in   thee   of   action   to-be   of-thee   son

74.3. The divine seed (water, generative life force energy) within you will be destined for actions that will come to pass through your life and struggles, oh my son…

EGYPTIAN BOOK OF THE DEAD HIEROGLYPH TRANSLATIONS Volume 6: Featuring The Osirian Resurrection

Verse 75.

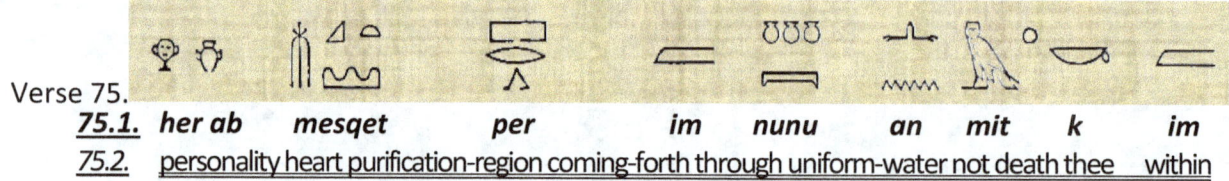

75.1. her ab   mesqet   per   im   nunu   an   mit   k   im
75.2. personality heart purification-region coming-forth through uniform-water not death thee within

75.3. ...who are from the innermost part of the purification region in heaven, from where purified personalities come into existence on earth, having proceeded from the undifferentiated primeval waters of Creation, beyond the ignorance and vicissitudes of ego and the vicissitudes of egoism. This means that you are from a region beyond death; So, no! Absolutely not, for these reasons there can be no death within you!

Verse 76..

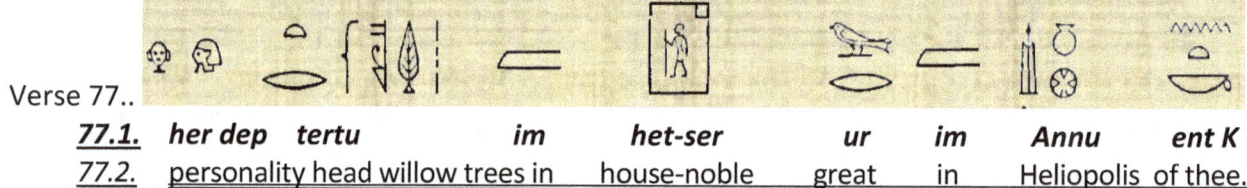

76.1. ta   na   mit   ent k   bennu   aah   mes
76.2. fire   that   poison   to thee   phoenix   great   born

76.3. The fire of that poison, is from a lower source and you are from a higher source; therefore, the fire being given to you is to one who is the great Phoenix, born of...

Verse 77..

77.1. her dep   tertu   im   het-ser   ur   im   Annu   ent K
77.2. personality head willow trees in   house-noble   great   in   Heliopolis of thee.

77.3. ...that personality who is the head, the chief, among the willow trees, *Asar(Osiris)*, in the house of the great noble elder who presides over the holy solar city of Heliopolis/Anu: the god *Ra, the Creator Spirit*, the source and sustainer of Creation. Of you ...

EGYPTIAN BOOK OF THE DEAD HIEROGLYPH TRANSLATIONS Volume 6: Featuring The Osirian Resurrection

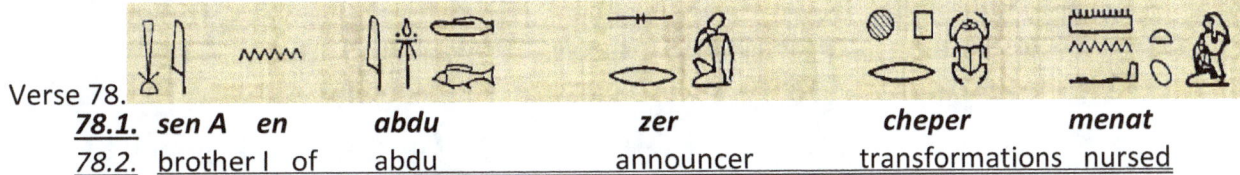

Verse 78.
78.1. sen A   en   abdu   zer   cheper   menat
78.2. brother I   of   abdu   announcer   transformations   nursed

78.3. ...we know that you *Heru(Horus)* are the brother of the Abdu fish, who guides the boat of that same noble of Heliopolis/Anu (the god Ra, the Creator Spirit, the source and sustainer of Creation), the same fish that announces the changes that are occurring as the boat of life engages the journey of life through seasons, weather and time changes. How can you be injured? How can you, who have this lineage and this guidance be harmed? You were nursed by...

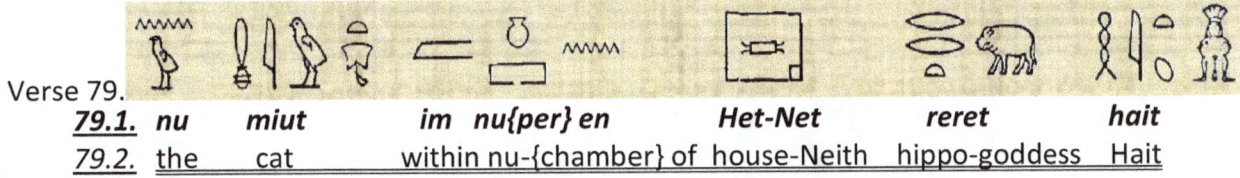

Verse 79.
79.1. nu   miut   im nu{per} en   Het-Net   reret   hait
79.2. the   cat   within nu-{chamber} of   house-Neith   hippo-goddess   Hait

79.3. ...the cat goddess, (*Bastet*), the wielder of feline force to vanquish snakes and scorpions, which represent inimical forces of spiritual evolution like anger, hate, greed, mental dullness, agitation, attachment, and other expressions of egoism that threaten spiritual aspiration. She is within the private inner chamber of the Temple of goddess Net/*Neith*, my mother and your grandmother, the great goddess of Creation who manifests as the hippopotamus goddess *Reret*, the fiery protector against those who are iniquitous and unrighteous. Also, you have been nursed by *Hait*, the goddess aspect of the god *Bes*, who comes from the southern pigmy peoples and who is an aspect of you, *Heru(Horus)*, ...

EGYPTIAN BOOK OF THE DEAD HIEROGLYPH TRANSLATIONS Volume 6: Featuring The Osirian Resurrection

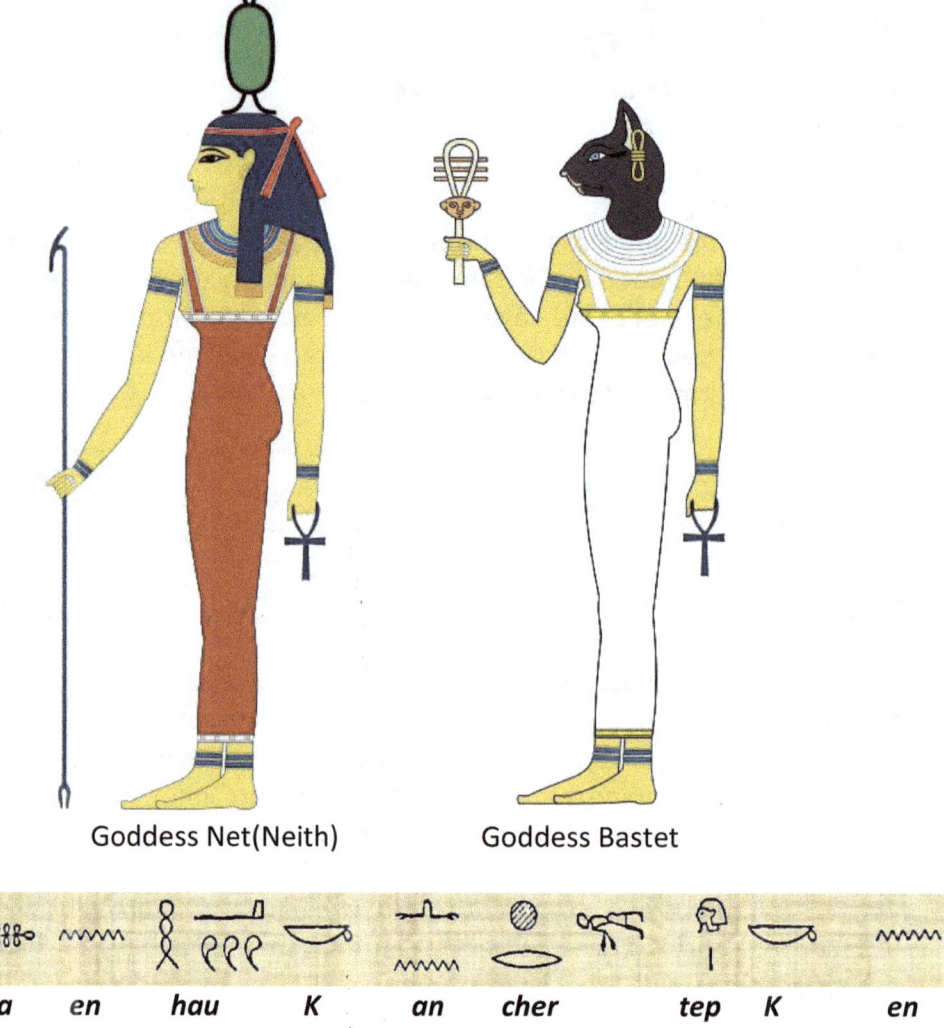

Goddess Net(Neith)   Goddess Bastet

Verse 80.
- 80.1. **im   sa   en   hau   K   an   cher   tep   K   en**
- 80.2. through protection of body-parts thine   not   fall   head thine   to

- 80.3. ...and through their protection of your body parts, your head shall not lose strength and tone and slump down to the ground.

EGYPTIAN BOOK OF THE DEAD HIEROGLYPH TRANSLATIONS Volume 6: Featuring The Osirian Resurrection

Verse 81.
81.1. udjat {mit}   im   K   an   seshep   hau   K   tay
81.2. enemy{death} within   thee   not   receive   body-parts thine burning.

81.3. The enemy, death, that is within you through the poison will not get to the inner body parts, your tissues, muscles, nerves etc., in order to burn them, damage and destroy their capacity to sustain life...

Verse 82.
82.1. en   mitu   K   an   hen   K   her   ta   an
82.2. of   poison   thine not   falter   thy   personality ground   not

82.3. ... by spreading the poison in you. Your personality will not falter and fall to the ground. No...

Verse 83.
83.1. khaz   K   her   mu   an   sekhem   ra   neb
83.2. feebleness thy   person water   not   power   reptile   any

83.3. ...shakiness, fragility, weakness will afflict your personality's water, its life essence and engendering capacity. There will be no effectiveness of the power of any reptile's...

Verse 84.
84.1. pezeh   im   K   an   rehen   may   neb
84.2. bite   in   thee   not   lean   lion   any

84.3. ...bite that may get into your body. No lion, including the lion-headed serpent from the fiend Apophis can lean on you,...

Verse 85..

85.1.	sekhemt	im	K	ent-K	sa	Neter	djesert
85.2.	power	in	thee	to –thee	son	Divine	sacred

85.3. ...can have power within you. For, you are the son of the sacred Divinity. Therefore, you are sanctified consecrated, blessed and protected.

Verse 86.

86.1.	per	im	Geb	ent-K	Heru	an	sekhem
86.2.	come-forth	through	Earth-God	to-thee	Horus	not	power

86.3. You proceed from, you are descended from the god *Geb*, my father, in a line that comes down through me to you in your name of *Heru* (*Horus*). No, there cannot be any way that there can be power...

Verse 87.

87.1.	mit	im	hau	K	ent-K	Geb	neter	djeser
87.2.	poison	in	body-parts	thine	to-thee	Earth-God	Divinity	sacred

87.3. ...of a poison in your body parts; for, you are from the earth god *Geb* and he is a sacred, holy, hallowed divine entity presiding over the earth and its creatures.

Verse 88..

88.1.	per	im	Geb	pa	entet	cher	dem	mit
88.2.	come-forth	through	Earth-God	that	exist	under	bite-cut	likewise.

88.3. You proceed from the lineage of *Geb,* my father, the god of the earth who presides over all animals including scorpions. Furthermore, any person who exists, and who is likewise injured by a bite that has cut into their body, any authentic Shemsu *Heru(Horus)*, follower of *Heru(Horus)*, who is afflicted with the poison of the inimical forces of egoism on the mind and body, having realized your lineage as their own, will be protected likewise. So, nothing on earth can hurt you, for, all proceeds from the earth, which you are a part of.

EGYPTIAN BOOK OF THE DEAD HIEROGLYPH TRANSLATIONS Volume 6: Featuring The Osirian Resurrection

Verse 89.

89.1.	*iu*	*fedu*	*shepsetu*	*im*	*sa*	*en*	*hau*	*K*
89.2.	it is	four	noble (goddesses)	form	protection	of	body-parts	thine

<u>89.3.</u>   Additionally, it is four, the number of those excellent, exalted, noble goddesses, including myself, *Aset(Isis),* Intuitional Wisdom, along with *Nebthet,* Physical Existence, *Net/Neith (Creatress Divinity), and Serqet* (scorpion goddess of protection and action), who perform the task of protecting your body parts, your limbs, head, torso, abdomen, etc. So how is it possible for you, my beloved son, to be harmed?

The Four Protective Goddesses Aset(Isis), Net(Neith), Serqet, Nebethet(Nephthys)
[left-Canopic shrine of Tutankhamun]

Above: the same goddesses protecting a sarcophagus from its four corners.

RUBRIC: ASET REFLECTS ON THE SITUATION AND HOW IT OCCURRED

Verse 90.

90.1.	nuk	Aset	aurti	im	tja	Se	baka tj	im	Heru
90.2.	I am	Isis	conceived	as	male-child	hers	pregnant she	with	Horus

90.3. "My name is *Aset (Isis)* and I conceived a male child; I was pregnant with a male child within my belly whose name is *Heru (Horus)*.

Verse 91.

91.1.	Netert	mes n-A	Heru	sa	Asar	im-khenu{per} sesh	en
91.2.	Goddess	birth of-me	Horus	son	Osiris	in-inner chamber nest	of

91.3. I am the Goddess who gave birth to *Heru (Horus)* who is also the son of *Asar (Osiris)*. This birth occurred in the interior part of a marshland of...

Verse 92.

92.1.	ha	haa	n-a	her Ze	ur	zep zen	her	maa n-A
92.2.	papyrus	rejoicing	of-I	person she	greatly	doubly	her person	seeing of-I

92.3. ...of papyrus. I rejoiced immensely, over and over, when I saw that personality, that male newborn child, come into time and space manifestation on the earth plane...

Verse 93.

93.1.	usheb	her	tef	amun Se	su	zedeg se su
93.2.	answer	her person	tef father	hide I	he	conceal I he

93.3. ...who would answer for the crimes that were done to *Asar* (Osiris) by *Set(Seth)*; someone who would respond to and seek justice to correct the injustice and stand up for and redeem his father, *Asar* (Osiris). So I hid *Heru (Horus)* in that papyrus marsh; I concealed him. Baby *Heru(Horus)* represents newly born Spiritual Aspiration that is defenseless and must be protected and kept safe and hidden from outside egoistic forces that can harm it-while it is young, and I *Aset(Isis)* as the goddess of Wisdom, do this task.

EGYPTIAN BOOK OF THE DEAD HIEROGLYPH TRANSLATIONS Volume 6: Featuring The Osirian Resurrection

Verse 94.
94.1. kher   send   antep   F   shema   A   im   {nut}   toau
94.2. under fear concealed he stranger I through{city} entreaties

94.3. I was anxious and fearful because as I had reached the city I was not familiar with the area and was seen as a stranger by most of the people there as I went about humbly and earnestly asking people for help…

Verse 95.
95.1. im   aped   arit Ka   ursh   A   her heh   nekhen
95.2. through geese beef action   watcher I   person seek   solar-child

95.3. …in the form of geese and beef, the *Hetep/Hotep* offering of non-duality. Also, I spent time keeping watch, as an observer, aware of my plight, the fate of my beloved *Asar (Osiris)*, the welfare of the child *Heru (Horus)*. Once I went out in search of sustenance, for the sake of the child, who is descendant of the solar legacy…

Verse 96.
96.1. her ari   kher   F   anen ent   er   hept   Heru   gem   en
96.2. person make under he   return to   about   embrace   Horus   found   of

96.3. Placing his tender body low, below the tops of the marsh, not showing him off or exposing him openly, so as to keep him concealed, I went out to the city to find provisions to take care of him. When I returned and went to embrace *Heru (Horus)* I looked to find the whereabouts of…

EGYPTIAN BOOK OF THE DEAD HIEROGLYPH TRANSLATIONS Volume 6: Featuring The Osirian Resurrection

Verse 97.
97.1. su   Heru   nefer   en   nub   nekhen   sug
97.2. him   Horus   beautiful/good   of   gold   solar-child   suckling-babe

97.3. …him, my beautiful and good *Heru (Horus)*, my golden solar-child, my tender, helpless suckling baby…

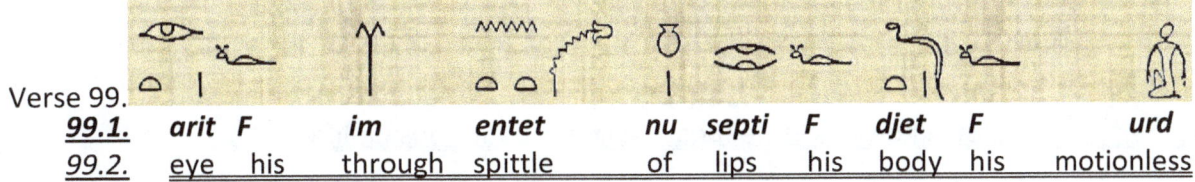

Verse 98.
98.1. antet F   ent-F mu   n-F   taiu   im   mu   nu
98.2. nothing him   of –his water of-his   ground   through   water   of

98.3. …but nothing came from him, no signs of life! The ground around his body was moistened; it had come from his body; it was liquid from…

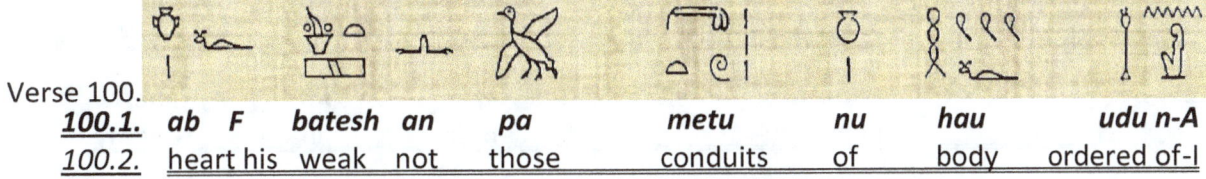

Verse 99.
99.1. arit F   im   entet   nu   septi   F   djet   F   urd
99.2. eye   his   through   spittle   of   lips   his   body   his   motionless

99.3. …his eyes and through the spittle that had leaked out from his little mouth, as his body lay slumped-over and completely motionless!

Verse 100.
100.1. ab F   batesh   an   pa   metu   nu   hau   udu n-A
100.2. heart his   weak   not   those   conduits   of   body   ordered of-I

100.3. His heart was weak, he was helpless and moribund! Those circulatory, digestive, urinary channels of the physical body and other subtle conduits of the astral body, whereby the life processes of the body move through and operate, were not functioning in his body. So I sent out an order.

EGYPTIAN BOOK OF THE DEAD HIEROGLYPH TRANSLATIONS Volume 6: Featuring The Osirian Resurrection

Verse 101.
101.1. ta   her   imu   adeh   rer   zen   n-A
101.2. cried-out persons   within   marshland-papyrus   turned they to-me

101.3. I cried out for help from anyone around, anyone who was in the marshland where we were hiding; they turned away from what they were doing and came to me…

Verse 102.
102.1. her a   iu   en   A   tahu   im   per   zenu
102.2. immediately   came   to   me   marshland-dwellers   in   houses theirs

102.3. …right away; they came to me from their homes in the marshland.

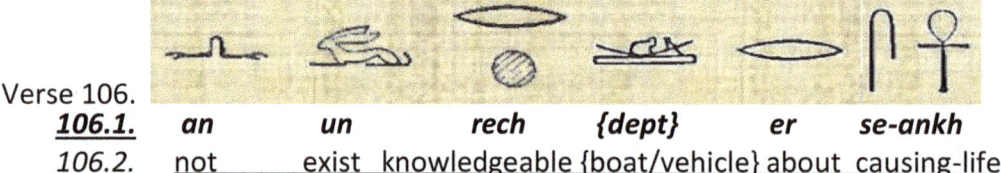

Verse 106.
106.1. an   un   rech   {dept}   er   se-ankh
106.2. not   exist   knowledgeable {boat/vehicle} about causing-life

106.3. However, there did not exist anyone among them who had actionable knowledge of or a means by which life could be caused to be restored.

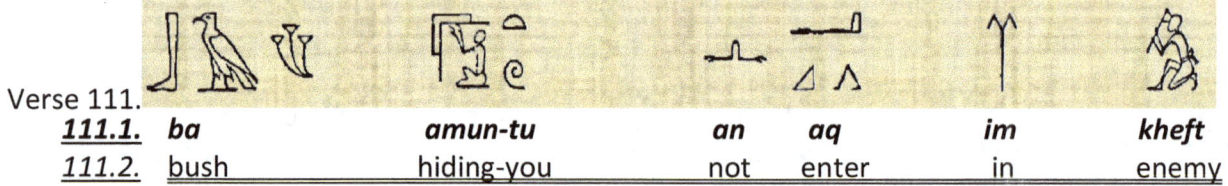

Verse 111.
111.1. ba   amun-tu   an   aq   im   kheft
111.2. bush   hiding-you   not   enter   in   enemy

111.3. In those papyrus bushes, where I hid *Heru (Horus)*, no enemy was supposed to be able to enter into there.

Verse 112.
112.1. er-ze   heka   en   Tem   tef   neteru
112.2. as to-it   words-power   of   Tem   father   gods/goddesses

112.3. That was because *Tem*, the father of the Gods and Goddesses and Maker of Creation, had blessed us with words of power, an energetic mental creative decree, which would act as an aura of protection around the area where we were located.

Verse 113.
113.1. enty   im   pet   im   ari   ankht   an   aq
113.2. of   in   heaven   through   making   life   not   enter

113.3. From there in the heaven, through his power of creating life, the protective aura did work and there was no entry…

Verse 114.
114.1. setep   er   uu   pen   an   rere   n-F   cheb
114.2. Seth   about   district   that   not   go-around of-he   papyrus-marshes

114.3. …for the god *Set (Seth)*, who was our enemy then, who had killed *Asar (Osiris)*, who had imprisoned me, and caused us to go into hiding. *Set (Seth)* was not able to go around freely throughout the area where we were in the papyrus marshes."

RUBRIC

Verse 115.

115.1.	**Heru**	**baq**	**er**	**khest**	**en**	**sena F**	**an**	**dechn**	**Se**
115.2.	Horus	fragrance	as to	foreigner	of	brother he	not	hid	she

115.3. However, despite *Aset's (Isis')* efforts to protect *Heru (Horus)* there was a vulnerability. The scent of the fragrance of *Heru (Horus)* caught the attention of his (Asar's/Osiris') brother (*Set(Seth)/Seth*), who was still a foreigner to their location. So at a distance, *Set (Seth)* sensed their whereabouts even though he himself could not go into their specific area because of the protective boon of the divine grace of *Tem* in the form of his protective words of power invocation. Additionally, there was another issue, namely that she (*Aset/Isis*) had not similarly asked to hide...

Verse 116.

116.1.	**Imu**	**shemsu**	**F**	**heh**	**zepzen**	**ra**	**enen**
116.2.	within	following	he	go-to	time {twice}	day	rushes

116.3. ...those within the following of *Heru (Horus)*, who were his servants, his worshipers, taking care of him while *Aset (Isis)* was away looking for food. They came to the papyrus rushes (grasses) twice daily and apparently they were followed; not by *Set (Seth)* but by something else.

END RUBRIC

DEATH OF HORUS

Verse 117.
117.1. Udjert {uhat}   her djem   F   aun-ab   her chun   en-medes F
117.2. Udjert {scorpion} person-cut   him   ravager-heart person bite   to- cut   him

117.3. The servants of *Heru (Horus)* said: "the *Udjert* scorpion has cut him, the poisonous ravager of greed, covetousness, and avarice has bitten him so as to cut him and kill him by envenoming his heart!"

Verse 118.
118.1. erta   en   Aset   fend   Ze   im   ra   F   her rech   zet   aru
118.2. gave of   Isis   nose   hers in   mouth his person know breathing about

118.3. *Aset (Isis)* gave her nose the task of searching for life as she brought it close to the mouth of *Heru (Horus)* to know if he was breathing.

Verse 119.
119.1. im   khenu   en   kar   F   wep   Ze   men   nu   auaa
119.2. in   inner   of   shrine his open   she   wound   of   heir

119.3. As he lay in the inner part of his shrine, *Aset (Isis)* opened the place where she found instability, a wound on the body of the young heir to the throne of *Asar (Osiris)*...

EGYPTIAN BOOK OF THE DEAD HIEROGLYPH TRANSLATIONS Volume 6: Featuring The Osirian Resurrection

Verse 120.

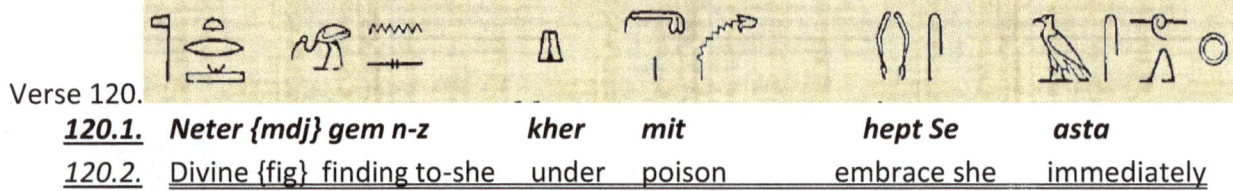

120.1.	Neter {mdj} gem n-z	kher	mit	hept Se	asta
120.2.	Divine {fig} finding to-she	under	poison	embrace she	immediately

120.3. …the Divine Child; underneath the cut she indeed found poison there. Then she embraced him right away.

The image above has been provided to give the reader a visual impression of the events and meaning at this stage in the text.

Verse 121.

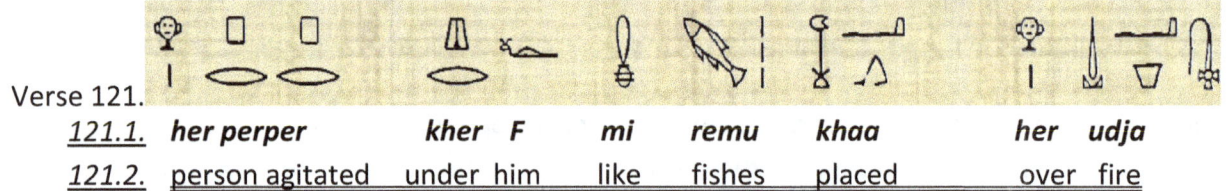

121.1.	her perper	kher F	mi	remu khaa	her udja
121.2.	person agitated	under him	like	fishes placed	over fire

121.3. *Aset (Isis)* became agitated, as anyone might be in her situation. She held him up and moved around the room, as if trying to not have her feet on the earth, she was acting in such a way so as to avert any further contact with earthly dangers, like fish that are placed over a fire so as to be cooked and they fliping around from side to side trying to get away from the heat; thus she proceeded and raising the child to the sky, as if away from the earth and for the Divine Father *Tem, in the sky,* to see what had occurred.

Verse 122.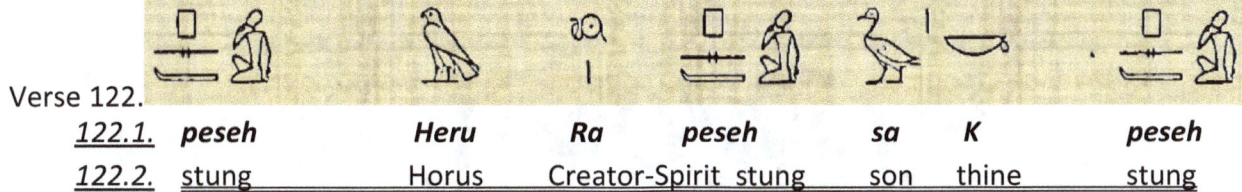

122.1.	peseh	Heru	Ra	peseh	sa	K	peseh
122.2.	stung	Horus	Creator-Spirit	stung	son	thine	stung

122.3. Aset (Isis) said: "It's a bite, it's a puncture! *Heru (Horus)* has been bitten and poisoned! Oh *Ra,* who are in heaven, Oh Divine Creator Spirit, your son has been stung; he has been bitten and wounded!

Verse 123.

123.1.	Heru	au	en	au	neb	sutu	en	Shu
123.2.	Horus	heir	of	heir	lord	domain/realm	of	Shu

123.3. *Heru (Horus)* is the heir of another heir, the lord of the realm, the domain of *Shu*, the God of conscious awareness through space and Ethereal Light that emanates from *Ra*, the Creator Spirit. Shu is the father of *Aset's(Isis') father*, Geb, and thus, Shu is *Heru's(Horus')* great grandfather.

EGYPTIAN BOOK OF THE DEAD HIEROGLYPH TRANSLATIONS Volume 6: Featuring The Osirian Resurrection

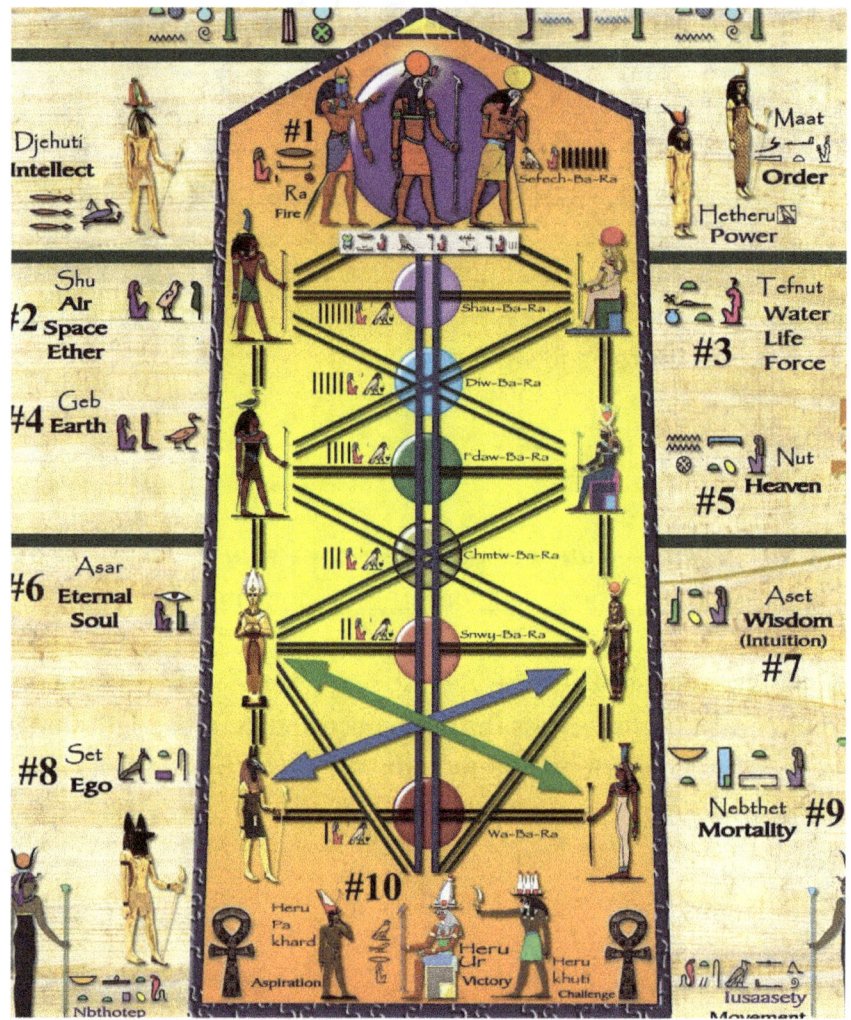

Gods and Goddesses of Anunian(Heliopolitan) Theurgy that emerged from the God Ra

Verse 126.

126.1. *peseh*   *nekhen*   *nefer*   *en*   *nub*   *nuu*

126.2. bitten/stung   solar-child   beautiful/good   of   gold   baby/infant

126.3. My beautiful child, who is descended from the sun, from *Ra*, the sun god and Creator Spirit of all, through *Shu* and then through to *Geb* and then through *Asar (Osiris)*; my child who is of the very golden essence of the sun, my baby, fresh from the Primeval Waters of Nun, has been stung.

Verse 127.

127.1.	sug	antet F	peseh	Heru	sa	Un-Nefer
127.2.	suckling-babe	nothing he	bitten/stung	Horus	son	existence-beautiful

127.3. My beautiful suckling baby, he shows no signs of life. *Heru (Horus)*, the son of Asar (*Osiris*), in his name: "Beautiful-Existence", has been bitten."

THE GODDESSES NEBEHET (NEPHTHYS) AND SELKET (SERQET) OFFER ASSISTANCE AND DIVINE INSPIRATION

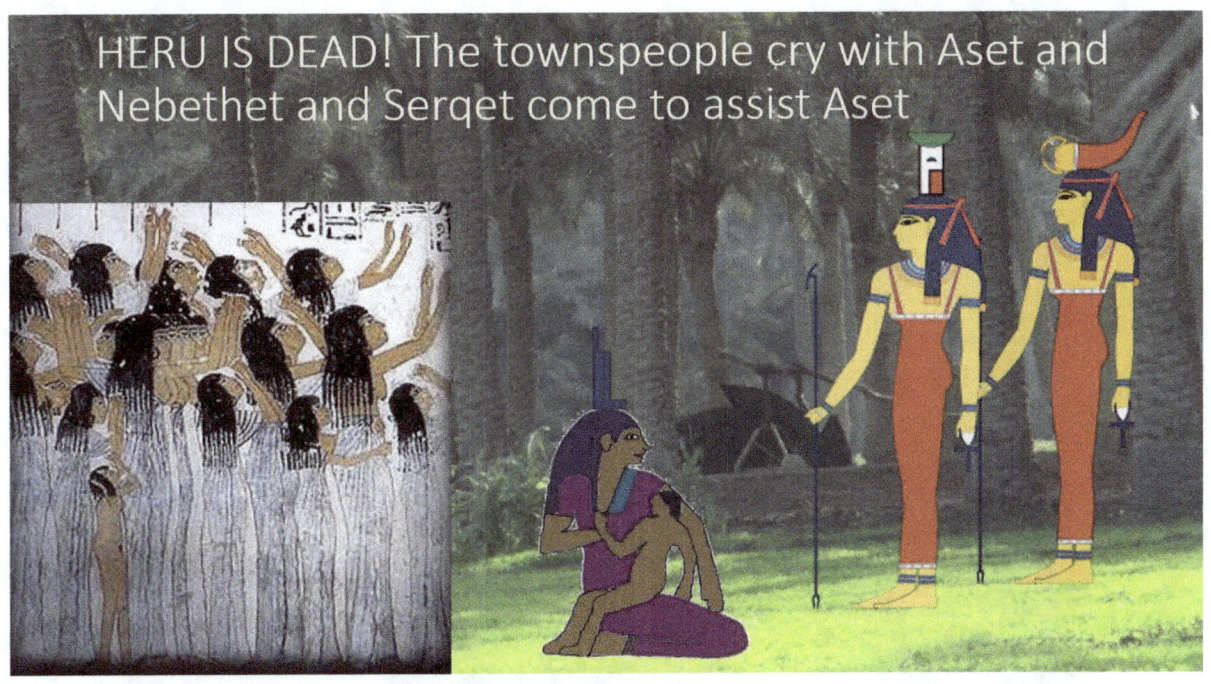

The image above has been provided to give the reader a visual impression of the events and meaning at this stage in the text.

EGYPTIAN BOOK OF THE DEAD HIEROGLYPH TRANSLATIONS Volume 6: Featuring The Osirian Resurrection

Verse 128.

128.1. iu   er- F   Nebethet   her remu   Ze   rer
128.2. came about-he Nephthys   person crying   she   turning

128.3. The twin sister of *Aset (Isis)*, the earth goddess *Nebethet (Nephthys)*, arrived to the location where *Aset (Isis)* was. Seeing the commotion *Nebethet (Nephthys)* started crying. Turning towards the location of *Aset (Isis)*…

Nebethet   **Serqet**

Verse 129.

129.1. **aadeh**   **Serqet**   **her**   **peter**   **zep zen nema ter**

129.2. swampland   Scorpion-Goddess person what?   twice   who?   what?

129.3. ...who was still in the swampland. The cousin of *Aset (Isis)*, the scorpion goddess *Serqet/Selket*, arrived to *Aset's (Isis')* location. She was not as emotional as her two cousins. Pointedly, she asked: "What has happened? What has happened? Who is involved? What has happened?"

Verse 130.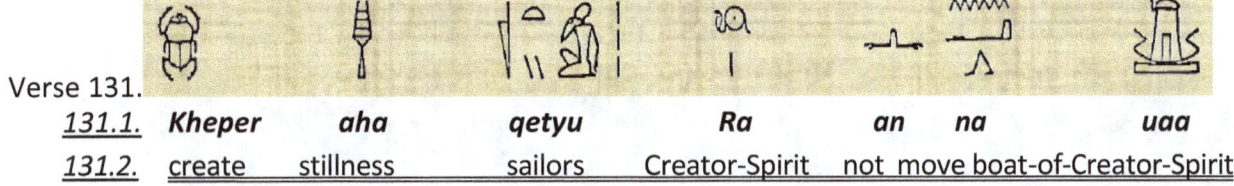

130.1. **er**   **sa**   **Heru**   **Aset**   **dua**   **er-T**   **er**   **pet**

130.2. about   son   Horus   Isis   adorations   as to-she   as to   heaven

130.3. If there is some trouble about *Heru (Horus)*, the son of *Aset (Isis)*, then *Aset (Isis)* should turn towards the heavens and make adorations...

Verse 131.

131.1. **Kheper**   **aha**   **qetyu**   **Ra**   **an**   **na**   **uaa**

131.2. create   stillness   sailors   Creator-Spirit   not   move   boat-of-Creator-Spirit

131.3. ...so as to create stillness among the sailors, the oarsmen of the boat of *Ra*, the Creator-Spirit; therefore, if this is done then the boat of *Ra* will not move,...

Verse 132.

132.1. en -Ra er sa Heru her im F udu
132.2. of Creator-Spirit about son Horus person in he commanded

132.3. …so that the boat of *Ra*, the Creator Spirit should see about his son *Heru (Horus)*, a person in himself. So *Aset (Isis)* began to utter a behest directed at the boat of *Ra* that sails through the heavens and whose movement creates the objects of Creation and sustains their fleeting appearance in time and space.

ASET (ISIS) MAKES AN INVOCATION TO STOP THE BOAT OF RA AND RESURRECT HERU (HORUS]

The image above has been provided to give the reader a visual impression of the events and meaning at this stage in the text.

Verse 133.

133.1.	Aset	kheru-Se	er	pet	zebh	Ze	er	uaa-en-Ra	en
133.2.	Isis	voice-hers	as to	heaven	invocation	hers	as to	boat-of-Creator-Spirit	of

133.3. *Aset (Isis)* directed her mind towards the heavens with an invocation. This was a special directed invocation, an appeal, a summoning, a beseeching, an entreaty to evoke, incite, arouse, to call to mind and call forth and induce, to draw out a response by *Ra*. Just as with the concept of *maa-kheru* "true of voice", which is not an audible expression, but rather a state of mind, this special invocation of *Aset (Isis)* is an expression of focused Conscious Awareness on the Divine. In this case, it is awareness of a realized truth that she had previously achieved in her past relations with Ra [an arrangement she had with *Ra* after she attained Spiritual Enlightenment, as detailed in the scripture of the myth of the *Aset (Isis)* and *Ra, a foreshadowing that in the future there will come a time when Heru(Horus) will be in need of being revived from poison, and Ra pledged that when that time comes, he will let the poison die and Heru(Horus) to live*][8] So, this invocation was directed/focused to the *Boat-of-Ra* and itsoccupants…

Verse 134.

134.1.	Heh	sechen	aton	im	aq	Ze	an	menmen	F
134.2.	millions	still	Sundisk	manner	coming-in	her	not	stopped	he

134.3. …the *Boat of Millions of Years* was now still; the *Sundisk*, the body of the god *Ra*, the sun that traverses through the heavens, as if traveling in a boat, was not coming along in its daily journey in the usual manner; rather, he, *Ra*, is now completely stopped. The invocation was the cause of the stilling of the boat.

Verse 135.

	her aset F	Djehuty	i u	aper	im	peh F
135.1.	person throne his	Thoth	came	provisioned	within	arrived he

135.2. *Ra* was like a person sitting, unmoved, on his throne in the stopped boat. *Djehuty (Thoth)*, the god of words of power, high intellect and hieroglyphic writing, who is the uncle of *Aset (Isis),* and who is

---

[8] See book Mysteries of Isis and Ra by Dr. Muata Ashby

Verse 136.

	kher	udu	aat	en	maa-kheru	peter	zep-zen	Aset
136.1.	kher	udu	aat	en	maa-kheru	peter	zep-zen	Aset
136.2.	possessing	command	great	of	spiritual-victory	what	twice	Isis

136.3. …possessing a great command that promotes Spiritual Victory (Enlightenment). His mission is to insure the Spiritual Victory of *Heru (Horus)* as per the command given to him by Ra. *Aset (Isis)* saw *Djehuty (Thoth)* and immediately started asking, repeating herself twice, "what is this, what is this that has happened?" Incredulous and anxious about what has occurred to her son, *Aset (Isis)* went on asking what is this and how could it be that the golden child, the one who would answer for his father, has fallen under such misfortune? What is this? What is this? Asking "What is it that has happened?" is a starting point for spiritual aspiration, that leads to the answer to life's problems which when answered relieves life's problems and leads to spiritual victory. Those who go along with life and do not ask why they suffer in life, do not discover the meaning of lif e and overcome the sufferings of life. They remain subject to death and cannot be redeemed and awakened to their spiritual nature *Asar(Osiris)*. *Aset (Isis)*…

Verse 137.

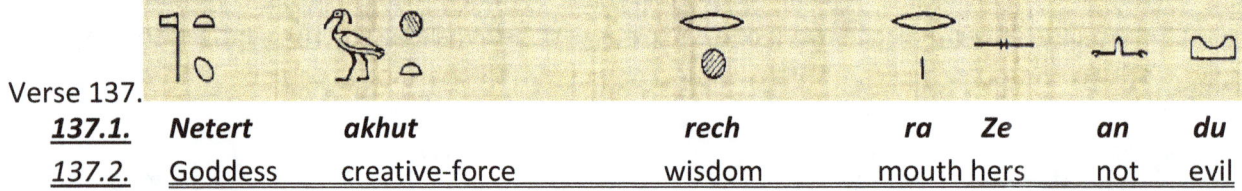

	Netert	akhut	rech	ra	Ze	an	du
137.1.	Netert	akhut	rech	ra	Ze	an	du
137.2.	Goddess	creative-force	wisdom	mouth	hers	not	evil

137.3. …the goddess, whose mouth possessed creative-force based on knowledge of all worldly disciplines and spiritual intuition, asked *Djehuty (Thoth)* this question, repeatedly and with spiritual force behind it, such as what she used to stop the progress of the boat of Ra. *Djehuty (Thoth)* started to speak: "Please do not be anxious about the fate of *Heru (Horus)* because, ultimately, no evil…

EGYPTIAN BOOK OF THE DEAD HIEROGLYPH TRANSLATIONS Volume 6: Featuring The Osirian Resurrection

Verse 138.

138.1.	as	er	sa	Heru	sa	F	en	uaa
138.2.	witness	about	son	Horus	protection	his	of	boat

138.3. …shall be witnessed in relation to the son, *Heru (Horus)*; it will be as if no malady ever struck him. I say this confidently because his protection is coming from the boat…

Djehuty(Thoth) and Aset(Isis) from the Temple of Aset(Isis)

Verse 139.

139.1. en	Ra	ay n-A	mi-en-ra	im dept	Aton
139.2. of	Creator-Spirit	come of-I	like-the-sun	through boat	sundisk

139.3. ...of Ra, the Creator-Spirit. I come to you like the sun does, daily, illuminating and doing away with the darkness; I am here today through the auspices of the boat of the Sundisk, Ra, which is the power that created Creation and which was orchestrated...

Verse 140.

140.1. im	aset-per F	en	zef {ra}	kek	chepr
140.2. through	abode his	of	yesterday	night	creation

140.3. ...through and from his abode of yesterday, which was like the nighttime before there was Creation and the Creation...

Verse 141.

141.1. zeshep{ra}	der	er	senab	Heru	en	mut F
141.2. light-radiance	drive-out	for	health	Horus	to	mother his

141.3. ...brought in the power of radiant light, from the Shining Spirit of *Ra*, which drove out the darkness of nothingness to bring into manifestation the things, the objects of Creation. In the same way, just as I have come to you now from yesterday and am here today, so too the darkness of evil, infirmity and death, that was experienced before my arrival, will be driven out by the radiance of the Creator Spirit. This I declare will happen, the power and radiance of the Creator Spirit will drive out the poison [***aun-ab***] [9], ravager of the heart poison from the Udjert Scorpion, in *Heru (Horus)* and will restore his health and return him to his mother...

---

[9] see verse 117

EGYPTIAN BOOK OF THE DEAD HIEROGLYPH TRANSLATIONS Volume 6: Featuring The Osirian Resurrection

Verse 142.

	Aset	Zenu	neb	ent	kher	medes	mitet
142.1.	Aset	Zenu	neb	ent	kher	medes	mitet
142.2.	Isis	they	all	of	under	knife	likewise

142.3. *Aset (Isis)*. I further declare, in accord with your earlier pact with *Ra*, that the same covenant and bond that you made with *Ra* when you learned his secret name, that he would help in the future to insure the health of *Heru (Horus)* and anyone else who is similarly under the cutting danger threatening their spiritual victory, will similarly be assisted. Therefore, all those who become souls on earth, and fall under the knife, the death of conscious awareness caused by egoism, will be assisted by the arrangement organized by goddess Aset, thet their Heru conscience will be saved from damage by their ego self and that they too will ultimately succeed in the struggle of life and redeem their own Asar nature (their soul).

EGYPTIAN BOOK OF THE DEAD HIEROGLYPH TRANSLATIONS Volume 6: Featuring The Osirian Resurrection

CONTENDINGS OF HERU(HORUS) AND SET(SETH) Version 1

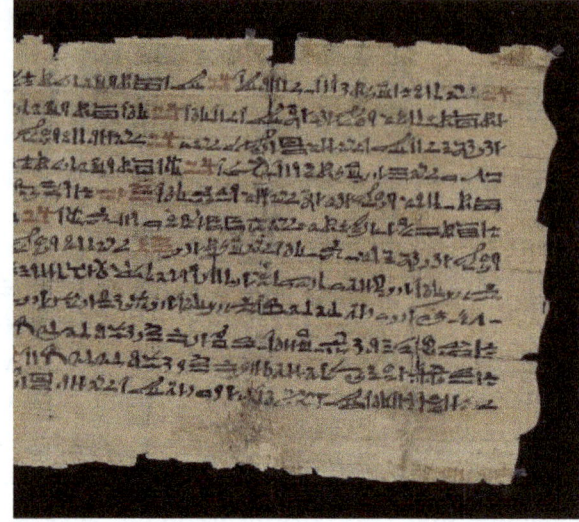

PAPYRUS CHESTER BEATY

THE TREE OF MYTHIC SCRIPTURES OF THE ASARIAN RESURRECTION MYTH RENDERED IN ANCIENT EGYPTIAN HIEROGLYPHIC TEXT:

EGYPTIAN BOOK OF THE DEAD HIEROGLYPH TRANSLATIONS Volume 6: Featuring The Osirian Resurrection

Trilinear translations contendings of Heru and *Seth* from Papyrus Chester Beaty (library) I recto.

Title:[10]

Contendings of Horus and *Seth* (recto), Beginning of the words of the great dispenser of entertainment (love-songs I) (verso), Sale of a bull (verso)

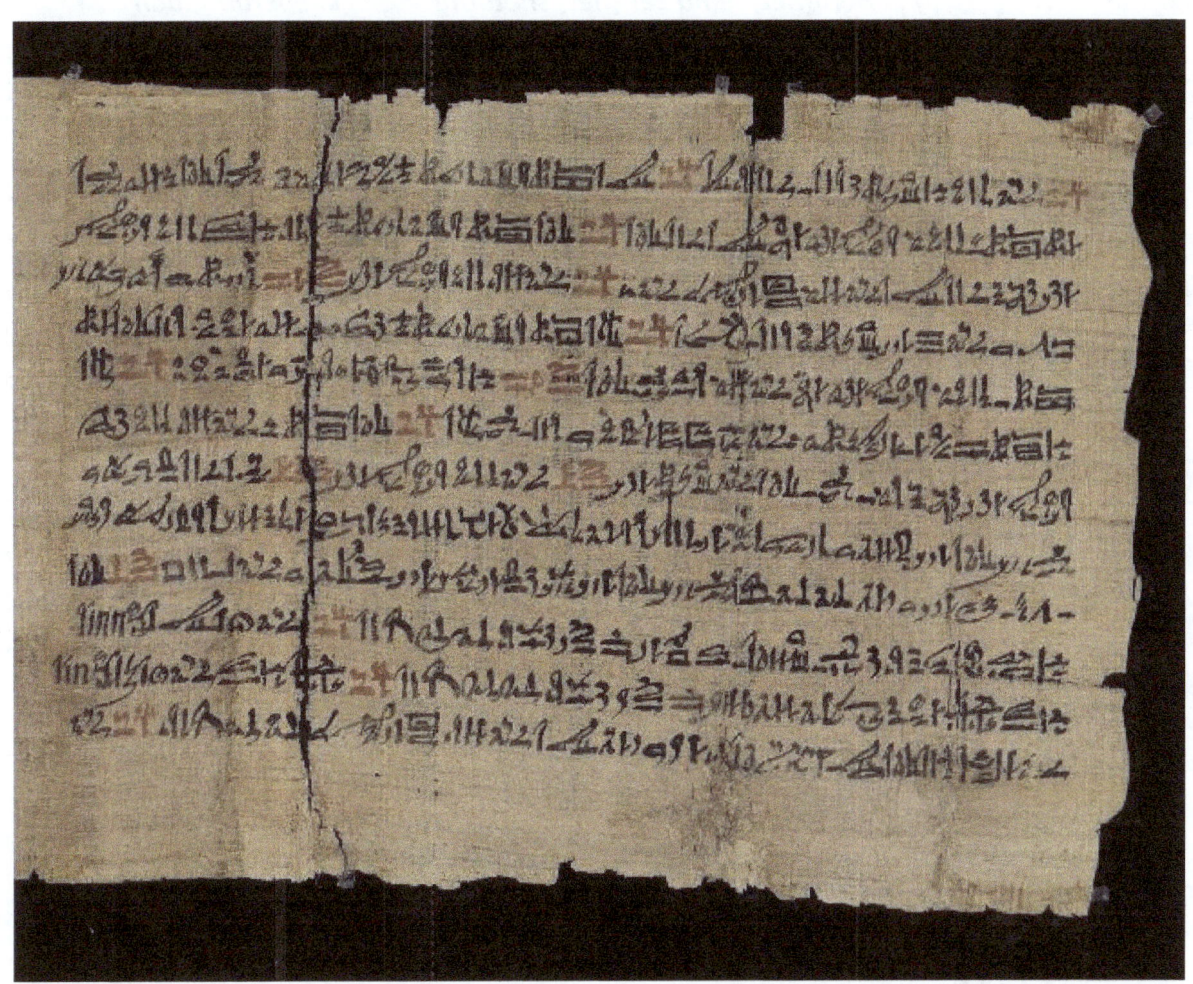

---

[10]Production date: c. 1160 BC Dimensions: 280 mm x 1195 mm (height x length) Material: Papyrus (material) Ink (material)

EGYPTIAN BOOK OF THE DEAD HIEROGLYPH TRANSLATIONS Volume 6: Featuring The Osirian Resurrection

The Conflict Between Heru (Horus) and Set (Seth)-Fundamental Problem and Confusion Between the Higher Self and the Lower Self

Verse 1.

1.1. *chena wep   se-djed Heru{net} hena Set {net} shetautu   kheperau   aah*

1.2. Thus verdict speech that Horus {divinity} with Seth{ divinity } secret forms   great

1.3. Thus, here opens the telling about the god *Heru (Horus)* and the god *Set (Seth)*, two divinities along with their great forms and appearances, characters and passions that operate in the human personality and the verdict all this leads to…

Verse 2.

2.1. *aytu {mdj} sensu   seru   ia   khepery {mdj}*

2.2. troubles {fig} nobles   elders   which create

2.3. …and also about their troubles. It is about nobles and elders and those who create those same troubles.

Verse 3.

3.1. *hemz   emba Neberdjer {net} her ucha chet   aautu{mdj}   en atef Asar*

3.2. sitting   before Lord-of-All {div} person enquire concern offices {fig} of father Osiris

3.3. Now. There is a person sitting in front of *Neberdjer,* the *Lord-of-All* divinity, the transcendental, absolute Supreme Being manifesting in the form of a director of the gods and goddesses in time and space. This person *Heru(Horus)* is enquiring about a concern they have about the office and position that belonged to their father *Asar (Osiris)*…

3.4. **nefer   chaay**
3.5. beautiful dawnings

3.6. ..he who is the one of beautiful appearances, like the never ending dawns of the sun that manifest in a myriad ways daily.

EGYPTIAN BOOK OF THE DEAD HIEROGLYPH TRANSLATIONS Volume 6: Featuring The Osirian Resurrection

Heru Comes to the Company of Gods and Goddesses seeking Justice

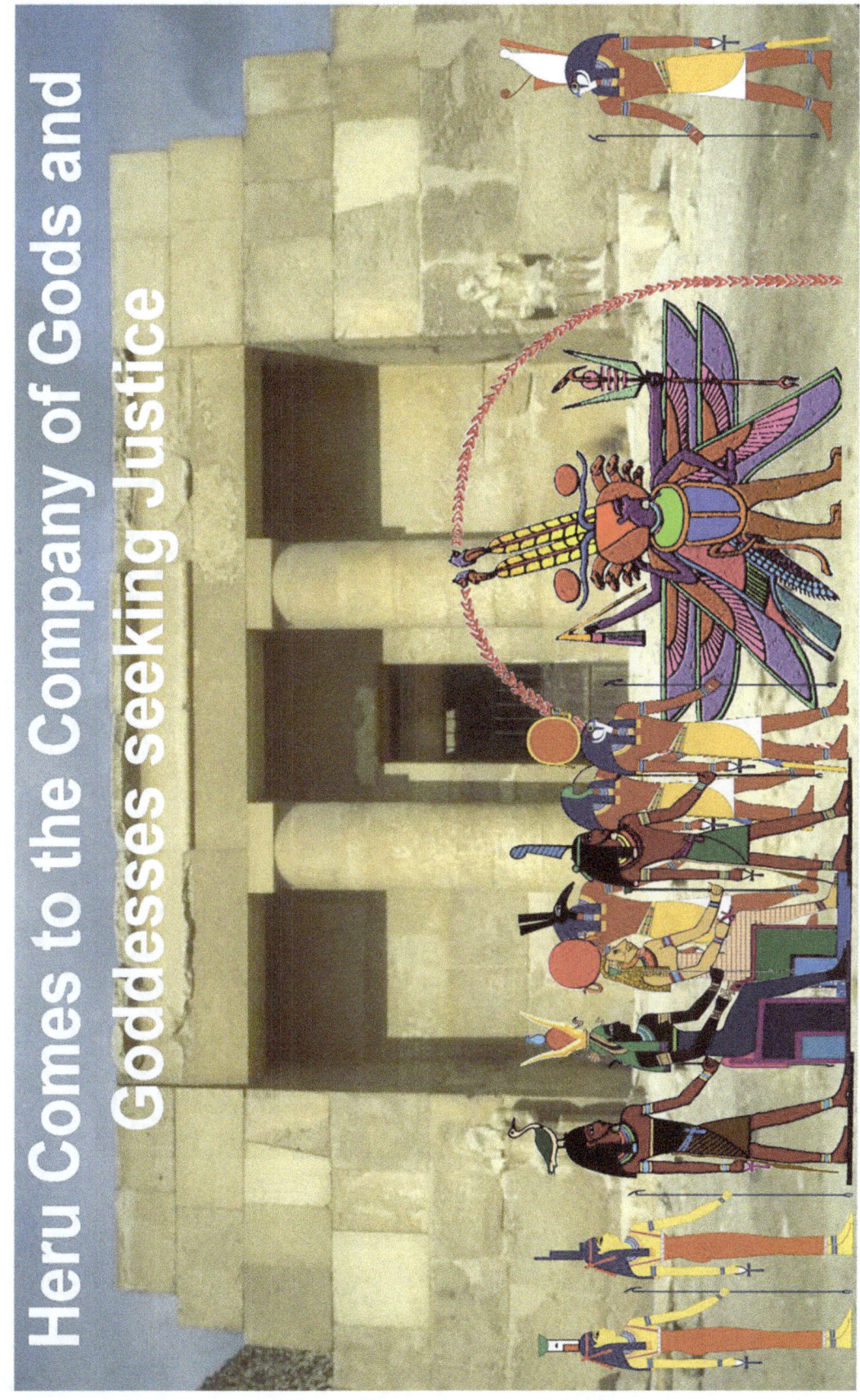

The image above has been provided to give the reader a visual impression of the events and meaning at this stage in the text.

Statue of the *Neberdjer,* The Lord-of-All

EGYPTIAN BOOK OF THE DEAD HIEROGLYPH TRANSLATIONS Volume 6: Featuring The Osirian Resurrection

Image from Papyrus of *Neberdjer,* The Lord-of-All

EGYPTIAN BOOK OF THE DEAD HIEROGLYPH TRANSLATIONS Volume 6: Featuring The Osirian Resurrection

Verse 4.

4.1. ***iu Djehuty{net} cherpu   udjat   sensu seru{net} imy Anu {net}***
4.2. it is Thoth{div} presenting   eye   noble elder{div}   within Heliopolis{div}

4.3. The divinity, the god *Djehuty(Thoth)* comes in presenting the Divine Eye, the Eye of wellness and power to the noble divine elder, the god *Ra-Herakty* (the Creator-Spirit-of-the-two-horizons [i.e. Creator-Spirit-mind, spanning from the beginning to end of time] and head of the Company of Gods and Goddesses of Creation who emerged from Nun, the Primeval Ocean at the beginning of time and under the auspices of *Neberdjer*, the *Lord-of-All*), whose seat of power is the divine city of Heliopolis (Anu, city of the sun).

Verse 5.

5.1. ***Djed in   Shu{div} maaytu{mdj} neb user***
5.2. Speech by   Shu{divinity} truthfulness lord dominium

5.3. The following words come from the divinity *Shu,* the first-born son of Ra, the god of air, space and Ethereal Light. He says: "Truthfulness, Oh Lord of dominion of Creation (speaking to Ra)...

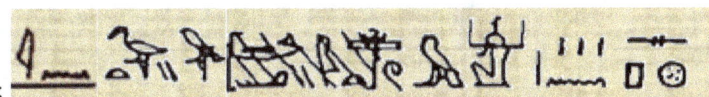

5.4.   {Heru}
5.5. **su   im   djed   amma   ta aaut   [Heru]**
5.6. you form saying give   that office   [Horus]

5.7. …indeed, truthfulness would be expressed if you emphatically proclaim that the office [of *Asar (Osiris)*] should be given to [*Heru (Horus)*].

Verse 6.
6.1. **in   Djehuty{net} maaytu{mdj} im hehu en   zep**
6.2. by   Thoth{div} truthfulness{fig} form millions of times-over.

6.3. Then Lord *Djehuty (Thoth)* spoke. Lord *Djehuty* (*Thoth*), the god of writing and intellect exclaimed, "Wow, I have heard no truer words spoken; this is true millions of times over.

Verse 7.   [dmg]
7.1. **aha   Aset{net} [dmg] segebu aah{mdj} iu st   reshutu   {mdj}**
7.2. rise-up Isis{div} [dmg] cried-out greatly{fig} it is she overjoyed{fig}

7.3. Now the divinity, goddess *Aset (Isis)*, rises up, coming forward and, in response to what has been said, she shouts out loudly {figuratively}. She is overjoyed at the prospect of her son being given the office of his father that was usurped by her brother, the god *Set(Seth)*, after *Set(Seth)* killed *Asar(Osiris)* to take his throne office.

Verse 8.[dmg]
8.1. [words] **ten Neb-er-djer{net} ya   ach   chena   tenu ary sechru{mdj} ua**
8.2. [About the words] yours Lord-of-All{div} hey what look-into your action planning alone

8.3. [About all that has transpired so far and the words that have been spoken up to now], the divinity *Neberdjer, Lord-of-All* divinity, in his manifestation as the god *Ra-Herakty*, the time and space personification of the Supreme Being, who is the source of all the gods and goddesses and foundation of all their creations, says: "Hey, wait a minute, what's going on here; are you all taking the action of planning the outcome of this issue by yourselves?

The images above has been provided to give the reader an impression of the test events and meaning at this stage.

EGYPTIAN BOOK OF THE DEAD HIEROGLYPH TRANSLATIONS Volume 6: Featuring The Osirian Resurrection

The High God Does Not Agree with The Other Gods and Goddesses that Heru (Horus) should be Given the Throne of His Father Asar (Osiris)

Verse 9.

- **9.1.** *ahan*   Neb-er-djer{net} ger im[dmg] aadt{ra} qendt   tay   Pesedjetu
- 9.2. attention-to Lord-of-All{div} silence within[dmg] moment anger at Company Gods
                                                                                                                    Goddesses
- 9.3. The attention then went to Neberdjer, the *Lord-of-All* divinity, in his manifestation as the god *Ra-Herakty,* because suddenly he went silent and remained as if in a paused state. It was realized that *Lord-of-All* divinity, in his manifestation as the god *Ra-Herakty,* was angry with the Company of Gods and Goddesses of Ra, the Creator-Spirit, whom he brought into manifestation at the beginning of Creation and who help him maintain Creation; he was angry with them for rushing to a conclusion and going forward, making plans for coronation etc., all by themselves without considering other issues.

Verse 10.
- **10.1.**   *un*   *in*   Set{net} sa {net} Nut   [{net}]
- 10.2.   presence by Seth{div} son{div} Nut   [{div}]

- 10.3. Now the god *Set (Seth)*, the son of the goddess *Nut,* the goddess that manifests as the sky and heavens, and the brother of *Asar (Osiris)* and *Aset (Isis)* and the one who usurped his brother's throne of office, made his presence felt after watching and listening to what has been transpiring so far.

10.4. **djed   amma   kha   tu F   er   bu   nu** [dmg] **ay   er   mau**
10.5. words give   leave you he as-to place any [dmg] who as to appearance

10.6. He bellowed the following: "let's give ourselves the chance to get out of this place to somewhere else. This court is no place for this decision; in some other place I will demonstrate who deserves the throne and...

Verse 11.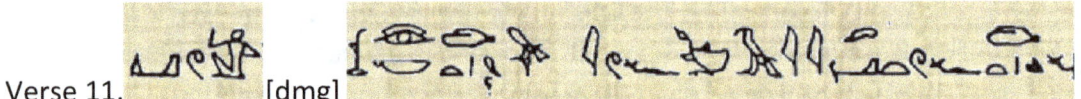
[dmg]
11.1. diu   petra k det {net} iu F tjay {necht} tu F det F
11.2. giving [damaged] seeing you hand {div} it is he male {force} to he hand he

11.3. ...will give [dmg] to you the seeing of the evidence of he whose divine hand is of a stronger male hand and how it will exert its force over his [*Heru's (Horus')*] hand...

Verse 12.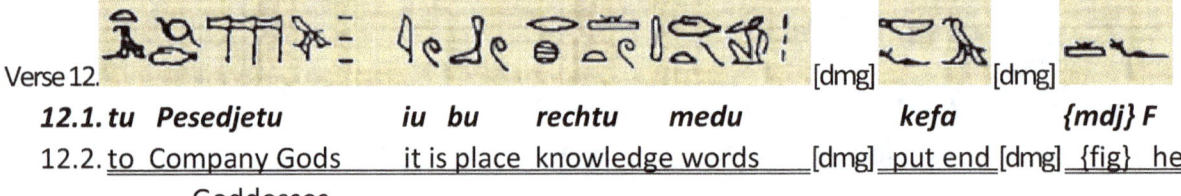
[dmg]   [dmg]
12.1. tu Pesedjetu   iu bu   rechtu   medu   kefa   {mdj} F
12.2. to Company Gods   it is place knowledge words [dmg] put end [dmg] {fig} he
       Goddesses

12.3. ...which will be shown to the Company of Gods and Goddesses. It is about having a place where it will be known how I put an end to him, *Heru(Horus)*.

Verse 13.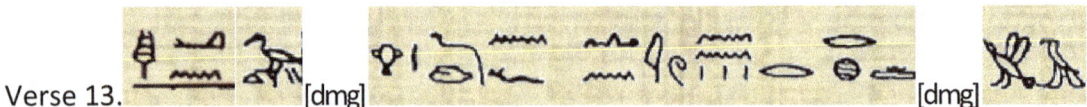
[dmg]   [dmg]
13.1. ahan Djehuty[dmg]**her djed n-F   an   iu   nenu   er rech(mdj)**[dmg] **chena**
13.2. attention-Thoth[dmg]person speaks to-him (Seth) not it is notice as-to know [dmg] enquire

13.3. The attention now went to the god *Djehuty(Thoth)*[dmg]. He is the person who now responds to what *Set(Seth)* just said. "Are you saying that we are to ignore and not enquire about...

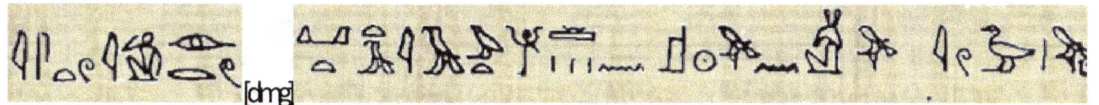

13.4. *astu   ay   aru   dit ta aautu   {mdj} en Asar   en Set {net} iu sa {net}*

13.5. notice who action[dmg] give that office {fig} of Osiris to Seth {div}it is son {div}

13.6. ...the fact that someone else is contending for the same office and to give that office of *Asar(Osiris)* to you, *Set(Seth)*, even though his son...

13.7. [dmg] *Heru* {net} *aha*

13.8. [dmg] *Heru (Horus)* {div} standing

13.9. [dmg] ...the divine god *Heru(Horus)* is standing right here in front of us?

Verse 14.

14.1.   *ahan   chena Ra{net}-Heru{net}-akhty{net}{net} qendt* [dmg] *er A qen(mdj) zepzenastu*

                                                                                                                                    ab en

14.2.   attention considering Ra{div}-Horus{div}two-horizons{div}{div} angered doubly about I greatly specifically

                                                                                                                                     heart of

14.3.   The attention now went to the consideration of the god *Ra- Heru (Horus)-Two-Horizons* (Creator-Spirit-of-the-two-horizons *{twice divine}*), *Ra-Herakty*. He, concurring with the divine *Lord-of-All,* became exceedingly angered towards what Lord *Djehuty (Thoth)* just said specifically because the heart (mind) of...

14.4. *chena Ra{net} er-dit ta aautu {mdj} en Set {net} aah pehty tu sa {net} Nut*

14.5. consideration Ra {div} give that office{fig} to Seth{div} great double- powerful to son Nut

14.6. ...the god Ra was of the disposition in consideration favoring Set. The divinity, Ra, says: "I think we should give the office of *Asar(Osiris)* to *Set(Seth)*; I mean, after all, *Set(Seth)* is doubly powerful and he, like *Asar(Osiris)*, is a son of goddess Nut, the sky divinity who constitutes outer space and the heavens, where shining spirits reside in their star forms.

Verse 15.

15.1. *iu Anhur {net} ash segabu   aah{mdj} her{net} en ta Pesedjetu*

15.2. <u>it is Onuris{div} calls-out cries-out greatly{fig} as to person {div} to the Company of Gods and Goddesses</u>

15.3. The divinity *Onuris(Anhur)*, an aspect of the divinity *Ra,* whose titles include *Slayer of Enemies* and *Rescuer* that exemplifies the combative attitude, defiance and indignant approach to dealing with injustice, he cried out loudly, protesting to the Company of Gods and Goddesses...

The God Anhur (Onuris)

Verse 16.

16.1. *er-djed ach chena enty iu nenu ary er F*

16.2. <u>as-to say how about dispossessing it is this doing as-to him</u>

16.3. ...about the issue of disinheriting *Heru (Horus),* which would be the outcome if they follow the previous suggestion by *Ra-Herakty* (Creator-Spirit-of-the-two-horizons), *Ra-Herakty*.

Verse 17.

17.1. *un   in   ta Pesedjetu   her djed en Djehuty{net} emba Neberdjer{net} ach{mdj} ary k*

17.2. presence of that Company person say to Thoth{div} presence Lord-of-All {div} what action thee of Gods and Goddesses

17.3. The presence of the Company of Gods and Goddesses was felt through their words to the god *Djehuty (Thoth)*, in the presence of the *Lord-of-All* divinity. They instructed him thus: "You are directed to take the following action:…

Sending a Letter to Goddess Net(Neith) for Her Advice

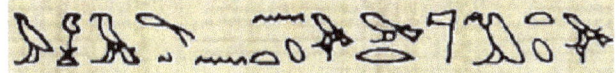

17.4. *ucha   en Net {net} ur Neter mut {net}*

17.5. letter   to Neith{div} great Goddess mother {div}

17.6. …send a letter to *Net (Neith)*, the Great Mother, the Divine Goddess of Creation. Then we may have guidance as to how to proceed with this matter.

Verse 24.

24.1. *chena   remtju   enty hemhen en repit*
24.2. considering people deprived 80   years

24.3. This matter requires special consideration as the dispute between these people has gone on for 80 years."

Verse 25.

25.1. *un   in   Net   ur   neter mut {net} habuy   ucha   en ta Pesedjetu{net}*
25.2. presence of Neith great goddess mother{div} message letter   to that Company Gods Goddesses

25.3. Now the presence of Great Mother Goddess *Net(Neith)* is being felt. What follows is her reply message that reached to the location of the Company of Gods and Goddesses.

Verse 26.
- **26.1.** er djed   amma   ta aautu{mdj} en Asar{net} en sa{net} F Heru {net}
- 26.2. as-to tell give   that office{fig} of Osiris{div} of son{div} his Horus {div}

26.3. "About this whole affair, I don't see what the quandary is? The answer is clear. Give the office, which belonged to the divine god *Asar(Osiris)*, give it to his divine son, *Heru(Horus)*! What's so hard about that? Do it now; right now!

Verse 27.
- **27.1.** im-an ary art n-a zepu   aahyu   en
- 27.2. do-not do offering to-me time great   {mdj} of

27.3. Listen; do not make an offering to me at this great time, in the midst of…

27.4.
- **27.5.** gery   enty ben set er aset-pertu im-an er pu iu A qendt   im tu ta
- 27.6. falsehood depriving not he as-to thrones do-not as-to this it is I angered means one this

27.7. …an untoward action, a fraud, by doing what is wrong based on a falsehood concerning to whom the throne belongs. Don't even think about it. Otherwise I would get angry and who knows, a person (directed at each member of the Company) may find that…

Verse 28.
- **28.1.** pet   tjehy   en chena   iu   metutu   her
- 28.2. heaven moves to then   conceived through one upon

28.3. …suddenly a situation may be conceived wherein the sky may start to fall in on top of one…!

Image of Goddess Net from tomb of Nefertary

EGYPTIAN BOOK OF THE DEAD HIEROGLYPH TRANSLATIONS Volume 6: Featuring The Osirian Resurrection

Verse 29.
- **29.1.** a   qebu   Set{net} im chetu tu   F   amma   n-F Anat   {netrt}   Aztayrtat*
- 29.2.   ia   double   Seth{div} form things to him give   to-him Anat   goddess Astarte

29.3.   I say, double the possessions of the god *Set(Seth)* and additionally, to satisfy his needs, also give him the goddesses *Anat* and *Astarte*…

EGYPTIAN BOOK OF THE DEAD HIEROGLYPH TRANSLATIONS Volume 6: Featuring The Osirian Resurrection

Goddess Anat   ***Goddess Aztjardet***   *(at Edfu, Egypt temple)*

Semitic related goddesses associated with war (Anat relates to Hetheru--- Astarte relates to Sekhemit)

144

EGYPTIAN BOOK OF THE DEAD HIEROGLYPH TRANSLATIONS Volume 6: Featuring The Osirian Resurrection

29.4. {netrt} tay K   sherauty   im tu K   dit Heru {net} er ta   aset-peru en atef{net} Asar{net}
29.5. {goddess} they your daughters   through you give Horus{div} that throne of divine father Osiris

29.6. …who is also a goddess. They are both your (Ra's) daughters. Furthermore, let justice be served through the action of giving to the divine god *Heru (Horus)*, that throne that belonged to his divine father, divine *Asar (Osiris)*.

Verse 31.

31.1. un in   Neberdjer{net} qendt er Heru {net} iu F her djed n-F tu K hur   tu
31.2. presence of Lord-of-All {div} anger as-to Horus{div} it is he person say-of he to thee pathetic to

31.3. Now, the presence of the divinity *Lord-of-All* was felt in a severe manner. He became angry at the god *Heru (Horus)* and started berating him by saying: "I say to you (to the Company of Gods and Goddesses) about this person *Heru(Horus)*, he is pathetic, a weakling in regard to;…

31.4.
31.5. im hatu   k   cher tay   aautu   aah   {mdj} tar k   chena adj   {nedjs} banuy
31.6. his body parts property those office   great {fig} ends thee consider boy {little} wretched

31.7. …just look at his pathetic weakling body and limbs! No, the possessions, belongings, goods, land, house estate and the authority and domain, etc. of this great office would come to a bad end. It would be too much for him to handle; just look at this little boy's body with wretched …

31.8.
31.9. **dept**   er   F
31.10. taste   about him

31.11. …taste about him, a bad taste and smell in the mouth…bad breath!

Verse 32.

32.1. iu BaBa   {net}
32.2. It is BaBa   {div}

32.3. Now it is the divinity *BaBa*, a son of *Asar (Osiris)* and the god of truth and virility who has a chance to weigh in on the proceedings...

The God BABA Berates the God Ra

BABA

Verse 33.

33.1. Djed en chena Ra{net}-Heru{net}-akhty{net}{net} kara{net}k shuy
33.2. Says to well-then Ra{div}-Horus{div}two-horizons{div}{div} sanctuary{div} hollow

33.3. ...he says to the god *Ra-Heru (Horus)-the-Creator-Spirit-of-the-two-horizo*ns{twice divine}, *Ra-Herakty*: "Well then, all I have to say is, after hearing what you said all I can think is that your sanctuary(throne), the authority you command it with, and the wisdom content of what I heard is just worthless, vacant, and hollow."

Verse 35.

35.1. iu F nemau aref F her pezed F {net} iu ab F er djuu aah{mdj} ur
35.2. It is he lie-down tangled he on back his {div} It is heart his as-to despondent greatly{fig} major

35.3. After hearing that rebuke, *Ra* went alone to his pavilion and lied down on his back feeling dejected and greatly despondent and remained in that condition.

EGYPTIAN BOOK OF THE DEAD HIEROGLYPH TRANSLATIONS Volume 6: Featuring The Osirian Resurrection

Goddess Hathor Comes in to Lift the Animus of Ra

Verse 39.
- 39.1.1. *un   in   Hetherut   {net} neb{t} neha   ter   her aayy*
- 39.1.2. presence of Hathor   {div}   mistress sycamore honoring person coming in

- 39.1.3. Now, the presence of goddess *Hetheru (Hathor)* is being felt. She is the mistress of the sycamore tree, which gives nourishing figs, and sustains life. She is the female expression of Ra, and is also represented as his daughter. As the right Eye of Ra, she is Ra's dynamic energetic expression in time and space. She is depicted as the serpent that surmounts his SunDisk which is also the fire spitting serpent, a beneficent destructive power of light, which destroys enemies of light and dispels the darkness (blindness) of ignorance. She comes into the presence of *Ra*, uttering praises of honor and making genuflections of appreciation in the area where *Ra* was.

The image above has been provided to give the reader a visual impression of the events and meaning at this stage in the text.

39.2.
- **39.2.1. *iu set her aha emba   atef{net} set Neberdjer{net} iu set kefauty***
- 39.2.2.   it is she person rising-coming before father{div} hers Neberdjer, the Lord-of-All it is she undothing

- 39.2.3. The goddess stepped up to the place where her divine father, *Lord-of-All,* was and she stood in front of him and disrobed.

147

39.3.

39.3.1. kat set er her {net} F ahan chena neter{net}aah{mdj} sebaa im set

39.3.2. vagina hers as-to person{div}he attention consideration Divinity{div} great{fig} laughs with her

39.3.3. She then displayed her nakedness and exposed herself to him. *Hetheru(Hathor)* symbolizes the power of Spirit that is the dynamic movement of Consciousness that causes the movements in matter, time and space, that appear as Creation. This dynamic cosmic energy, represented by the goddess, finds its most pure mythic expression in the imagery of sexual polarity, whose attraction for itself (*Ra* for *Hetheru* and vice versa) causes interest in life and the aesthetics of human evolution, which occurs when the dynamics of sexual expression become sublimated into the mystic movement of spiritual aspiration, *Heru(Horus)*. When the sex-polarity tends towards egoism there is favoritism for ego desires (Seth). When sex-polarity tends towards spiritual evolution there is favoritism for Heru. Upon seeing this display, the attention from the great divinity was drawn to her and his animus, his disposition, was uplifted as he laughed with her.

The image above has been provided to give the reader a visual impression of the events and meaning at this stage in the text. The image of the goddess *Baubo*, a goddess from ancient Greco/Roman of mythology, who is recognized as an expression in of goddesses Isis and Hathor, is presented here as she was known to lift her skirt and show her genitals, as is described about goddess Hathor in the Ancient Egyptian scripture.

Verse 41.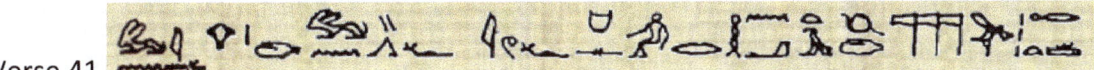
- **41.1.1.** *Un in* her di uny F iu F hemz er hena ta Pesedjetu {net} aaht{mdj}
- 41.1.2. presence of person gives hurry he it is he sitting as-to with Company of Gods and Goddesses

- 41.1.3. Now, the presence of the divine father was felt as he hurried back over to the place where the Company of Gods and Goddesses was and sat down with them.

Verse 43.
- 43.1. *un in* Set{net}aah{mdj} pehty sa{net} Nut   {net}
- 43.2. presence of Seth{div} great{fig} double power son{div} Nut{div}

- 43.3. Now, the presence of the god *Set (Seth)* is felt. He says: "I am the great god *Set (Seth)* and I am the doubly powerful son of goddess Nut, powerful of body and mind (ego-personality).

Verse 45.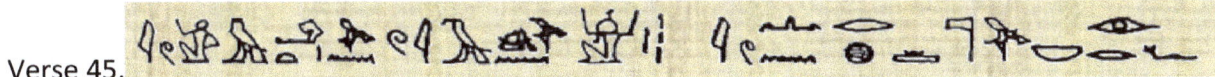
- **45.1.** *iu A im hat{net} en uia{net} en hehu   iu an rech{mdj} Neter{net} neb ary F*
- 45.2. it is I in front{div} of boat{div} of millions   it is not known{fig} Divinity{div} actions he

- 45.3. Listen to what I have to say. I am the one who stands in the front of the divine boat of millions of years, the *Boat of Ra* that sustains Creation. I protect it from its enemies and I don't know of any other god or goddess who can do what I do."

From Ancient Egyptian Book of Coming Forth by Day- of *Heruben*, XXI Dynasty

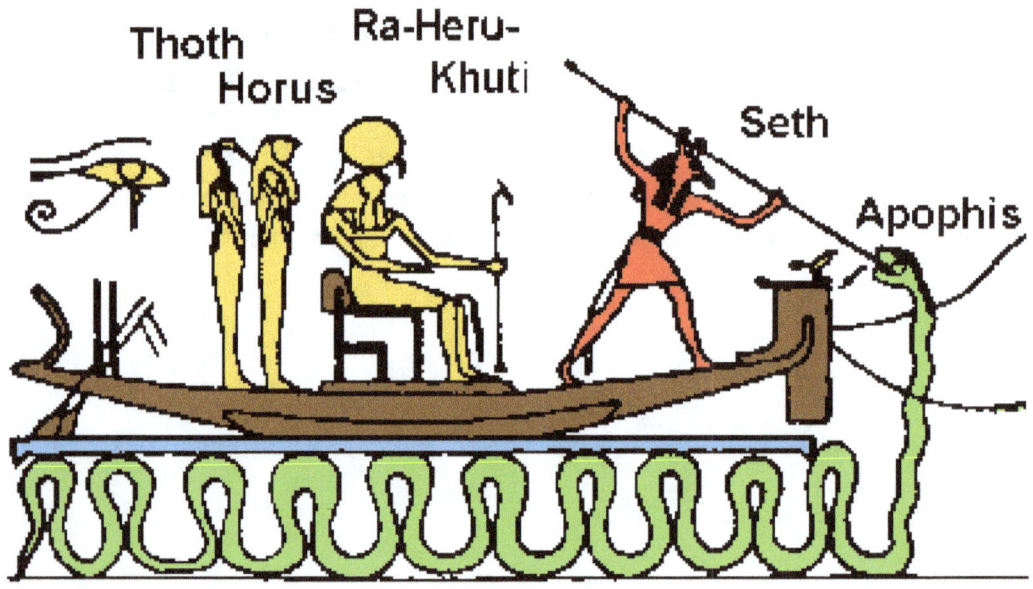

Djehuty(Thoth), Heru(Horus), Ra-Herukhuty (Creator Spirit-Two Hrizons), Set(Seth), Apep(Apophis)

EGYPTIAN BOOK OF THE DEAD HIEROGLYPH TRANSLATIONS Volume 6: Featuring The Osirian Resurrection

Verse 47.
47.1. Un   in senu her djed maatu{mdj} Set{net} sa{net} Nut   {net}
47.2. presence of them (Company) person said truthful Seth{div} son{div} Nut {goddess}

47.3. Now, the presence of the Company of Gods and Goddesses was felt as they all, to a person, said "What the god *Set (Seth)*, the divine son of goddess Nut, has said is true."

Verse 48.
48.1. Un in Anhur{net} hena Djehuty{net} ash segabu   aah er djed ia   ary er tu dit
48.2. presence of Onuris{div} and Thoth{div}   call-out shouting   great as-to saying doing the giving

48.3. Now, the presence of the gods *Anhur (Onuris)* together-with *Djehuty (Thoth)* was felt as they started to loudly call out, shouting about and asking a rhetorical question: How can we give...

Verse 49.
49.1. ta   aautu   {mdj} en sen mut{net} iu sa {net} en khat {net} aha
49.2. those   offices   of brother mother{div} it is son{div} of body{div} standing

49.3. ...the throne offices to the divine uncle while the divine heir, the divine son of the divine body of the original office holder of the office is standing right here in front of us?

The Oaths of Aset (Isis) and Set (Seth)

Verse 55.

55.1.
55.1.1. *ahan* Aset{net} qendt   er ta Pesedjetu {net}   iu set her aryt ankh en
55.1.2. attention Isis{div} angered as-to that Company {div} it is she person doing life oath to

55.1.3. Now attention turns to goddess *Aset (Isis)*. She is angry at the Company of Gods and Goddesses so she decided to take a life-oath; she is swearing on her life and on...

55.2.

55.2.1. *Neter{net} embah ta Pesedjetu{net} im djed ankh*

55.2.2. Divine{div} front-of that Company {div} form-of speaking living

55.2.3. …the Divine Divinity in front of the divine Company invoking her living…

55.3.

55.3.1. *Mut{net} Net{net} Netert   ankh Ptah{net} ta-tu-nen{net}{net}*

55.3.2. Mother{div} Neith{div} goddess living Ptah{div} earth architect of divine divine

55.3.3. …divine mother, goddess *Net (Neith),* and the living god *Ptah-ta-tunen*, the twice divine architect of Earth-Creation, both of them high divinities among the ranks of all divinities.

Verse 56.

56.1.1. *iu   tu   uah   nay   medtu   embah   Temu {net}*
56.1.2. it is   to   swear   by   speech   before   Temu {div}

56.1.3. It is an oath that I am swearing, by my own life, which is about my outrage that I will impart through my speech in front of the god *Temu*, the aspect of *Ra* that relates to dissolution as ender of Creation…

56.2.

56.2.1. *sensu seru imy Anu mitet{mdj} Khepera{net} hery ab uia {net} F*
56.2.2. nobles and elders in Heliopolis {fig} likewise Creator-of-Forms{div} boat{div} he

56.2.3. …who is the noble elder in the city of Anu(Heliopolis), the city of the Sun divinity Ra Tem; likewise I will impart my thoughts, about this unethical process, to the god *Khepera*, the Creator of Creation aspect of *Ra,* and we will see what they say about the travesty that is being discussed and proposed here now.

EGYPTIAN BOOK OF THE DEAD HIEROGLYPH TRANSLATIONS Volume 6: Featuring The Osirian Resurrection

Verse 60.

60.1.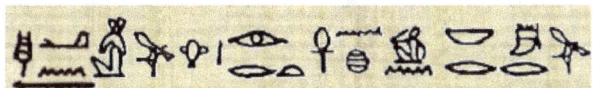

60.1.1. *ahan   Set{net} her art-ankh en Neberdjer{net}*
60.1.2. attention Seth{div} her do-living-oath to Lord-of-All{div}

60.1.3. Now the attention turns to momentous words by the god *Set (Seth)*. This person takes the severe action of doing a life-oath, swearing on the divine *Lord-of-All* himself…

60.2.

60.2.1. *er djed ben iu A   er se chenu   im ta qenebtu   iu   Aset{net} im set*
60.2.2. as-to say bad it is I a   s-to cause isolate through the assemblies it is   Aset (Isis) within she

60.2.3. …by swearing the following; I *Set (Seth)* say it is bad to have these assemblies the way they are presently constituted; we should isolate them at a different location where this woman (*Aset (Isis)*), cannot be allowed access to it.

Verse 79.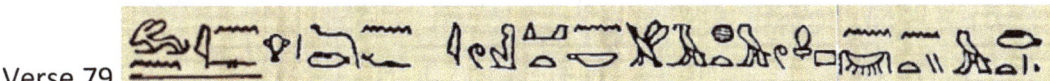

79.1. *un   in ze her djed en-F   iu a dit en-K chena chetmu   en nub enty im det*
79.2. presence by she person says to-him it is I give to thee consider value of gold empty hand

79.3. Now, the presence of the goddess is felt as she says to the boatman called **Nemnty,** who is a god that facilitates transportation: "Here, I am giving you the gold that was in my hand which is not empty."

The image above is included to give an impression of a scene where Isis, disguised as an old lady, meets the boatman.

Aset (Isis) and the Boatman

Verse 81.

81.1.1. *un in F udjay   set er chenay   hery {ab} chera er su im nay*

81.1.2. presence of the boat-voyage she as-to consideration content before as-to him in his

81.1.3. Now, the presence of the boatman is felt as he accepted her gold and grants her the boat ride to the island location of the Company of Gods and Goddesses. He felt hesitant about transporting any woman to the island where the court was meeting, but was content, having received the payment in gold.

81.2.

81.2.1. *aqs khery{mdj} na menu*

81.2.2. walk under{fig} some trees

81.2.3. The boat reaches its destination, the isolated island where *Set (Seth)* demanded that the deliberations should be held without the presence of *Aset (Isis)*. The goddess starts walking among some trees.

Verse 82.

82.1.

82.1.1. *un   in ze nu   iu set petra   ta Pesedjetu*

82.1.2. presence of she observes. It is she surveying   that Company of Gods Goddesses

82.1.3. Now the presence of *Aset (Isis)* is felt as she observes her surroundings and then she spots where the Company of Gods and Goddesses is located.

82.2.

82.2.1. *iu   senu hemz her imy   aqu   embah Neberdjer{net}*

82.2.2. it is them sitting persons within-eating breads   presence Lord-of-All{div}

82.2.3. She spotted them within an area eating bread together in the presence of the divine *Lord-of-All*.

EGYPTIAN BOOK OF THE DEAD HIEROGLYPH TRANSLATIONS Volume 6: Featuring The Osirian Resurrection

Aset (Isis) Tricks Seth into Speaking Truth and Decreeing His Own Fate

Verse 87.

    87.1.   un in ze her shenty im hekauy   set

    87.2.   presence of she person pronouncing form words-power she

    87.3.   Now the presence of Aset (Isis) is felt again as she begins uttering words of power on herself.

Verse 88.

    88.1.   iu set aryt Kheperu{mdj} set im ua   sherau   nefert{mdj} en hatu   set

    88.2.   it is she doing transforming{fig} she form one maiden beautiful{fig} of body hers

    88.3.   She makes her body transform into one with the appearance of a maiden with an irresistibly beautiful physical body that would be appealing to Set (Seth).

Verse 89.

    89.1.   iu an unu   mi qednu{mdj} set im chena ta er djer F

    89.2.   it is not existing like design{fig} woman consider earth as to anywhere he
                                  constructed
                        formed, qualities

    89.3.   Aset (Isis) created a body that was so beautiful in its design, form, proportions and qualities that he, Set (Seth), would not have seen anywhere in the world.

EGYPTIAN BOOK OF THE DEAD HIEROGLYPH TRANSLATIONS Volume 6: Featuring The Osirian Resurrection

The image above has been provided to give the reader a visual impression of the events and meaning at this stage in the text.

Verse 90.
- 90.1. *ahan en F mer*   ta set er   djuu   aah en   ur
- 90.2. attention to him desire that woman as-to greatly of enormously

- 90.3. Now attention goes to *Set (Seth)*, who, upon seeing her, immediately desired her badly, so much as to be smitten and obsessed with lust.

Verse 95.
- **95.1.** *iu F her djed en-ze tua*   *im sheraut {mdj} nefert*
- 95.2. it is he person saying to her: you form maiden beautiful

- 95.3. Now *Set (Seth)* speaks to her: "Hey, you there, I call to you who are the very perfect form of a beautiful maiden."

Verse 96.

96.1. iu set djed en F kay   chenay   neb{net} aah{mdj}
96.2. it is she speaking to him reflect consideration lord{div} great{fig}

96.3. *Aset (Isis){as maiden}* began to speak to *Set (Seth)*. She started by explaining her situation for the consideration of *Set (Seth)*, who she, as the beautiful maiden, addresses as a "great lord."

Verse 97.

97.1. Ar anuk   unu   A im hem madayt {mdj}   ua   menau
97.2. as-to I   existing I as wife together-with{fig} one herdsman

97.3. As for myself, I lived as the wife of a herdsman and we were together.

Verse 98.

98.1. iu A mesu n-F ua   sa   tjay
98.2. it is I birthed for-him one child   male

98.3. It is I who birthed one male child for him.

Verse 99.

99.1. iu chenay   A hay   mit
99.2. it is considering my husband dead

99.3. Now, consider my plight, that my husband, unfortunately, died and I, along with my young child were left alone.

EGYPTIAN BOOK OF THE DEAD HIEROGLYPH TRANSLATIONS Volume 6: Featuring The Osirian Resurrection

Verse 100.

100.1.

100.1.1. **iu chena a-djed nemh khepru im sa nay aautetu {dher} en**
100.1.2. it is considering I-say orphan transform into educate he position {cattle} of

100.1.3. Now consider the situation; my little boy is an orphan, my son has had be educated in and forced to take on the role, and assume the position of tending cattle for...

100.2.

100.2.1. **chenay F atef {net}**
100.2.2. consideration he father{div}

100.2.3. ...fulfilling the position of his {divine} father. Set does not notice the use of the title divine when the maiden referred to her husband.

Verse 101.

101.1. chera er ua remtju djeradjeru {mdj} iay
101.2. assuredly as-to one person border-crossing{fig} came

101.3. Assuredly, I will tell you about a certain person, a man who crossed the borders of our property.

Verse 102.

102.1. iu F hemz im chenay A ia haytu-per
102.2. it-is he siting in consider he my estate-buildings

102.3. Think about it, then he sat himself down in our property, without permission or being invited!

Verse 103.

103.1. cher F mi nay her djed-en chenay A sherau   {net}
103.2. presence him like their person says-to then my boy {div}

103.3. Then what happened next is that in the presence of my son this person said to the {divine} boy. Again, Set does not notice the use of the title divine when the maiden referred to her son. *Aset(Isis)* continues telling her story, relating what that man, who crossed the borders of her property, said to her son.

Verse 104.

104.1. iu A qenqen K atef {net} mit tua   nehemu   na aautetu   en chenay K
104.2. it is I   beating thee father{div} dead me snatching   his position of concerning your

104.3. "It is I who am going to beat you. Your father is dead so nobody can stop me, and you are young and feeble. So I am taking over and grabbing the offices, position, and possessions of yours,...

104.4. atef {net}
104.5. father{div}
104.6. ...from your divine father."

Verse 105.

105.1. cher   A-er dit   ary K n-F necht   tu
105.2. with   me as-to give doing thee to-he strength   to

105.3. Now I say to you great sir [*Aset (Isis)* speaking to *Set (Seth)*], who are with me, I give you permission to apply your strength to this man so as to protect us from him. Will you help me and my son?

EGYPTIAN BOOK OF THE DEAD HIEROGLYPH TRANSLATIONS Volume 6: Featuring The Osirian Resurrection

Verse 106.
106.1.1. ahan Set{net} her djed n-Ze   ia   arytu   dit na
106.1.2. attention Seth {div} person says to-her I-say doing giving his

106.1.3. Now attention goes to the god *Set (Seth)*, the person who now replies to *Aset (Isis)*. This is what I say, about the action of giving himself…

106.2.
106.2.1. aautetu {mdj} en chena remtju djeradjerau   {mdj}
106.2.2. position   {fig} of considering person border-crossing{fig}

106.2.3. …the position {fig} of his own volition and to cross a border into someone else's property and take over and…

Verse 107.
107.1. iu chena   sherau   en   chena   ahauty   aha
107.2.   it is considerable boy-child   to   then   fighting   standing-up

107.3. …then forcing the boy-child to get into a fight with him. I will stand up for you, oh beautiful maiden; you can count on me to fight on your behalf against such injustice perpetrated by such a despicable bully, a thug who forces himself on a helpless widow and a young child.

Verse 108.
108.1.1. ahan   Aset {net} her aryt   kheperu{mdj} set im ua djerat
108.1.2. attention Isis{div} person does transformation{fig} she into one kite

108.1.3. Now attention turns to *Aset (Isis)*, who transformed her body again. This time, she transformed from the beautiful but illusory maiden into the body of a kite, a female hawk.

108.2.

108.2.1. *iu set   puyt*

108.2.2. it is she taking-flight

108.2.3. Then *Aset (Isis)*, in her form as a kite, took flight…

The image above has been provided to give the reader a visual impression of the events and meaning at this stage in the text.

Verse 109.
109.1. *iu   set   hemz   her   udjay   tep en   ua en shentyu*
109.2. it is she sitting person safe / strong top of   one of acacias

109.3. …from her position standing in front of *Set (Seth)*, to a position of safety, sitting, in a position of strength, atop some acacia trees.

EGYPTIAN BOOK OF THE DEAD HIEROGLYPH TRANSLATIONS Volume 6: Featuring The Osirian Resurrection

Verse 110.

110.1.1. iu set ash   en Set{net} ia tjemu   en-K   in   im ra-K

110.1.2. it is she calling-out to Seth{div} hey crying of-thee by through mouth-thine

110.1.3. It is *Aset (Isis)* now calling *Set (Seth)* out on his hypocrisy. And he started crying when he realized what was happening, as if he was the one who was wronged, and feeling embarrassed at being caught in his hypocrisy. *Aset (Isis)* says: "Hey, don't bother crying about it; the words came out of your mouth.

110.2.

110.2.1. ia   djed su   djez-K

110.2.2. hey   speech your own-thine

110.2.3. Hey, you admitted it was wrong about what I told you that happened to the widow which is what you yourself are trying to do to me and *Heru (Horus)*. Ha! So, you are caught by your own words, and you have pronounced the judgment upon your own self."

Seth Complains to Ra about What Isis has done but Gets No Relief and Still Does Not Accept His Fate

Verse 123.

123.1.1. ia n-Z n-A   un   in chena   Ra{net}-Heru{net}-akhty{net}{net}

123.1.2. Hey-I, said to she of me presence of consideration Ra{div}-Horus{div}two-horizons{div}{div}

123.1.3. Now *Set (Seth)* goes to the god *Ra-Herakty*. *Set (Seth)* tells him that he said to goddess *Aset (Isis)* that he would help her and that it is wrong what the man wanted to do to her family, taking over their property and beating her son, etc. But that was based on a deception from *Aset (Isis)* so *Set (Seth)* is making that complaint. Then the presence of the god *Ra-Horus-Two-Horizons (Creator-Spirit-of-the-two-horizons [twice divine])*, *Ra-Herakty* was felt in consideration of this matter (the deception of *Aset (Isis)* perpetrated on *Set (Seth)*)...

EGYPTIAN BOOK OF THE DEAD HIEROGLYPH TRANSLATIONS Volume 6: Featuring The Osirian Resurrection

Seth Complains to Ra about What Isis has Done but Gets No Relief and Still Does Not Accept His Fate

The image above has been provided to give the reader a visual impression of the events and meaning at this stage in the text.

123.2.

    123.2.1.   **Her djed n-F   iu-K   djed n-Ze ach**

    123.2.2.   person said to him it is you said to her what?

    123.2.3.   ...this person(*Ra*) said to *Set (Seth)*: "Hey, it was you who said that to her. So, what can I do about it? What's done is done. So you are going to have to deal with it!"

Verse 129.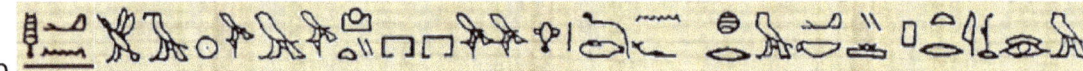

    129.1.1.   *ahan*   **chena Ra{net}-Heru{net}-akhty{net}{net} Her djed n-F   cher ma Ky {mdj} petra im**

    129.1.2.   attention consideration Ra{div}-Horus{div}two-horizons{div}{div} person says to him presence behold
                                                                                                        moreover observe

    129.1.3.   Now attention turns to the god *Ra-Horus-Two-Horizons (Creator-Spirit-of-the-two-horizons[twice divine], Ra-Herakty)*, who, after considering *Set's (Seth's)* statements replies: "come to your senses and look at yourself, your actions, motivations, feelings and intents; then observe the fact that...

EGYPTIAN BOOK OF THE DEAD HIEROGLYPH TRANSLATIONS Volume 6: Featuring The Osirian Resurrection

129.2.

129.2.1. **ent-K ia weput tu djez-K ach cher-K an**

129.2.2. of-thee you-say judgment to your-self what before-you rejected

129.2.3. ...you yourself have judged yourself and you have done so with your own volition; so your complaint, that you have brought to me, about what your sister goddess *Aset (Isis)* did to you, is rejected."

Verse 130.

130.1. *ahan* Set{net} her djed en-F amma an tu Nemty{net} chena ma kheny

130.2. attention Seth {div} person says to him give bring to Nemty{div} consider ferryman

130.3. Now attention turns to *Set (Seth)*; he says to Ra "well forget about *Aset (Isis)*, just bring me Nemty. He is the unrighteous ferryman who brought her to our private court session so he is the one at fault for my problems." So *Set (Seth),* avoiding facing his own unrighteousness, criminality, hypocrisy, and guilt over what he had done to Asar, redirected his aggression from *Aset (Isis)* onto or Nemty, the boatman, and punished him, as he could not punish anyone else other than himself.

Nemnty (the boatman) is punished by Seth for ferrying Isis to the Island where the Company was sequestered.

Ra Decrees That The Crown Should Be Given to Heru (Horus)

Verse 135.

135.1. *un in* chena Ra{net}-Heru{net}-akhty{net}{net} hena Temu{net} neb tawy Anu {net}

135.2. presence of then Ra{div}-Horus{div}two-horizons{div}{div} with Temu{div} Lord two-lands Heliopolis{div}

135.3. Now the presence of the god *Ra-Horus-Two-Horizons (Creator-Spirit-of-the-two-horizons[twice divine], Ra-Herakty),* and that of the god *Temu*, the aspect of *Ra* that relates to dissolution as ender of Creation, Lord of the Two Lands of Upper and Lower Egypt, whose seat of power is the city of the sun divinity (Anu/Heliopolis) is being felt.

EGYPTIAN BOOK OF THE DEAD HIEROGLYPH TRANSLATIONS Volume 6: Featuring The Osirian Resurrection

The image above has been provided to give the reader a visual impression of the events and meaning at this stage in the text.

Verse 138.

138.1.

138.1.1. *iu tenu dit hedjt{net} her tep{net} en Heru{net} sa{net} Aset{net}*
138.1.2. it is you-all give white{div} person head-top{div} of Horus{div} son{div} Isis {div}

138.1.3. …The decree for you (speaking to the Company of Gods and Goddesses) now is to give the Divine White Crown signifying legitimate rulership of Kemet (Ancient Egypt), and place it on the divine head of divine *Heru/Horus*, who is the divine son of goddess *Aset (Isis)*…

138.2.

138.2.1. *im tu tenu tenhaty F er ta aset-peru en atef Asar{net}*
138.2.2. through to you-all wings he as-to this throne of father Osiris {div}

138.2.3. …by you-all placing wings on him so that he may take flight as the sovereign sitting on the throne of his divine father the divine *Asar (Osiris)*.

Set (Seth) Does Not Agree with the Decree to Give the Throne to Heru (Horus) and Vows to Fight On by Taking an Oath

Verse 142.

142.1. **ahan Set{net} ash segabu   aah{mdj} her en tay Pesedjetu {net}**
142.2. attention Seth{div} cry-out   great{fig} person to Company{div}

142.3. Now attention turns to Set (Seth) {div}. He cries out bitterly at what has happened. The god Heru (Horus) has been crowned. Set (Seth) turns his attention to the Company of Gods and Goddesses.

Verse 146.

146.1.1. **un   in n-F aryt ankh   im djed   ia ruay   hedj{net} her tep en{net} Heru{net}**
146.1.2. presence of from him action life-oath by speaking I reverse   white{div} person head-top{div} of
                                                                                          Horus{div}

146.1.3. Now his presence is felt as he takes the action of uttering a life-oath by speaking the following words: "I will reverse what has been done with the white crown, the putting of it on the top of the head of the god Heru (Horus)...

146.2.
146.2.1. **sa{net} Aset{net} metutu   chaa   F er chena mu ary   se-chenu**
146.2.2. son{div} Isis {div}   (some)one topple him as-to then water actions cause-advancing

146.2.3. ...the son of goddess Aset (Isis). I reject what has happened and someone [i.e. Set (Seth)] will knock the crown from his head and he will fall over like a hippopotamus that has been struck down.

146.3.
146.3.1. **iay   er   mau   F   er ta   aautetu   {mdj}**
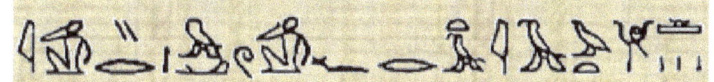
146.3.2. I   say   struggle   he   as-to that office/position {fig}
146.3.3. I say that I will continue to struggle with him, so it's not over; I will fight him for control of the offices and position of the throne of Kemet (Ancient Egypt)."

EGYPTIAN BOOK OF THE DEAD HIEROGLYPH TRANSLATIONS Volume 6: Featuring The Osirian Resurrection

Horus and Seth Fight as Hippopotamuses

The image above has been provided to give the reader a visual impression of the events and meaning at this stage in the text.

Verse 148.

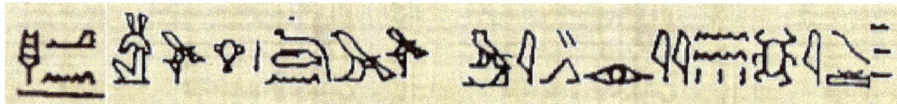

148.1.
148.1.1.   *ahan*   **Set{net} her djen en Heru{net} maay ary nenu {mdj}**
148.1.2.   attention Seth{div} person says to Horus{div} permit doing ourselves transformation

148.1.3.   Now attention turns to the god *Set (Seth)*; this person *Set (Seth)* says to the god *Heru (Horus)*: "Lets allow ourselves to go fight by transforming ourselves…

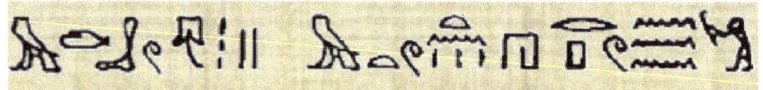

148.2.
148.2.1.   *im debu*   *im tu tenu herpu*
148.2.2.   form hippopotamuses in to those submerging

148.2.3.   … into hippopotamuses going into those waters and submerging ourselves and fighting underwater." This battle between Heru (Horus) and Set (Seth) that is occurring submerged in the waters is a metaphysical metaphor for the Sekhet Hetep realm of the Duat, the Netherworld, that metaphysically refers to the

EGYPTIAN BOOK OF THE DEAD HIEROGLYPH TRANSLATIONS Volume 6: Featuring The Osirian Resurrection

subconscious mind (under the surface of the conscious mind) where the battle of *Heru (Horus)*, Spiritual Aspiration, and *Set (Seth)*, Egoism, takes place, to claim the throne of Kemet (Ancient Egypt), that is, Spiritual Victory, Spiritual Enlightenment.

Verse 154.

154.1. **iu   set   tjezu   n-F   chena   ma   chau**
154.2.   it is she tying   to-he then   behold rope
154.3. *Aset (Isis)* tied, a piece of copper that she formed into a harpoon, with some rope.

Aset sends a harpoon intended to hit Set

The image above has been provided to give the reader a visual impression of the events and meaning at this stage in the text.

Verse 155.

155.1.
155.1.1. **iu   set   hep   tu   F   er   chena   mu**
155.1.2.   it is she fetter-strike to   he   as-to then   water

155.1.3. *Aset (Isis)* is worried about the fight and the possibility of *Set (Seth)* hurting her son. So she prepares to throw the copper harpoon to fetter *Set (Seth)*, into the water…

EGYPTIAN BOOK OF THE DEAD HIEROGLYPH TRANSLATIONS Volume 6: Featuring The Osirian Resurrection

155.2.
155.2.1. er   ta aset-per herpu   ia   aru   Heru{net} hena Set{net}
155.2.2. as-to that abode submerged   I   do   Horus{div} and Seth{div}

155.2.3. ...in order to have it go to where divine *Heru (Horus)* and divine *Set (Seth)* had earlier submerged themselves into the waters.

Verse 158.
158.1. ia   ashu en tjebu   sefech   im   A   anuk Heru{net} sa{net} Aset{net}
158.2. hey cries-out to copper-weapon loosen me   I-am Horus{div} son{div} Isis{div}

158.3. Instead of striking and fettering the god *Set (Seth)*, the weapon, instead, hit the god *Heru (Horus)*. He cried out in pain saying: "the copper weapon has hit me; loosen it since, I am divine *Heru (Horus)*, the son of the divine *Aset (Isis)*."

> Goddess Aset(Isis) calls out to her harpoon to release Heru and it does. She then releases the weapon again and this time it hits Seth.

Verse 161.
161.1.1. un   in Ze [dmg]   er hui   tu   F
161.1.2. presence of Isis [dmg] as-to fetter   to   him

161.1.3. Now the presence of *Aset (Isis)* is felt as she releases the weapon again and this time it is directed to fetter him [*Set (Seth)*]...

161.2.
161.2.1. an   er chena mu   iu   F dep   medi hem {net} en Set{net}
161.2.2. contradict as-to then water it is he taste means-of servant{div} to Seth{div}

161.2.3. ...so as to contradict what he is doing in the waters; the weapon bites and tastes the body of the god *Set (Seth)* so as to make him into a servant (i.e. sublimate his feelings, intents and actions) and thus restrict what he is doing.

Verse 164.

164.1.1. **ahan** Set{net} her ash n-Ze er djed in iu mertu {set} chena Ze-A

164.1.2. attention Seth{div} person cry-out to-she as-to say that it is loving thus she-he

164.1.3. Now the presence of the god *Set (Seth)* is felt as this person cries out to *Aset (Isis)* saying: "by sending your weapon to me, does that mean that you love him…

164.2.

***164.2.1.* djerdjerau {mdj} er sen{net} en mut Set {net}**

164.2.2. boasting   {fig}   as-to brother{div} of mother Set{div}

164.2.3. …but what about me?" Arrogantly: "Aren't I your own brother who has the same mother as you?"

Verse 165.

165.1. **ahan** Aset{net} ashu en chenay set tjebu im djed   sefech   im F

165.2. attention Isis{div} call-out to then her copper form speaking loosen   in him

165.3. Now the presence of goddess *Isis* is felt as she calls out to her copper weapon by speaking the words: "loosen, release from biting into him."

Verse 167.

167.1. **un in her{net} sa{net} Aset{net}** qendt   er   mut tu F Aset{net}

167.2. presence of Horus{div} son{div} Isis{div} anger   as-to mother of his Isis{div}

167.3. Now the presence of the god *Heru (Horus)*, the divine son of the divine goddess *Aset (Isis)*, who is a serpent goddess, became exceedingly angry at his mother, the divine *Aset (Isis)*.

EGYPTIAN BOOK OF THE DEAD HIEROGLYPH TRANSLATIONS Volume 6: Featuring The Osirian Resurrection

Heru (Horus) Cuts Off the Head of Aset (Isis) and a Deep Truth is Revealed About Her Nature

Verse 171.

    171.1. *iu   F   ruay   udjay   en {net} mut to F Aset{net}*

    171.2. it is he reversal cut-head{div}   of {div}mother his Isis{div}

    171.3. It is he *Heru (Horus)* who, in his great anger, reversed himself from the fight with *Set (Seth)* and turned to his divine mother *Aset (Isis)* and cut off her divine head.

Verse 174.

    174.1. *un   in   Aset{net} her aryt kheperau set im ua en repyt   {net} en dez*

    174.2. presence of Isis{div}   person does transformation she into on of statue   {div} of   flint
                                                                                                                noble
                                                                                                             woman

    174.3. Now the presence of divine *Aset (Isis)* is felt as this personality makes a transformation from animated goddess into a statue of a noble woman/goddess that was made of flint, a very hard finely grained mineral quartz stone.

Granite Statue of Aset (Isis)

Ancient Egyptian Flint Ancient Egyptian Neolithic Period

Verse 175.

175.1. iu an unu   im dez set udjay   {net}
175.2. <u>it is without existing in statue hers head   {div}</u>

175.3. This statue is with the body only and does not have a head. This revelation about the goddess displays her catalyst nature that sparks the process of resurrection and births the process of spiritual evolution through her service to the soul, *Asar(Osiris)* and her nurturing of the redeemer of the soul, *Heru(Horus)*.

Heru (Horus) Leaves the Battle and Goes to the Mountains to Find Rest from the Fight

Verse 183.

183.1.
183.1.1. ***ast   ar Heru{net} su sedjer   khery   ua neha   shenusha***
183.1.2. <u>behold as-to Horus{div} he sleep   under   one sycamore   grove</u>

183.1.3. Now look at what is happening to *Heru (Horus)*. After the recent events of fighting with *Set (Seth)* but each one not winning over the other, as well as the incident of *Aset (Isis)* trying to help *Heru (Horus)* but being unable to help him or stop *Set (Seth)*, *Heru (Horus)* left the fight and went to reflect, recuperate and rest under a sycamore tree that was in a grove…

Ancient Egyptian Tomb of Sennedjem at Dier-el-Medina showing worship of goddess Nut as the Sycamore Tree

EGYPTIAN BOOK OF THE DEAD HIEROGLYPH TRANSLATIONS Volume 6: Featuring The Osirian Resurrection

183.2.

183.2.1. im chena   ta   en uaht
183.2.2. in at that time land of oasis

183.2.3. ...that was at that time located in an oasis land, away from the fight and away from the Company of Gods and Goddesses.

Heru (Horus) is Found by Set (Seth) and he Injures Heru (Horus)

Verse 184.

184.1. un   in   Set{net} her   gem   imu {mdj} tu F   iu   F   mehy im F
184.2. presence of Seth{div} person found within {fig} to   him   it is   he   full   in   he

184.3. Now the presence of the god *Set (Seth)* was felt as he found *Heru (Horus)*. He found him *Heru (Horus)* as he was feeling disheartened and full of himself in a pitiful state, as if everything is about him, his troubles, his sorrows, his life.

Verse 185.

185.1. iu F   hui   tu F her aty   F her chena   dju
185.2. it is he fettering-strike to him person without{back} he person then mountain

185.3. So, the god *Set (Seth)*, finding the god *Heru (Horus)* in such a state, did strike out at him, and was able to hurt and fetter him, temporarily incapacitating the god *Heru (Horus)*, as he was lying on a mountain, resting.

Verse 186.

186.1. iu   F   ruay   udjat   {net} F {snwj} im aset-per tu
186.2. it is he reverse   eyes   {div}his{two} in abode to

186.3. Then the god *Set (Seth)* carried out the reversal he had vowed previously by gauging out the two divine eyes, which represent the sun (right eye) and the moon (left eye), of the god *Heru (Horus)* from their abode in his eye-sockets.

EGYPTIAN BOOK OF THE DEAD HIEROGLYPH TRANSLATIONS Volume 6: Featuring The Osirian Resurrection

Verse 188.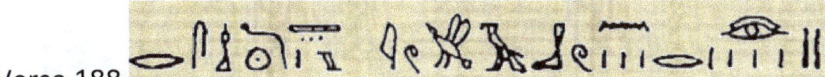

188.1.1. **er se-hedj ta   iu chena bu enu er artu {snwj}**
188.1.2. about dawn earth it is thus   place we as-to eyes {two}

188.1.3. When the sun started coming up over the horizon, the two eyes...

188.2.

188.2.1. **en arty-F{net} kheperu   im ze-cha reret {snwj}**
188.2.2. of eyes-his{div} transform into pill/bulb {two}

188.2.3. ...the eyes of his, reverted to their germinal forms and turned into two pill like spheres.

Verse 189.

189.1.   **iu senu redu   {mdj} im zesheny**
189.2.   it is they springing-up{fig} as lotuses

189.3.   Then those same two pill or bulb like spheres transformed into their natural forms and sprouted into two lotuses.

Above: image of two Blue Lotuses

Above: images of the sun and moon- which are the eyes of Heru (Horus) and of Ra

Goddess Hetheru (Hathor) Finds Heru (Horus) and Heals Him

Verse 192.

192.1. *un   in   Hethert   {net} neb{t} nehat   {net} resy   her   shemt*
192.2. presence of Hathor   {div} mistress sycamore   {div} southern person guide

192.3. Now the presence of goddess *Hetheru (Hathor)* is being felt. She is the mistress of the divine southern sycamore and she was searching for the god *Heru (Horus)* seeking to honor him and serve as his guide.

Verse 193.

193.1. *iu set gemu   {mdj} Heru{net}*
193.2. it is she finding {fig}   Horus{div}

193.3. The goddess *Hetheru (Hathor)* "found" the god *Heru(Horus)*.

Verse 194.

194.1. *iu   F   sedjer   her remu   her ta uaht*
194.2. it is he resting   person crying   person this oasis

194.3. He was laid-out, disheartened, resting but as a person crying and alone in the oasis where he had sought refuge from the conflict with *Set(Seth)* and the burst of anger at his mother. As she who is the source of boundless energy which sustains the universe, making contact with *Hetheru (Hathor)* implies the development of inner will-power which engenders clarity of vision to discern what is righteous from what is unrighteous.

EGYPTIAN BOOK OF THE DEAD HIEROGLYPH TRANSLATIONS Volume 6: Featuring The Osirian Resurrection

Verse 195.

195.1. un in Ze mehy im ua   gah-set V196⇒ iu set har   set
195.2. presence of she full in one gazelle-female   it is she measure-milk she

195.3. Now the presence of goddess *Hetheru (Hathor)* is felt again as she finds a female gazelle. V196⇒ Hetheru (Hathor) is "*mehy*" or fullness of Consciousness, which is a reference to her form as Mehurt, the cow goddess that is brimming with life essence that symbolizes the female embodiment of the Primeval Ocean, *Nun*, from which the substance of the world is formed. Fullness refers to her full udder that is full of milk, symbolic of life giving essence. The gazelles are robust creatures as they can live in desert without water, run at high speeds and they dig up *bulbs* from the ground. So Hetheru (Hathor) finds a female gazelle that is likewise full of milk, symbolic of life giving essence and fullness of Consciousness. She then proceeds to milk the gazelle until she gets a measure of its milk from it.

Left-Dorcas Gazelle of North Africa, Right-Ancient Egyptian Gazelle divinity in wood carved statue

Verse 197.

197.1. iu   set her   djed-en Heru{net}
197.2. it is she person says-to   Horus{div}

197.3. It is goddess *Hetheru (Hathor)* now saying to the god *Heru(Horus)*:

Verse 198.

198.1. ia un   aryt K   di-A nay   ia   artetu   im
198.2. I-say open   eye thine give-I his   I   milk   in

198.3. It is me, *Hetheru (Hathor)*, I am asking you to open your eyes so that I may put some special milk into them.

180

EGYPTIAN BOOK OF THE DEAD HIEROGLYPH TRANSLATIONS Volume 6: Featuring The Osirian Resurrection

The gazelle milk given by the goddess *Hetheru (Hathor)* worked and the eyes of the god *Heru(Horus)* were healed. She guided him back to the place where Ra-Herakty was and she explained to him what had happened.

Verse 205.

205.1.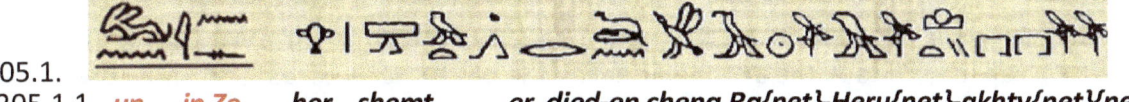

205.1.1. un   in Ze   her   shemt   er djed-en chena Ra{net}-Heru{net}-akhty{net}{net}
205.1.1. presence of Hathor was felt guide   about says-to consider   Ra{div}-Horus{div} two-horizons{div}{div}

205.1.2. Goddess *Hetheru (Hathor)* healed the god *Heru(Horus)*. *Hetheru(Hathor)* restored his two eyes that *Set (Seth)* had gauged out, restoring *Heru's (Horus')* fullness of Consciousness. She then acted as a guide for him and led him to the place where her father, the king of the gods, *Ra-Horus-Two-Horizons* (Creator-Spirit-of-the-two-horizons{twice divine}),]), *Ra-Herakty*, was located, for his consideration of all these issues and recent events.

The image above has been provided to give the reader a visual impression of the events and meaning at this stage in the text.

205.2.

205.2.1. gem im{mdj} Heru{net} iu gabuy   su   Set {net} im aryt F   cher ary A se aha
205.2.2. found in {fig}   Horus{div}   it is wearied   he Seth {div}   in doing he   before action I cuase standing

205.2.3. *Hetheru(Hathor)* tells *Ra*: I, *Hetheru(Hathor)*, found the god *Heru(Horus)* in a wearied state, especially after what *Set(Seth)* did to him, hurting his vision capacity; "I took the action of healing the divine *Heru(Horus)* and I now present him before you and so he is standing here in your presence and none the worse for wear."

> The *Lord-of-All*, in the presence of the Company of Gods and Goddesses told *Heru(Horus)* and *Set(Seth)* to stop fighting and leave them alone and go away and eat and drink and work out their problems and stop fighting. So *Heru(Horus)* and *Set(Seth)* left from the area of the Company and at the suggestion of *Set(Seth)* they went to rest together.

The Gods Heru (Horus) and Set (Seth) are Sent Away and told to Stop fighting. They Go Away Together as Set (Seth) Makes Overtures of Friendship with Ulterior Motives

Verse 212.

212.1. chera ar im chet   tra   en   ruhauy   iu   tu   zesh   en   senu
212.2. before about form going-away time of evening   it is   to   lie-down   of   them

212.3. The two were before, that is in front of, being in the presence of the Company of Gods and Goddesses; from there the two combatants go away together and evening time comes. It is time for them to lie down to sleep.

Verse 213.

213.1. *iu   sedjer   im chena   za {snwj} chera ar im   gerhet*
213.2. it is sleeping   in consider the-two{two} before about form nighttime

213.3. So, now consider that the two combatants are lying down together and it is the middle of the night, the time of sleeping.

Verse 214.

214.1. *iu   Set{net} dit   necht   hannu   F*
214.2. it is Seth{div} allows strong   phallus   his

214.3. Then it was the god *Set(Seth)* who allowed his penis to become strong and stiff.

Verse 215.

215.1. *iu   F   dit hannu an-zenen er aud   menty   red en Heru{net}*
215.2. it is he(Seth) puts penis to-move as-to between thighs   leg of Horus{div}

215.3. Then the god *Set(Seth)* moved his penis to a position in between the thighs of the god *Heru(Horus)*.

Verse 216.

216.1. *un   in   Heru{net} her dit tay   F det   er   aud   menty redy F*
216.2. presence of Horus{div} person gives that his hand   as-to between   thighs legs his

216.3. Now, the presence of the god *Heru(Horus)* is felt as he instinctively placed his hand between his thighs and legs.

EGYPTIAN BOOK OF THE DEAD HIEROGLYPH TRANSLATIONS Volume 6: Featuring The Osirian Resurrection

Verse 217.

217.1. *iu   F   shesep   ta   metut   en   Set{net}*
217.2. it is   he(Horus) receiving that seed   of   Seth{div}
217.3. So, it would appear that the god *Heru(Horus)* is receiving the semen from the god Set.

Verse 218.

218.1.

218.1.1. *un   in   Heru{net} her shemt   er-djed en mut tu F   Aset {net}*
218.1.2. presence of Horus{div} person marching to-tell   to mother of his Isis   {div}

218.1.3. Now, the presence of the god *Heru(Horus)* is felt as he instinctively went directly to his mother, the goddess *Isis*.

> The god *Heru(Horus)* explained to *Aset(Isis)* about what had happened, how they went to bed and *Set(Seth)* had done what he had done. *Aset(Isis)* asked him to open his hand where he had received the seed of *Set(Seth)*.

Verse 221.

221.1. *iu set ash   segabu   aah*
221.2. it is she(Isis) cries-out shouts-out   greatly

221.3. Realizing what has happened *Aset(Isis)* became extremely dismayed; she cries out, then shouts out and so loudly that anyone in the area would have heard the screams.

Verse 222.

222.1. *iu   set   tjay   {necht}   chenay   set   tjebu*
222.2. it is she(Isis) male   {force}   considering   she   copper-weapon

222.3. Now the goddess *Aset(Isis)* takes action to protect the maleness of *Heru(Horus)*. Considering what has happened she takes a copper weapon in hand.

EGYPTIAN BOOK OF THE DEAD HIEROGLYPH TRANSLATIONS Volume 6: Featuring The Osirian Resurrection

Verse 223.
    223.1. *iu set shad   det F {net}*
    223.2. it is she(Isis) cut-off   hand his {div}

    223.3. Then the goddess *Aset(Isis)* swiftly, without warning, cut off the hand of the divine *Heru(Horus)*.

Verse 225.
    225.1. *iu set shedy   en-F det {net} im shau   {mdj}*
    225.2. it is she(Isis) draw-forth of-him hand{div} through command{fig}

    225.3. Then the goddess *Aset(Isis)* proceeded to draw out of the god *Heru(Horus)* a new hand. This she did through a command uttered by her.

Verse 226.
    226.1. *un in Ze an en-Ketu {mdj} en sega en-en {qerhet} nedjm{mdj}*
    226.2. presence of Isis bringing item s {fig} of carry of-to {jar} sweet {fig}

    226.3. Now, the presence of *Aset(Isis)* was felt as she proceeded to bring some items to the god *Heru(Horus)*. The items included a jar containing some sweet ointment.

Verse 227.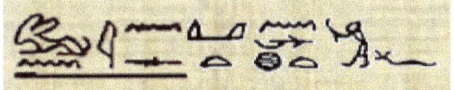
    227.1. *iu set ditu F er hannu   en Heru{net}*
    227.2. it is she(Isis) giving he as-to phallus   of Horus{div}

    227.3. Then the goddess *Aset(Isis)* proceeded to give the ointment to the god *Heru(Horus)* by applying it to his penis. Thus, accessing one's intuitional wisdom capacity, that goddess *Aset(Isis)* represents, facilites the generative power (symbolized by the phallus) of the spiritual aspirant's *Heru(Horus)* capacity to defeat egoism, *Set(Seth)* .

Verse 228.
    228.1. *un in Ze dit necht   F*
    228.2. presence of Isis giving strong   he
    228.3. Now, the presence of *Aset(Isis)* was felt in that she caused the penis of the god *Heru(Horus)* to get "strong", i.e. stiff.

EGYPTIAN BOOK OF THE DEAD HIEROGLYPH TRANSLATIONS Volume 6: Featuring The Osirian Resurrection

Verse 229.

229.1. iu ditu F as ua udjay {qerhet}
229.2. it is giving he as-to one vital {jar}

229.3. Then it was the god *Heru(Horus)* who proceeded to give one portion of his generative vital life force in the form of semen that went into the jar.

Verse 230.

230.1. iu F dit hay tay F metut er-Ze
230.2. it is he give embarks that he seed to-she

230.3. So, it is the god *Heru(Horus), the cosmic principle of spiritual aspiration,* who gives of his semen which was collected by the goddess *Aset(Isis), the cosmic principle of Intuitional Wisdom and knowledge of one's true Transcendental Self.*

Verse 231.

231.1.1. un in Aset{net} her shemt khery ta metut
231.1.2. presence of Isis{div} person guiding custody that semen

231.1.3. The presence of Goddess *Aset(Isis), the goddess of Intuitional Wisdom,* was felt in her having custody of and guiding the seed…

231.2.

231.2.1. en Heru{net} im tra en duau er
231.2.2. of Horus{div} in time of morning as-to

231.2.3. …of the god *Heru(Horus) the cosmic principle of spiritual aspiration,*. In the morning time, about…

231.3.
- 231.3.1. **chena   hesebu   pettu   en   Set   {net}**
- 231.3.2. considering calculating treading of   Seth {div}

231.3.3. ...then and in consideration of the god *Set(Seth)*, the cosmic principle of egoism and the ego-personality (identity as the body-mind complex)...

Verse 232.
- 232.1.1. **iu set her djed-en chena karyu   {mdj}   en   Set   {net}**
- 232.1.2. it is she(Isis) person saying to then gardener {fig}   of   Seth {div}

232.1.3. ...it is *Aset(Isis)*, the person who was talking with the gardener of the god *Set(Seth)*.

232.2.
- 232.2.1. **ach   im   sy   mu   chena**
- 232.2.2. what   in   his   plants   considering-then

232.2.3. She asked him: "what are the type of plants, please consider carefully before answering ...

232.3.
- **232.3.1. enty Set{net}   imy   F   dy   im   diu-K**
- 232.3.2. any   Seth{div} take-in(eats) he here form give-you

232.3.3. ...any ones that the god *Set(Seth)* eats here every day, that are given to him by you?"

> The goddess *Aset(Isis)* finds out from *Set's(Seth's)* gardener that he eats lettuce so the goddess proceeds with her plan to use the semen of *Heru(Horus)* with a specific plan to reverse the plan of Set who was trying to compromise *Heru(Horus)*.

EGYPTIAN BOOK OF THE DEAD HIEROGLYPH TRANSLATIONS Volume 6: Featuring The Osirian Resurrection

Verse 234.

234.1. *iu*   Aset   {net} dit   ta   metut   en   Heru{net} reru
234.2. it is Isis   {div} gives that semen   of   Horus{div} upon

234.3. After finding out, from the gardener, that the god *Set(Seth)* likes to eat lettuce every day, she proceeded to place the seed of the god *Heru(Horus)* on that very same lettuce.

Verse 235.

235.1.1.1. *ahan*   Set{net} her iay   im   chena   F
235.1.1.2. attention   Seth{div} person comes   in   then   he

235.1.1.3. Now attention rises to the god *Set(Seth), the god of egoism and the ego-personality,* who comes into the scene.

235.1.2.
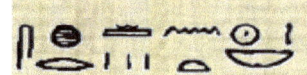
235.1.2.1. *secheru{mdj} ent ra-neb*
235.1.2.2. arrangement{fig} of daily

235.1.2.3. According to the arrangement that the god *Set(Seth)* had, of eating lettuce daily:

Verse 236.

236.1.1. *iu*   F   *imy*   *na*   *ab-tu*[11]   *enty*   *su*   *imyu*
236.1.2. it is he eat   that   pure/holy   any   he   eating

236.1.3. He came in as usual to eat some lettuce. That holy lettuce, being laced with the seed of *Heru(Horus)*, the generative life force of the cosmic principle of spiritual aspiration and redeemer of the Soul, *Asar(Osiris)*, his father, was there and any of

---

[11] NOTE: Verse 236-
The word ab refers to lettuce. The word abt refers to that which is holy and pure – therefore a play on words that incorporate the two terms into one-sanctifying the seed of *Heru(Horus)*

it, even a small portion containing the essence of *Heru(Horus)*, that he would eat, would have the desired effect, and he was eating...

236.2.

236.2.1. im de unuy   zepzen
236.2.2. form hand hurriedly double-time
236.2.3. ...in a rushed manner, double-time.

Verse 237.

237.1. ahan F aha au - ur   im ta metut   en Heru{net}
237.2. attention he stepping-up pregnant greatly through that seed   of Horus{div}

237.3. Now the attention turns to the god *Set(Seth)*, the cosmic principle of egoism and the ego-personality, in who, unbeknownst to himself, a conception has taken place and he has become pregnant with the seed of the god *Heru(Horus)*, the cosmic principle of spiritual aspiration and redeemer of the Soul, *Asar(Osiris)*, his father.

Set(Seth) then challenges *Heru(Horus)* to go in front of the court of Gods and Goddesses to plead their cases.

Verse 241.

241.1. iu   aha   im embah ta Pesedjetu {ntru} aaht{mdj}
241.2. it is stepping-up in presence Company Gods Goddesses great{fig}

241.3. Now it is the two contenders who are stepping up in front of the great Company of Gods and Goddesses.

Verse 243.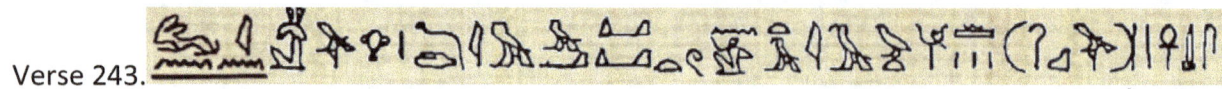

243.1.1. **un** | **in** | **Set{net} her djed amma {snwj} tu** | **n-A ta aautu{mdj}** | **(heq{net})** | **ankh-udja-senab**

243.1.2. presence of | Seth{div} person says give give | to for-me that office{fig} | (sovereign{div}) | life-vitality-health

243.1.3. The presence of the god *Set(Seth)* is felt as he makes demands: "give me, give to me the office and position of being the divine sovereign⟩ Ruler of Egypt with Life-Vitality-Health.

243.2.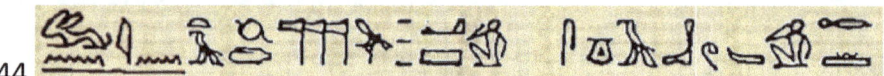

243.2.1. **chena** | **unu** | **ar Heru{net} chena enty aha ary** | **katu** | **ahaty** | **er-F**
243.2.2. consider being | that Horus{div} then null stepping-up action vagina | force | as-to him

243.2.3. Now, you in the Company of Gods and Goddesses should consider that this person stepping up before you, called the god *Heru(Horus)*, is a void, invalid, empty personality because a sexual act such as done to a vagina by a male, has been done on him, by force (by me). I, *Set(Seth)*, egoism, have impregnated the cosmic principle of spiritual aspiration, *Heru(Horus)* with my generative force of egoism, so now he cannot redeem the soul, *Asar(Osiris)*.

Verse 244.

244.1. **un** | **in** | **ta Pesedjetu {net} ash** | **segabu** | **aah{mdj}**
244.2. presence of | that Company of Gods and Goddesses cries-out shouts-out | greatly

244.3. The presence of the Company of Gods and Goddesses was felt now, realizing what has happened, according to what the god *Set(Seth)* said. They became extremely dismayed; they started to cry out; then they started shouting out with a great uproar.

EGYPTIAN BOOK OF THE DEAD HIEROGLYPH TRANSLATIONS Volume 6: Featuring The Osirian Resurrection

Verse 245.

245.1. **un   as senu her besh   pugasu   er her{net} en Heru{net}**
245.2. presence astonishment theirs persons sick/vomit spit about person{div} to Horus{div}
245.3. The presence of the Company of Gods and Goddesses was really strongly felt now because of their astonishment. They, to a person, became ill when they thought about what *Set(Seth)* had said; more than that, they became physically ill and were gagging and throwing up. Then they could not contain their disgust and began spitting at the god *Heru(Horus)*, for allowing himself, the cosmic principle of spiritual aspiration and redeemer of the Soul, *Asar(Osiris)*, to be overtaken by the generative force of the cosmic principle of egoism, *Set(Seth)*, and thus now, be unable to continue the spiritual journey to redeem the father, *Asar(Osiris)*, the Soul. Thus, the Soul would now remain torn into pieces, and unredeemed; individuated ego consciousness, and *Heru(Horus)* the spiritual aspiration cosmic principle is now unable to discover its true Transcendental Self. Truly an upsetting scenario!

Verse 246.

246.1. **un   in Heru{net} sebaat   im   senu**
246.2. presence of Horus{div} laughing   through them
246.3. The presence of the god *Heru(Horus)* was felt now because he started laughing at the gods and goddesses in the Company due to what they were manifesting, having a reaction instead of acting on thoughtful sense, towards him.

Verse 247.

247.1.

247.1.1. **un   in Heru{net} her aryt ankhu   en Neter{net} im djed**
247.1.2. presence of Horus{div} personality doing life-oath of Divinity{div} form saying
247.1.3. The presence of the god *Heru(Horus)* was felt again as his person turned serious when he decided to take a life-oath, swearing on divine Divinity itself through saying…

247.2.

247.2.1. **adjay   chena   djed neb Set{net}**
247.2.2. lies   consider words all Seth{div}
247.2.3. … "I declare emphatically that all the words that the god *Set(Seth)* has said are wicked, evil lies!"

Verse 249.

249.1.

249.1.1. *un   in Djehuty{net} neb Neter{net} medu{net} sesh Maatu {mdj} en Pesedjetu {net} her*
249.1.2. presence of Thoth{div} lord Divine{div} words{div} scribe Truths {fig}   of Company Gods Goddesses persons

249.1.3. The presence of the god *Djehuty(Thoth)*, the lord of divinity and divine words, cosmic principle of purified mind and Cosmic mind, and the scribe of the truths of the Company of Gods and Goddesses…

249.2.

249.2.1. *sekh {mdj} det F her qaht   en Heru{net}*
249.2.2. grasp {fig}   hand his person shoulder   of Horus{div}
249.2.3. …used his hand to grasp the shoulder of the god *Heru(Horus)*.

Verse 250.

250.1. *iu F   her djed   maay   er bu en er wa ta metut   en Set{net}*
250.2. it is he person saying grant-move as-to place where as-to separate that seed   of Seth{div}

250.3. It is he, *Djehuty(Thoth/Hermes)*, he is the person who is saying "I grant the command that the seed/semen of *Set(Seth)* should move and separate itself from the body of *Heru(Horus)* from the place where it is."

Verse 251.

251.1. *iu set   ushebt   en-F im chena mu im khenu   chena   an- ba net seb zepzen*
251.2. it is seed answers   to-him in consideration water in interior thus constricted canal marsh

251.3. It is me, the seed of the god *Set(Seth)* answering you. Please consider that I am over here in the canal of marshy water so I am not in the body of the god *Heru(Horus)*.

EGYPTIAN BOOK OF THE DEAD HIEROGLYPH TRANSLATIONS Volume 6: Featuring The Osirian Resurrection

Verse 252.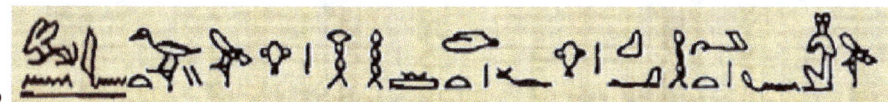
252.1. un   in   Djehuty{net}   sekh {mdj} det F   her qaht   en Set{net}
252.2. presence of Thoth {div}   grasp {fig}   hand his person shoulder   of Seth{div}

252.3. Now the presence of the god *Djehuty(Thoth/Hermes)* was felt as he grasped the shoulder of the god *Set(Seth)*.

Verse 253.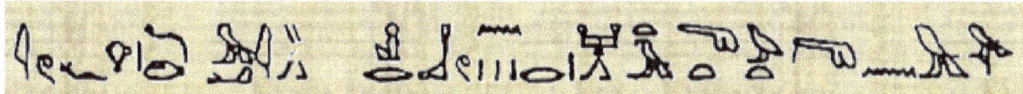
253.1. iu F her djed maay   er bu en er wa ta metut   en Heru{net}
253.2. it is he person saying   grant-move as-to place where as-to separate that seed of Horus{div}

253.3. It is he, *Djehuty(Thoth/Hermes)*; he is the person who is saying "I grant the command that the seed/semen of *Heru(Horus)* should move and separate itself from the body of *Set(Seth)* or from the place where it is."

Verse 254.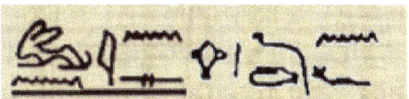
254.1. un   in ze   her djed n-F
254.2. presence of it, the seed personality says to him

254.3. Now the presence of the seed of *Heru (Horus)* is felt as it says to *Djehuty(Thoth/Hermes)*:

Verse 255.
255.1. iu   A   er iay   ten   nu kemau
255.2. it is I   as to coming   your to creating

255.3. "It is I inquiring about coming out as per your command but where can I create a path to come out through?"

Verse 256.

256.1.

256.1.1. **un   in   Djehuty{net} her djed n-Z maay**
256.1.2. presence of   Thoth{div}   person saying to-it permit-come
256.1.3. Now the presence of the god *Djehuty*(Thoth/Hermes) was felt as he said: "I grant you permission to come...

256.2.

256.2.1. **er   bu   en   er   wa   im mesdjert   F**
256.2.2. as to place where as-to separate through ear   his
256.2.3. ...out and separate yourself from the body of Set, through his ear."

Verse 257.

257.1.

257.1.1. **ahan set   her djed n-F   as tu ia   aru   pery**
257.1.2. attention seed person saying to-him notice to me doing coming-forth
257.1.3. Now attention turns to the seed, who replied: "take note that you are asking me to come forth...

257.2.

257.2.1. **er   bu   en   er   wa   im mesdjert   F**
257.2.2. as to place where as-to separate through ear   his

257.2.3. ... out and separate yourself from the body of Set, through his ear...

Verse 258.

258.1. iu   nuk mu   netery{mdj}{net}
258.2. it is I   seed   divine {fig} {div}

258.3. ... it is proper for me to do that, I who am the divine seed from divinity?"

EGYPTIAN BOOK OF THE DEAD HIEROGLYPH TRANSLATIONS Volume 6: Featuring The Osirian Resurrection

Verse 259.

259.1. un in Djehuty{net} her djed n-Z maay er bu en er wa im wept F{net}

259.2. presence of   Thoth   {div} person saying to-it permit-come as to place where as-to separate through forehead his{div}

259.3. Now the presence of the god *Djehuty(Thoth/Hermes)* was felt as he reflected on what the seed of *Heru(Horus)* had replied; then *Djehuty(Thoth/Hermes)* said: "alright, then I grant you permission to come forth through the point between the eyebrows from the forehead of *Set(Seth)*."

Verse 260.

260.1. un in pery im ua en aten nu Ra{net} en nub her tep en Set{net}

260.2. presence of   coming-forth as one of Sundisk of Ra{div} of gold person top-of-head of Seth{div}

260.3. Now the presence of the seed of *Heru(Horus)* is felt as it comes forth through the forehead of *Set(Seth)* in the form of a golden Sundisk proceeding from the god Ra that then moves to the top of the head of the god *Set(Seth)* and perches there as a crown on his head, demonstrating that the egoistic lower aspects of the personality, *Set(Seth)* has been mastered by the higher aspects of the personality, *Heru(Horus)*, and further, Heru's(Horus') spiritual generative power that has been raised to the 6th and 7th *psychospiritual energy centers (Sefech Ba Ra or chakras)*. The movement of Heru's(Horus') seed to the forhead and the point between the eyebrows is reflecting an awakening of Intuitional Wisdom of goddess *Aset(Isis)*, whose abode is represented by the 6th *psychospiritual energy center (Sefech Ba Ra or chakra)* located in the subtle astral body in the location of the point between the eyebrows on the forehead, and then also, the further movement of Heru's(Horus') seed to the crown of the head, the location of the 7th *psychospiritual energy center (Sefech Ba Ra or chakra)*, expressing as the golden Sundisk of Ra (Neberdjer), is reflecting Heru's(Horus') Transcendental experience of himself as Ra, the Transcendetnal Self, Neberdjer. Thus, what is being demostrated by *Heru's(Horus')* spiritual generative power as it expresses in the body of Set(Seth), is that his (Heru's/Horus') Arat Sekhem, Serpent Power Life Force Energy has been raised to the 6th and 7th *psychospiritual energy centers (Sefech Ba Ra or chakras)*, the centers of "Knowing Thyself" or Spiritual Enlightenment, Nehast.

EGYPTIAN BOOK OF THE DEAD HIEROGLYPH TRANSLATIONS Volume 6: Featuring The Osirian Resurrection

Verse 261.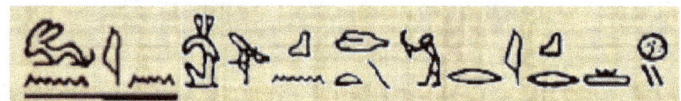

261.1. un in Set{net} qendt er aqer {mdj} zepzen

261.2. presence of Set(Seth){div} angered as-to perfection{fig} doubly

261.3. Now the presence of the god *Set(Seth)* was felt as he became exceedingly angry, especially considering the perfection of the Sundisk and how perfectly he had been outmaneuvered, coopted and presided over by the divine; furthermore, he was angry because the Sundisk proceeded from Ra, whom *Set(Seth)* thought was on his side all along. Now Set sees that Ra, the Creator Spirit and head of the company of gods and goddesses, is on the side of *Heru(Horus)* and not him.

Verse 262.

262.1. iu F auy det -F er meh{mdj}em chena aton nu Ra{net} en nub

262.2. it is he(Seth) stretching arms hand-his as-to fill{fig} inlay then Sundisk of Ra{div} of gold

262.3. It is he, then, the gods *Set(Seth)*, who started raising his arms and tried to grasp the Sundisk of the god Ra, that was on his head; he was trying to grasp, to fill his hands with the Sundisk, of gold, so as to permanently inlay it in his body.

Verse 263.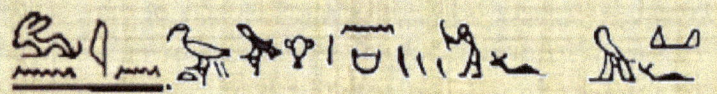

263.1. un in Djehuty her nehemu F im di-F

263.2. presence of god Djehuty person snatching he by giving-himself

263.3. Now the presence of the god *Djehuty(Thoth/Hermes)* was felt as he was the one who snatched the Sundisk from the head of *Set(Seth)* before he was able to grab it. Djehuty then kept the Sundisk for himself.

EGYPTIAN BOOK OF THE DEAD HIEROGLYPH TRANSLATIONS Volume 6: Featuring The Osirian Resurrection

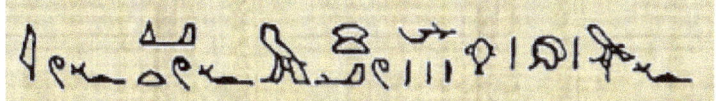

Verse 264.
    264.1. ***iu F di-tu F im chau   her tep {net} F***
    264.2. <u>it is he(Djehuty) giving to himself as crown person top-head {div} his</u>
    264.3. It was *Djehuty(Thoth/Hermes)*, the cosmic principle of Cosmic Mind (mind of the Creator Spirit, *Ra-Neberdjer*), who gave the Sundisk to himself by placing it on his own head as a crown, as this expression of *Heru's(Horus')* seed as the golden Sundisk of Ra represents *Heru's(Horus')* spiritual achievement of triumph of Spirit over ego and intuitional wisdom and Transcendental Consciousness, which now also means his mind is now also one with Cosmic mind.

CONCLUSION OF EPISODE

Verse 265.
    265.1. ***un   in   ta Pesedjetu {net} her djed maat{mdj} tu Heru{net} adjau {mdj} Set{net}***
    265.2. <u>presence of that Company   {div} person saying truth{fig} to Horus{div} lies   {fig} Seth{div}</u>

    265.3. Now the presence of the divine Company of Gods and Goddesses was felt as they, to a person, said: "The truth goes to the god *Heru(Horus)* and the deceits, dishonesties, mendacities, defamations, libels, are coming from the god *Set(Seth)*."

Set (Seth) Again Vows to Reject any Attempt to Give the Throne to Heru (Horus) and Challenges Him to Fight With Ships on the Water

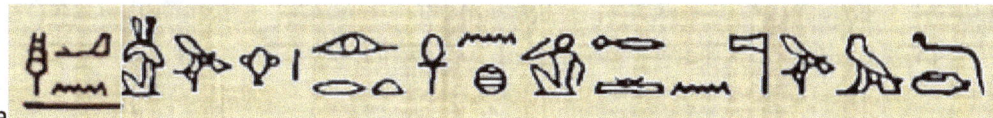

Verse 268.a
    268.1.1. ***ahan Set{net} her   aryt   ankh   aah{mdj} en Neter{net} im djed***
    268.1.2. <u>attention Seth{div} person doing life-oath great{fig} of Divine{div} by saying</u>

    268.1.3. Now the attention is commanded by the divine personality *Set(Seth)* as he makes an oath on Divinity itself by saying:

268.2.

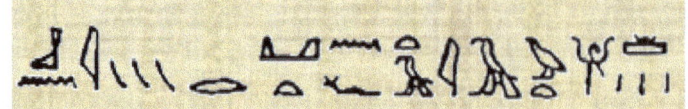

268.2.1. **benau   er   dit   n-F   ta   aautet   {mdj}**
268.2.2. <u>absolutely not about giving to-him that office {fig}</u>

268.2.3. "Absolutely not; I refuse and reject any attempt to give the office {fig} of King of Kemet (Ancient Egypt) to him." This signifies an important point in a spiritual aspirant's spiritual evolution. Even upon experiencing the higher states of consciousness, as *Heru(Horus)*, there is still a lag time to when the *Setian(Sethian)* ego-personality becomes purified and integrates with regards to those higher attainments. So, initially the personality will still present egoistic challenges for the spiritual aspirant.

Verse 269.

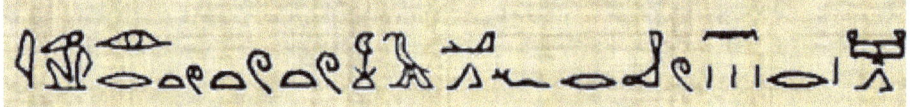

269.1. ia   aryt   tu tutu   chaa   F   er   bu   en   er   wa
269.2. <u>I say action to reject   topple   him as-to place of   as-to removal</u>

269.3. "Furthermore, I vehemently reject the idea and I will topple him and show you how I am stronger than him. Then *Set(Seth)* directs his speech to *Heru(Horus)*; so let us remove ourselves from here and…

Verse 270.

270.1.1. im   tu   ten   medeh nenu nehay   nau
270.1.2. <u>in   to   your   cut   those some   that</u>

270.1.3. …through mine and your resources let's cut some of that…

EGYPTIAN BOOK OF THE DEAD HIEROGLYPH TRANSLATIONS Volume 6: Featuring The Osirian Resurrection

270.2.

    270.2.1. *ahauy*   *en*   *aneru*
    270.2.2. battle-ships   of   stone

    270.2.3. ...stone into the form of battle ships so we can do battle and I will show everyone how I am better than you.

Verse 274.

    274.1. *un*   *in*   *Heru{net} her medeh*   *e-F*   *ua*   *dept*   *en*   *ash*
    274.2. presence of Horus{div} person cut   for-he one ship of cedar

    274.3. Now the presence of the person of the god *Heru(Horus)* is felt as he proceeds to make a boat by cutting cedar wood to put it together into the form of a ship.

EGYPTIAN BOOK OF THE DEAD HIEROGLYPH TRANSLATIONS Volume 6: Featuring The Osirian Resurrection

Above: image of the sacred boat of red cedar found buried next to the Great Pyramid, which is also the same type of material used by *Ra* for his mythic sacred boat(Sundisk that tracerses the heavens.

Image: Artist rendering of a resptred Ancient Egyptian boat.

Verse 275.

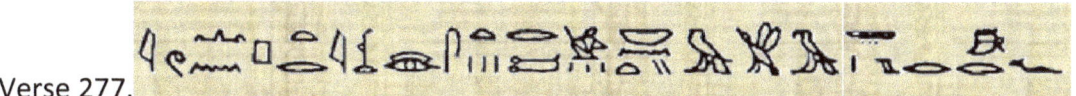

275.1. iu F seqah   F im qa   udja

275.2. it is he plastering   his through   strengthen

275.3. After putting the boat together, out of cedar, he proceeds to plaster over the cedar in order to strengthen the construction and prevent leaks.

Verse 276.

276.1. iu F chaa   F er chera mu im tra   en ruhauy

276.2. it is he pushing himself as-to then water in time   of   evening

276.3. Then the god *Heru(Horus)* proceeded to push the ship over into the water, during the evening time.

Verse 277.

277.1. iu an petra   setu remtej neb-enty im chena ta   er djer F

277.2. it is not survey   them people all-any   in consideration earth as-to when he

277.3. Since it was in the evening time, when the god *Heru(Horus)* placed the ship into the water, there was not even one person around to see what he was doing, as he was completely alone at the time.

Verse 278.

278.1. ahan Set{net} her petra   chena dept   en Heru{net}

278.2. attention Seth{div} person looking concerning boat of Horus{div}

278.3. Now attention turns to the person of the god Set(*Seth*) as, on the next morning, he steps up and looks at the boat of the god *Heru(Horus)*.

EGYPTIAN BOOK OF THE DEAD HIEROGLYPH TRANSLATIONS Volume 6: Featuring The Osirian Resurrection

Verse 279.

279.1. iu F her djed aneru er-F
279.2. it is he person saying stone as-to-he

279.3. Now, it is the personality Set(*Seth*) who assumed and then developed the delusion that the boat of *Heru(Horus)* was made of stone.

Verse 280.

280.1. iu F shemt er chena dju
280.2. it is he guiding to then mountain

280.3. It is he, *Set/Seth*, who then guided himself to the mountains.

Verse 281.

281.1. iu F shad ua tehan pen dju
281.2. it is he cut-off one head-to-earth that mountain

281.3. It is he, *Set(Seth)*, who then cut off one piece of that mountain by butting his head on it.

Verse 282.

282.1. iu F medeh n-F ua dept en aneru
282.2. it is he cut for-he one ship of stone

282.3. It is he, *Set(Seth)*, who then cut the piece of mountain into a ship for himself that was made completely of stone.

Verse 283.

283.1. un as en hay er nay senu ahauy embah ta Pesedjetu {net}
283.2. presence behold them oncomers as-to-their them boat -in-front-of that Company {div}

283.3. Now, the presence of the two of them, the gods *Heru(Horus)* and *Set(Seth)* with their ships, was present in front of the Company of Gods and Goddesses.

EGYPTIAN BOOK OF THE DEAD HIEROGLYPH TRANSLATIONS Volume 6: Featuring The Osirian Resurrection

Verse 284.

284.1. **un   in   chena dept en Set{net} her herpu   im chena mu**
284.2. presence by the   boat   of Seth{div} person sink   in   therefore water

284.3. The attention turned to the presence of the ship of the personality of the god *Set(Seth)* as his boat sank into the water.

The image above has been provided to give the reader a visual impression of the events and meaning at this stage in the text.

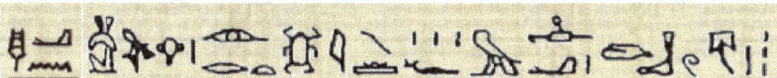

Verse 285.

285.1. ahan Set{net} her aryt kheperau F im   ua   debu
285.2. attention Seth{div} person doing transform he into one hippopotamus

285.3. Now the attention really turned to the god *Set(Seth)* as he became enraged and transformed himself into the form of a hippopotamus.

Verse 286.

286.1. *iu F dit chena gay   chena dept en Heru{net}*
286.2. it is he cause then tear-down   consider ship of Horus{div}

286.3. It is he, *Set(Seth)*, who then banged into the ship of the god *Heru(Horus)*, demolishing it.

Verse 287.

287.1. *un in Heru{net} her tjay {necht} tjebu F*
287.2. presence of Horus{div} person male{force} copper he

287.3. Now the presence of the god *Heru(Horus)* was felt as his personality became indignant, seeing the rage of *Set(Seth)*. The god *Heru(Horus)* then took a copper harpoon and using his male vital life-force hurled the harpoon at the god hippo *Set(Seth)* and struck him.

Verse 288.

288.1. *iu F hui   tu F er hem {net} en Set{net}*
288.2. it is he fettering-striking to he as-to servant {div} to Seth{div}

288.3. It is he, *Heru(Horus)*, who is hitting the god *Set(Seth)* so as to fetter him, causing him to become a divine servant. In metaphysical terms, the ego-personality eventually becomes subdued by the Enlightened Heru consciousness, that is no longer an aspirant, but now established as a self-realized personality.

Verse 289.

289.1. *un in ta Pesedjetu {net} her djed n-F im an ary hui   tu F er-F*
289.2. presence of that Company{div} person said to-him refrain/renounce/give up striking to him as-to him

289.3. Now, the presence of that Company of Gods and Goddesses, that was witnessing all, was felt as they ordered the god *Heru(Horus)* to stop hitting the god *Set(Seth)* and release him on his own recognizance.

EGYPTIAN BOOK OF THE DEAD HIEROGLYPH TRANSLATIONS Volume 6: Featuring The Osirian Resurrection

HERU TRAVELS TO SAIS TO TALK TO HIS GRANDMOTHER

Verse 292.

292.1. iu   F   ched   er   zay   er-djed Net{net} ur Neter-mut {net}
292.2. it is he (Horus) sailing-north to Sais   to-tell Neith{div} great Divinity-mother{div}

292.3. Feeling frustrated at the indecisiveness and intransigence of the Company of Gods and Goddesses, *Heru(Horus)* left the scene and sailed downstream, northwards to the city of Sais where resided his "grandmother" goddess *Net (Neith)*, the divine great mother goddess, and female expression of Neberdjer, the Supreme Transcendental True Self, though beyond gender and duality, expresses and manifests creation in terms of gender and polarity/duality. Again, this visit to hisrelates to *Heru's(Horus')* spiritual attainment of Transcendental Enlightened Consciousness.

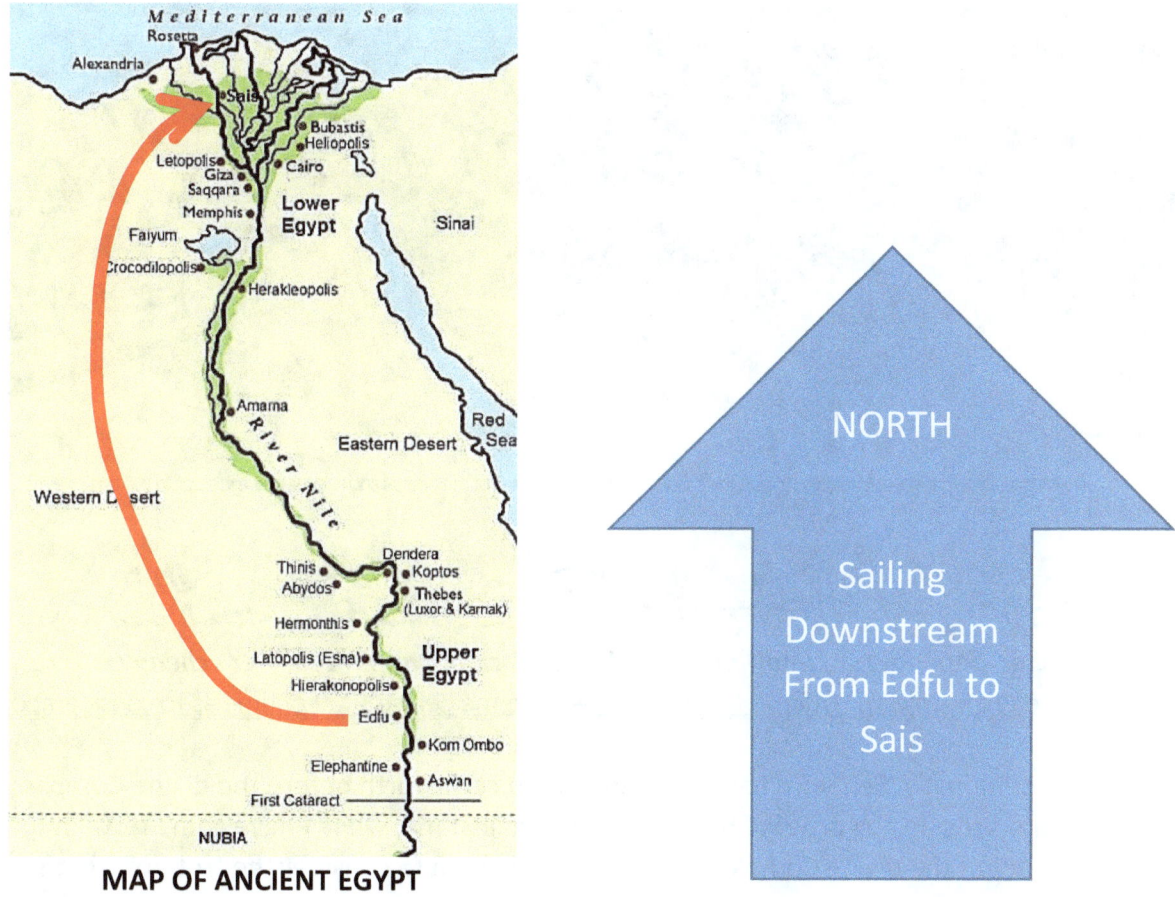

MAP OF ANCIENT EGYPT

NORTH

Sailing Downstream From Edfu to Sais

Verse 294.

294.1. **cher ben tutu   rech{mdj} udja   {mdj}   nenu**
294.2. by   not anyone   know{fig} judge   {fig}   this

294.3. *Heru(Horus)* told her that by no means does anyone (in the divine Company) know how to judge the situation between him and *Set(Seth)* so as to arrive at a final conclusion to the issue.

The image above has been provided to give the reader a visual impression of the events and meaning at this stage in the text.

Verse 295.

295.1. **cher ben dayt   {mdj} maat {mdj} F er A cher cha-en zep   er   chenay**
295.2. before not given   {fig} truth   {fig} he as-to me before 1000-of time as-to consideration

295.3. Additionally, *Set(Seth)* has not been able to come forth before the divine Company and provide any proof of his statements against me; while I have come forth in front of the divine Company 1000 times for them to consider the truth of what I have said.

Verse 296.

296.1. **iu A maatu {mdj}{net} er-F ra-neb**
296.2. it is I truthful {fig} {div} about-him day-every

296.3. Oh divine Mother, it is I, *Heru(Horus)*, who have been in the right and truthful in the things that I have said about him day after day! Yet there is no resolution.

Verse 297.

297.1. **cher iu ben su nu er-djed neb ta Pesedjetu {net}**
297.2. before it is not he see what-say all/any that Company{div}

297.3. Coming before the divine Company, he, *Set(Seth)* does not see any of their points of view or understands what they are saying about how I, *Heru(Horus)*, am right and he is wrong.

RA-of-Two-Horizons Commissions Djehuty (Thoth, Hermes) to Write a Letter to Asar (Osiris)

Verse 305.

305.1. **iu ta Pesedjetu {net} djed Shu{net} sa{net} Ra{net} maaytu im ia djed tu F neb Heru{net} sa{net} Aset{net}**
305.2. it is that Company{div} said Shu{div} son{div} Ra{div} truth in he who speaks to he all Horus[12] {div} son {div} Isis{div}

305.3. It is the divine Company of Gods and Goddesses that is speaking here as they say to one of their own, the god *Shu*, the divine son of the divine god *Ra*; they say: "truth is in all of what is being said by he who is the divine god *Heru(Horus)*[13], the divine son of the divine goddess *Aset(Isis)*.

---

[12] In some Ancient Egyptian texts the god Horus/Heru is refered to by the glyph:
[13] ibid

Verse 307.

307.1. djed ary-en Djehuty{net} en Neberdjer{net} amma habuy ta ucha en Asar{net}

307.2. saying action-to Thoth{div} to Lord-of-All{div} give message support letter to Osiris{div}

307.3. The god *Djehuty (Thoth, Hermes)* speaks to the divine *Lord-of-All*. He tells him that perhaps they should send a letter to the divine god *Asar(Osiris)* for his opinion and input into what should be done at this point since there is still indecision amongst the Company of Gods and Goddesses.

Verse 309.

309.1. un in Neberdjer{net} her djed-en Djehuty{net} hemz ia aru ucha en Asar{net}

309.2. presence of Lord-of-All{div} person said-to Thoth{div} sit-down I-say form do letter to Osiris{div}

309.3. Here the presence of the divine *Lord-of-All/Neberdjer-neter* was felt with a request to the god *Djehuty (Thoth, Hermes)* to sit down and write a letter, in the following way/format to the god *Asar(Osiris)* explaining the situation and their current dilemma.

{ **REPLY FROM THE GOD ASAR (OSIRIS)** }

Verse 319.

319.1. un in-F secheft tu F asta zep zen er chena enty Neberdjer{net} im hena er ta Pesedjetu {net} zep zen

319.2. presence of he (Osiris) undue to he hastening double-time as-to consideration empty Lord-of-All{div} in together double-time with as-to that Company{div}

319.3. Here the presence of *Asar(Osiris)* was felt as he hastily, in quick (double) time, replied to the letter from the divine *Lord-of-All* together with (i.e. in conspiracy with) the Company of Gods and Goddesses, urging their consideration because of the vacuous arguments and reticence to do what is right, in other words, their inability or refusal to uphold truth.

Verse 320.

320.1. er-djed ia   ar   tu   gabuy   sa {net} Heru{net} her ach{mdj}

320.2. as-to say I see   to   wearied   son{div} Horus{div} person what{fig}

320.3. As concerns this matter I, *Asar(Osirs)*, say the following: "I can see now what kind of treatment my wearied son has been receiving in this matter.

Verse 321.

321.1. iu anuk   ia   aru tenu im necht   chera

321.2. it is me   saying deed you-all in strength with

321.3. Now, think hard about what I am going to say. It is my action, my deed; it was I who gave strength to your forms, your manifestations, as cosmic forces, known as Neteru, the gods and goddesses. Indeed, you all operate with my strength and therefore, I am the source from which you owe your vitality, the capacity to be carrying on as the comic principles or forces of the spiritual aspirant, gods and goddesses, to begin with; and this is how you treat my son, who is spiritual aspiration and my redeemer!

Verse 322.

322.1. iu anuk   aru   bedety   er se-ankh neteru{net} mi na aautet her sa neteru{net}

322.2. it is me   doing   barley & grains as-to life Gods/ like their cattle upon nourish Gods/
                                                      Goddesses{div}   Goddesses{div}

322.3. It is me who made the barley and the grains that sustain the life of the gods and goddesses as well as their cattle, upon which their life is nourished and thus sustained.

EGYPTIAN BOOK OF THE DEAD HIEROGLYPH TRANSLATIONS Volume 6: Featuring The Osirian Resurrection

Verse 323.

323.1. iu bu   gem   im{mdj} su Neter{net} neb Netert{net} neb er ar F

323.2. it is not found in {fig} he God {div}   all   Goddess{div} all as-to do he

323.3. There is nowhere to be found any God or Goddess that can do what I have described above. So I am disturbed at the disrespect that has been accorded to me as evinced by the treatment that my son has received."

Verse 326.

326.1. ahan au   ash   F embah{mdj} F hena ta Pesedjetu {net}

326.2. attention hey cry-out he before{fig} he with that Company{div}

326.3. Now attention turns to the god *Ra-Herakty (Creator-Spirit-of-the-two-horizons{twice divine}),])*, *Ra-Herakty,* who, along with the divine Company of Gods and Goddesses received the letter from the god *Asar(Osiris)*.

{ **REPLY FROM Ra-Herakty (Creator-Spirit-of-the-two-horizons)** }

Verse 327.

327.1. iu   chena   Ra{net}-Heru{net}-akhty{net}{net} her djed

327.2. it is   then Ra{div}-Horus{div}two-horizons{div}{div} person saying

327.3. Now, it is the god *Ra-Heru(Horus-Two-Horizons (Creator-Spirit-of-the-two-horizons {twice divine}), Ra-Herakty,* who is saying that...

Verse 328.

328.1. ha   na   bu   kheper -Kua   ha   na   bu   mesu-K

328.2. Oh!   proclamation negation create thee Oh proclaim not born-thee

328.3. "Whoa! Wait a minute; you say you created these things (barley and the grains) and are the source of power of us gods and goddesses? But these were not created by you because you were not even born!

EGYPTIAN BOOK OF THE DEAD HIEROGLYPH TRANSLATIONS Volume 6: Featuring The Osirian Resurrection

Verse 329.

329.1. iu   bedety   kheperu   mera
329.2. it is barley & grains created   surely

329.3. Come on now; the barley and the grains that you are talking about were surely created before you were even born. So what are you talking about? You, Asar/Osiris, are acting as if you are some god that is more special or greater than any of us and deserve some special honor or respect or deference and that we should therefore accord your son some special dispensation when none of that is warranted.

EGYPTIAN BOOK OF THE DEAD HIEROGLYPH TRANSLATIONS Volume 6: Featuring The Osirian Resurrection

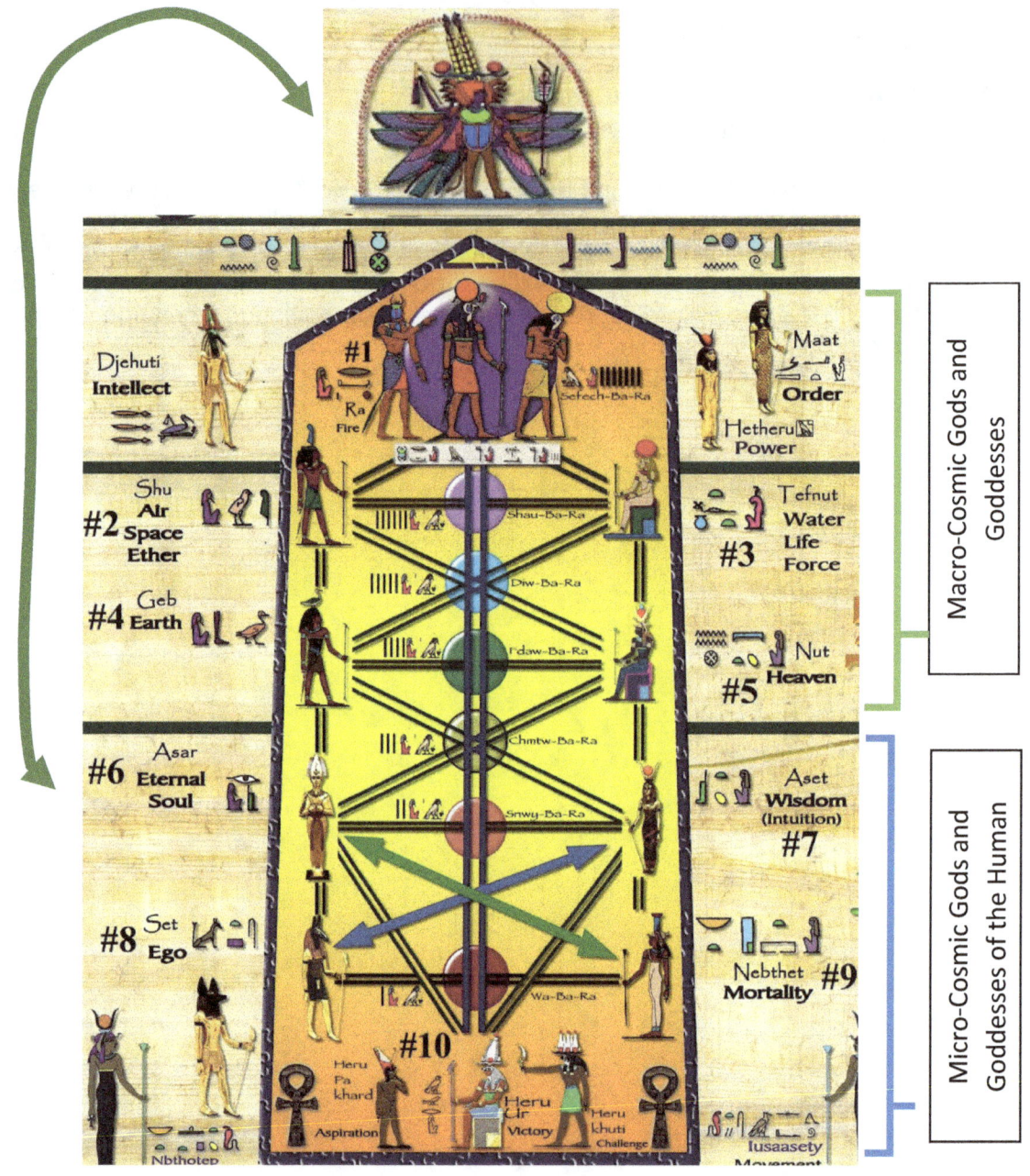

NOTE ON THE REPLY FROM RA TO ASAR: Poster of Gods and Goddesses of Anunian(Heliopolitan) Theurgy shows that **Ra** emanates from **Neberdjer**. In the Ancient Egyptian Creation myth scripture we are informed that *Neberdjer* (Supreme Being) and *Asar*(Osiris), the Universal Soul, are the same entity, one Transcendent and Absolute(Neberdjer) beyond time and space and the other (Asar/Osiris), symbolizing the plight of the incarnated soul, in time and space. So, even though Asar(aspect of Neberdjer) incarnates into the Anunian tree of gods and goddesses, and seems to come after *Ra-Herakty*, as the son of *Geb*, he is in reality just using that timeline and hereditary POSITION/OFFICE(as son of Geb[see green arrow-line]). Nevertherless, Asar, being essentially Neberdjer, has primacy and power over *Ra-Herakty* and the Company of Gods and Goddesses, being that he (being one with

Neberdjer) is the original source of Creation and all the gods and goddesses. This communication between *Ra-Herakty* and *Asar(Osiris)* also points out the similar nuances between *Neberdjer (transcendental aspect of Ra as an all encompassing Divinity)* and the emanated or incarnated, time and space, form of *Ra-Herakty*. Both *Neberdjer* (Supreme Being) and *Ra-Herakty* are the same entity, one Transcendent and Absolute (Neberdjer) beyond time and space and the other aspect (*Ra-Herakty*), in time and space. Thus, from a deeper metaphysical perspective, we are to understand that *Ra-Herakty* and *Asar (Osiris)* are aspects of each other and emanations of Neberdjer. Further, in reference to the name of Ra-Herakty, Herakty means *Heru (Horus)* in the horizons, and thus, relates that Heru, as well, is an aspect of Ra, and thus, is also of *Asar (Osiris)* and Neberdjer.

SECOND REPLY FROM OSIRIS

Verse 331.
- **331.1. iu   F   ash   F   embah   F**
- 331.2. it is he (Osiris) proclamation he before him

- 331.3. Now, it is the god *Asar(Osiris)* who has received the defiant proclamation from the god *Ra-Horus-Two-Horizons* (Creator-Spirit-of-the-two-horizons{twice divine}), *Ra-Herakty*, on behalf of the divine Company. The letter from the Company was placed before the god *Asar(Osiris)* for his review.

Verse 332.
- **332.1.1. un   in F   habuy   en chena   Ra{net}-Heru{net}-akhty{net}{net} ahan im-an**
- 332.1.2. presence of he(Osiris) message-letter to consideration Ra{div}-Horus{div}two-horizons{div}{div} turn-back refrain

- 332.1.3. Now the presence of the god *Asar(Osiris)* is being felt as he prepares a letter to be sent to the god *Ra-Horus-Two-Horizons* (Creator-Spirit-of-the-two-horizons{twice divine}), *Ra-Herakty*, urging him and the divine Company to turn back, refrain/renounce/give up their current course of action.

332.2.
- **332.2.1. djed nefer er aqer   zep zen chena ua aru K neb chena gem {mdj} ta**
- 332.2.2. (I) say beautiful-good as-to perfect excellent twice consider decry actions yours all the finding {fig} that

- 332.2.3. *Asar (Osiris)* writes, sarcastically: "Wow, I say, this is just beautiful, the best; this is perfection, excellence, excellence! Considering what you have said I hereby denounce all your actions and the thought processes that led you to arrive at the findings that…

332.3.
    332.3.1. **Pesedjetu {net} art**
    332.3.2. <u>Company   {div} done</u>

    332.3.3. ...you and the other gods and goddesses in the divine Company have arrived at to support the actions you are performing.

EGYPTIAN BOOK OF THE DEAD HIEROGLYPH TRANSLATIONS Volume 6: Featuring The Osirian Resurrection

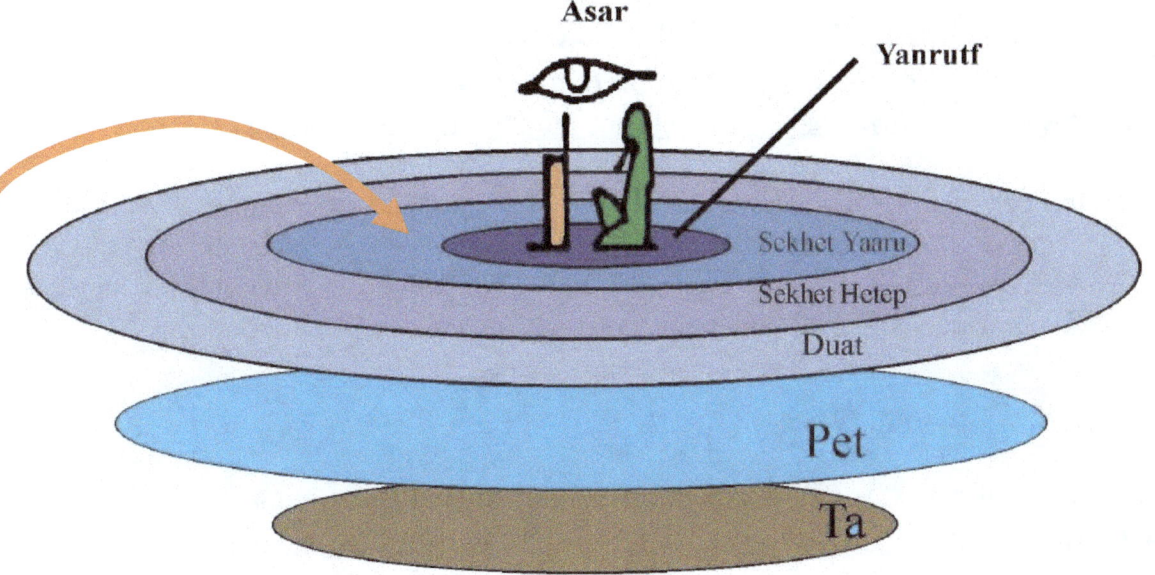

The Field of Purified Souls the Ancient Egyptians according to the Papyrus of Ani

SUMMARY: 1. Ani adoring the gods of Sekhet-Aaru. **3.** Ani ploughing in the Other World. **2.** Ani reaping in the Other World. **4.** The abode of the perfect spirits, and the magical boats.

DETAIL: 1. Ani making an offering before a hare-headed god, a snake-headed god, and a bull-headed god; Djehuty confirms the reading of the Maat scales as Ani makes the offering to the divinities collectively referred to as "Pauti" or "company". Ani traverses over water with a Hetep, arrives and makes the "Offering of peace in the Field of Peace."

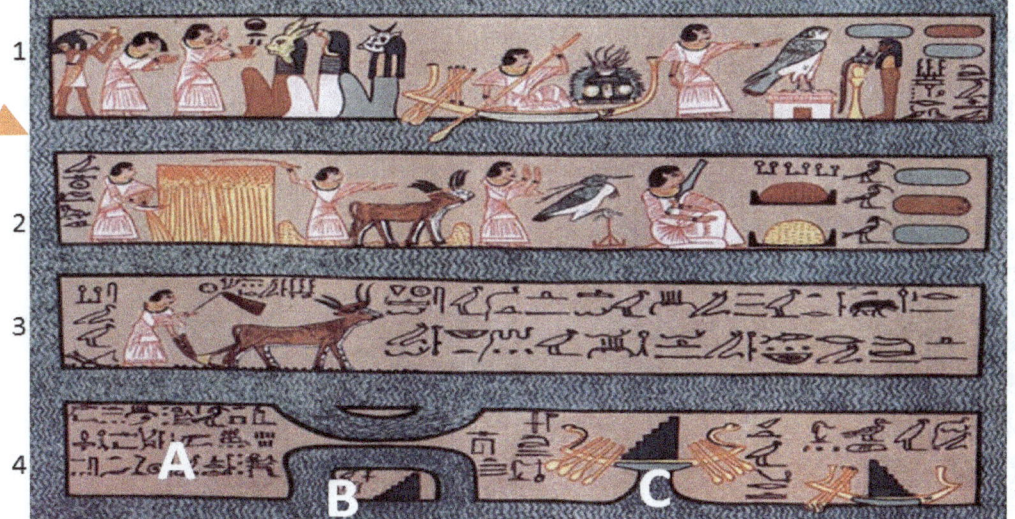

DETAIL: 2. Ani reaping corn, Ani driving the oxen which tread out the corn; Ani adoring a Bennu bird perched on a stand; Ani seated holding the *kherp* sceptre-mastery and power-sekhem-dominion; a heap of red and a heap of white corn; three KAU and three KHU,, "the food of the Kas of the Shining spirits.

DETAIL: 3. Ani holding the nekaku (flail) ploughing a field near a stream which contains neither fish, nor serpents, in the region Sechit yanru.

4. DETAIL: A abode of the AKHU-Shining spirits, the enlightened. a region called the "place of the spirits" who are seven cubits high, where the wheat is three cubits high, and where the SĀHU, or Glorious spiritual bodies, reap it   B-The birthplace of the "gods and goddesses" an island on which is a flight of steps; C-The place where the god therein is Un-nefer (*Asar*) in a boat with seven steps, lying at the end of a canal and having two serpents at the bow and stern (Aset and Nebethet); and a boat floating on a canal. The name of the first boat is Behutu-tcheser, the sacred steps and throne and that of the second Djefau the boat of the God who is movement and divine food sustaining all life.

215

Verse 333.

333.1. iu didi tu harpu   Maat {net} im khenu   duat
333.2. it is given to drowning   Themis {div} into interior Netherworld

333.3. It is becase of what you have given, that has caused that the daughter of *Ra*, the goddess of Truth (*Maat {Themis}*), should be as if drowning in the depths of the Netherworld and therefore, the outer-worlds, where you are, abound with injustice and untruth instead of Truth being upheld in all realms of Creation.

Verse 334.

334.1. ach   petra   K   chena sacheru{mdj} ger{mdj} im   ent K
334.2. what   see   thee then   plan   {fig} additionally within of thee

334.3. Furthermore, what you should see and should plan to do and understand within yourselves…

Verse 335.

335.1. ar   chena   ta   entytu {net} im F   su meh im wepu   hesiu   her
335.2. as-to consider land   his to{div} in he his full in messenger fierce-looking personalities

335.3. …and about which you should consider, is the fact that in this divine land there is a fullness of messengers that can be sent instead of missives like this one I am sending and that you are reading. This land is full of those messengers that I am speaking about now and they are fierce-looking personalities that you would rather not want to meet in person.

Verse 336.

336.1. iu ben set sendu   en Neter{net} neb Netert{net}
336.2. it is not he fear   to Gods{div}   any Goddess{div}

336.3. Be clear on this point; one particular beast, among those that I am speaking about, he does not fear any god or goddess!

EGYPTIAN BOOK OF THE DEAD HIEROGLYPH TRANSLATIONS Volume 6: Featuring The Osirian Resurrection

The image above has been provided to give the reader a visual impression of the events and meaning at this stage in the text.

Verse 337.

337.1.

337.1.1. iu a dit pery   senu im tu senu an haty en chena

337.1.2. it is I give going-forth them in to them bring heart to then

337.1.3. It is I who have the power to let these beasts go forth to the place where you are right now. Furthermore, I can have them bring to me your hearts, which you are using to think up the unrighteousness. Then…

337.2.

337.2.1. enty neb aryt zepu   im tu senu kheperu dy er hena a

337.2.2. any all action calamity   in to them live detain-here as-to with me

337.2.3. …any and all actions that were done will lead to a time of the experience of calamity in those hearts, untold mental sufferings that will be experienced. Furthermore, those hearts that have engaged in unrighteousness will be detained and will have to remain here with me in the Netherworld and will not be permitted to go to the outer realms!

EGYPTIAN BOOK OF THE DEAD HIEROGLYPH TRANSLATIONS Volume 6: Featuring The Osirian Resurrection

Verse 338.

338.1. ya   ach   chenay{net} kheperu dy hetepu{mdj} k her waset
338.2. hey   what considering{div} being here peace{fig} you person west

338.3. Hey! Consider where I am coming from. What am I doing here, being in the netherworld, resting in peace, thinking of you doing unrighteousness there while I am here in the Beautiful West?

Verse 339.

339.1. iu tenu en bu en   er wai er djeru{mdj} zep-zeny ny ma im sen
339.2. it is you of place of as-to away border{fig} doubly thereby permit in them

339.3. And this, while it is you, who are of the place far away, on the physical plane of Creation acting without upholding Maat. Think twice now about the fact that you are being permitted, allowed, to manifest as gods and goddesses where you are.

Verse 340.

340.1. iu F necht er-a cher ma-Ky gem {mdj} senu gery   im aryt
340.2. it is he strong as-to I before behold another finds their falsehood in action

340.3. Finally, it is he (*Asar {Osiris}*) who is the strong one; but look at all of you there, instead of looking for ways to uphold truth you are taking the action of looking for and finding ways to facilitate and rationalize falsehoods with your minds (hearts)."

{ **THE COMPANY OF GODS AND GODDESSES RECEIVED THE LETTER FROM ASAR (OSIRIS)** }

Verse 347.

347.1. un   in   Djehuty{net} seshep   chena   ucha
347.2. presence of Thoth{div}   receiving   then   letter

347.3. Now the presence of the god *Djehuty (Thoth)* is being felt as he received the letter from the god *Asar(Osiris)*.

218

Verse 348.

348.1. iu F ash   F embah chena Ra{net}-Heru{net}-akhty{net}{net} hena Pesedjetu {net}
348.2. it is he invoking he presence consideration Ra{div}-Horus{div}two-horizons{div}{div} with Company{div}

348.3. It is he ({*Djehuty(Thoth)*}), who is invoking, reading the words of *Asar(Osiris)* for the consideration of the god *Ra-Heru(Horus)-Two-Horizons* (Creator-Spirit-of-the-two-horizons {*twice divine*}), *Ra-Herakty*, together with the Company of Gods and Goddesses.

Verse 349.

349.1. un as en   her djed maat{mdj} tu zep-zen im ia djed tu F neb
349.2. presence attention them person saying truth{fig} he doubly through speech said by him all

349.3. Now the presence and attention of the Gods and Goddesses is the focus as they, after hearing what *Asar(Osiris)* had to say, all of them, to a person exclaimed: "what he has said is the truth; all of what *Asar(Osiris)* has said is the truth!"

Verse 351.

351.1.
351.1.1. un   in   Temu{net} neb tawy Anu{net} habuy   en Aset{net} er-djed an Set{net}
351.1.2. presence of Temu{div} Lord two-lands Heliopolis{div} message to Isis{div} about-saying bring Seth{div}

351.1.3. Now the presence of the God *Temu* is felt. He is the aspect of *Ra* that carries out the function of dissolution, the end of Creation, meaning, the end of egoism that perceives Creation as something other than Divine Consciousness, and thus, brings the spiritual journey to a completion, which paves the way for Spiritual Awakening, Nehast. Temu is also the Lord of the divine city Heliopolis, the capital of the Sun divinity, Ra. Temu sends a message to the goddess *Aset (Isis)* that the god *Set (Seth)* is to be brought to him.

351.2.
351.2.1. iu   F hanu   {mdj} im qahau
351.2.2. it is he(*Temu*) commanding{fig} manner fettered

351.2.3. Thus, the god *Temu* ordered that the god *Set(Seth)* be brought in to the god *Temu's* location but bound and tied, in other words, under arrest.

EGYPTIAN BOOK OF THE DEAD HIEROGLYPH TRANSLATIONS Volume 6: Featuring The Osirian Resurrection

The Gods Temu Issues an arrest order

The image above has been provided to give the reader a visual impression of the events and meaning at this stage in the text.

EGYPTIAN BOOK OF THE DEAD HIEROGLYPH TRANSLATIONS Volume 6: Featuring The Osirian Resurrection

Heru and his four sons stand before Asar with knives. The Set headed man is bound to a steak with knives in him. This is a representation of Heru and his Shemsu (followers) defeating Set.

In the image above, from the temple of Hetheru, Set is depicted as being tied and presented to the god Asar. Themple of Hetheru

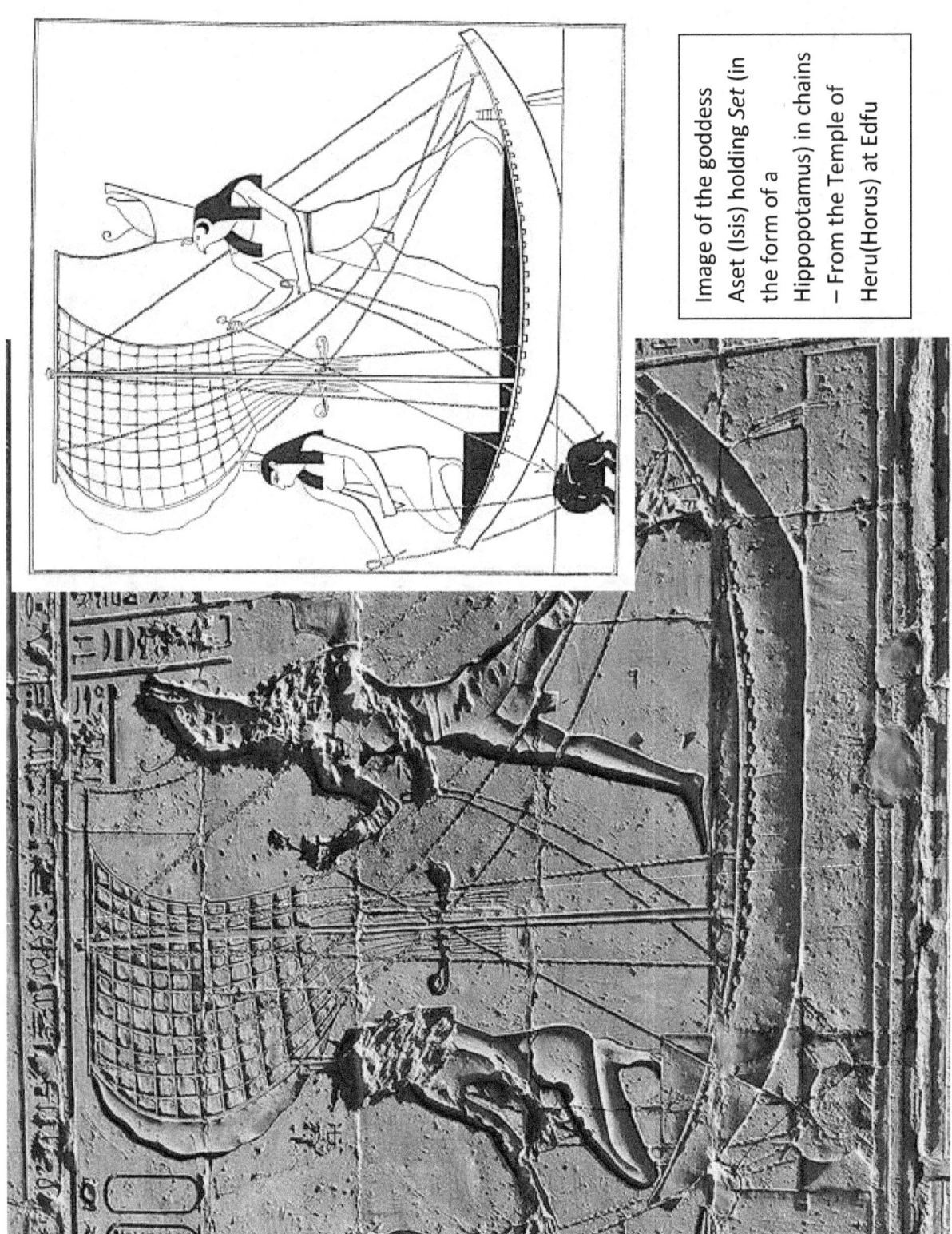

Image of the goddess Aset (Isis) holding Set (in the form of a Hippopotamus) in chains – From the Temple of Heru(Horus) at Edfu

Verse 352.

352.1. un   in   Aset{net} her   an Set{net}
352.2. <u>presence of Isis{div} person brings Seth{div}</u>

352.3. Now the presence of the goddess *Aset (Isis)* is being felt as she immediately carries out the order of the god *Temu*. She carries out the order and brings the god *Set(Seth)* to the presence of the god *Temu*.

Verse 353.

353.1. iu   F   hanu   {mdj} im qahau
353.2. <u>it is he command {fig} means fetterings</u>

353.3. It is indeed the god *Set(Seth)* who was brought in, by the goddess *Aset(Isis)*, as was commanded by the god Temu, in restraints.

Verse 355.

355.1. un   in   Temu{net} her djed en-F ia   aru-K   temt   ditu udja
355.2. <u>presence of Temu{div} person says to-him I-say action-thine not   give   judgment</u>

355.3. Now the presence of the god *Temu* is being again felt as he says to *Set(Seth)*, your actions did not give the judgment properly to the god *Heru(Horus)*.

Verse 357.

357.1.
357.1.1. un   in   Set{net} her djed en-F mbaa   chenay   neb{net} nefer{net}
357.1.2. <u>presence of Seth{div} person saying to-him on-contrary   consider   lord{div}   good{net}</u>

357.1.3. Now the presence of the god *Set(Seth)* is commanding attention as he replies to *Temu*. *Set(Seth)* says: "On the contrary, please take note my divine Good Lord...

357.2.
- **357.2.1.** *amma   ash   tu   en Heru{net} sa{net} Aset{net}   metutu*
- 357.2.2. <u>award   invoke to of Horus{div} son{div} Isis{net} one</u>

357.2.3. ...go ahead and make the award; I, the god *Set(Seth)*, invoke that, about the god *Heru(Horus)*, the divine son of goddess *Aset(Isis)*, that someone...

357.3.
- **357.3.1.** *dit en-F ta aautet {mdj} en   atef{net} Asar{net}*
- 357.3.2. <u>give to-he that office{fig} of   father{div} Osiris{div}</u>

357.3.3. ...should give to him that office of his divine father the god *Asar(Osiris)*."

Verse 358.
- 358.1. *un   intu   her an Heru{net} sa{net} Aset{net} au dit hedjt her tep{net} F*
- 358.2. <u>presence of he personality brought-in Horus{div} son{div} Isis{div} hail give white- person head{div} his crown</u>

358.3. Now the presence of the god *Heru(Horus)*, the divine son of the goddess *Aset(Isis)*, is felt as this exalted personality is brought into the presence of the Company of Gods and Goddesses. He is hailed and the white crown of Upper Egypt, the symbol of the source of Creation, the south, from which sustenance and strength comes to help the north to flourish, and which is the seat of power that had belonged to his father, is now placed on *Heru's(Horus')* divine head; and there are no objections from anyone.

Verse 359.
- **359.1.** *iu   tu   di-tu F er ta aset-per en atef{net} Asar{net}*
- 359.2. <u>it is for give-to him as-to that throne/abode of father{div} Osiris{div}</u>

359.3. This is the giving, to the god *Heru(Horus)*, that which concerns rulership, the throne of his divine father, the god *Asar(Osiris)*, which is the god *Heru's(Horus')* rightful abode.

EGYPTIAN BOOK OF THE DEAD HIEROGLYPH TRANSLATIONS Volume 6: Featuring The Osirian Resurrection

Verse 360.

360.1.

360.1.1. *iu   tu   her   djed n-F   tu-K im suten{net} nefer{net} nu ta-meri tu-K   im neb{net}*

360.1.2. it is to person saying to-him to-you as sovereign{div} good{div} of land-beloved to-you as Lord{div}

360.1.3. The situation is now that it is to him, to his personality, he, *Heru(Horus),* is being told in no uncertain terms, that he is the divine sovereign, the good divinity of the beloved land (Kemet/Ancient Egypt) and that he is also the Lord of Kemet (Ancient Egypt), i.e. he is THE god presiding over the earth and also he is its human ruler.

360.2.

360.2.1. *Ankh-Udja-Senab nefer{net} en ta neber shaa{mdj} heh hena   djeta*

360.2.2. Life—Vitality-Health good{div} of land Lord as-to piloting{div} eternity with forever

360.2.3. To you, *Heru(Horus),* as Lord of the land, we wish good Life-Vitality-Health and may you be the divine pilot leading all the people on the right path of life for eternity and forever.

Verse 361.

361.1.

361.1.1. ahan *Aset{net} ash   segabu*

361.1.2. rising-forward, attention Isis{div} invoke shout-out

361.1.3. Now attention turns to *Aset(Isis),* who rises forward and starts summoning and shouting to all about the...

361.2.

361.2.1. *aah{mdj} en-Sa{net} set Heru im djed   tu-K im Suten{net} nefer{net}*

361.2.2. greatness{fig} of son{div} hers Horus{div} by proclaiming to him as sovereign{div} good{div}

361.2.3. ...greatness of her divine son, *Heru(Horus),* by proclaiming that he is "The Good King".

EGYPTIAN BOOK OF THE DEAD HIEROGLYPH TRANSLATIONS Volume 6: Featuring The Osirian Resurrection

361.3.

361.3.1. abt netert im reshut   {mdj} se-hedj-K im annu -K

361.3.2.   heart goddess in rejoicing {fig} because-light up thee complexion –thine

361.3.3.   The heart of the goddess is rejoicing because of this attainment, by *Heru(Horus)*, has caused his physical appearance to take on a radiance, like the sun, which is his higher true nature, which illumines the planet and causes there to be light and life, health and goodness. Now that true nature is unconstrained and in full splendor.

The image above has been provided to give the reader a visual impression of the events and meaning at this stage in the text. The god Heru takes on a radiant glow.

Verse 363.

363.1.

363.1.1.   un   in   chena   Ra{net}-Heru{net}-akhty{net}{net} djed

363.1.2.   presence of then   Ra{div}-Horus{div}two-horizons{div}{div} saying

363.1.3.   Now the presence of the god *Ra-Heru(Horus)-Two-Horizons* (Creator-Spirit-of-the-two-horizons{twice divine}), *Ra-Herakty,* was then felt as he began to speak:

363.2.
- 363.2.1. **Amma didi tu n-a Set{net} sa{net} Nut {net} hemz F er hena A**
- 363.2.2. assign given to for-I Seth{div} son{div} Nut   {div} sitting he as-to with me

363.2.3. "Let the god *Set(Seth)*, the divine son of the divine goddess Nut, be given to me to sit with me.

Verse 364.
- **364.1. iu F im di-a im sherau {net} im tu F neferu im ta pet   metutu   sendu   n-F**
- 364.2. it is he as give-me form son{div} form to he lookout through that heaven one feared of-he

364.3. He (Set/Seth) will be as my divine son and he will act in the form of a lookout in my boat that traverses the heavens daily. He will protect the boat from inimical forces and he will be one who is feared by them."

Verse 365.

365.1.
- 365.1.1. un   in tu   her shemert er-djed en chena Ra{net}-Heru{net}-akhty{net}{net} Heru{net} sa{net}
- 365.1.2. presence of he person journey as-to say to consider Ra{div}-Horus{div}two-horizons   Horus{div}
                                                                                                    {div}{div}   son {div}

365.1.3. Now the presence of some personality is felt as a statement is directed at the god *Ra-Heru(Horus)-Two-Horizons (Creator-Spirit-of-the-two-horizons{twice divine})*, *Ra-Herakty*. "The divine *Heru(Horus)*, the divine son of…

365.2.
- 365.2.1. **Aset{net} aha im (heqa{net}) Ankh-Udja-Senab**
- 365.2.2. Isis {div} rises-forward form (sovereign{div}) Life-Vitality-Health

365.2.3. …goddess *Aset(Isis)* rises in the form of a sovereign, legitimate ruler with the power to govern all of Kemet (Ancient Egypt). To him I wish Life-Vitality-Health."

EGYPTIAN BOOK OF THE DEAD HIEROGLYPH TRANSLATIONS Volume 6: Featuring The Osirian Resurrection

Verse 366.

366.1. *ahan* chena Ra{net} her reshut {mdj} er aqer{mdj} zep-zen

366.2. rising-forward, attention then Ra{div} person joyous {fig} as-to perfection{fig} doubly

366.3. Rising forward, the attention turns to the god Ra, whose personality is in a state of unqualified joy; "This rising of *Heru(Horus)* to the throne of Kemet (Ancient Egypt) is wonderful, wonderful, excellent, excellent, perfect, perfect."

Verse 367.

367.1. iu F her djed en ta Pesedjetu {net} nehamu tenu er ta-wy en Heru{net} sa{net} Aset{net}

367.2. it is he person saying to that Company{div} cry-joy you-all about two-lands of Horus{div} son{div} Isis{div}

367.3. Then it was he, Ra, who said to the Company of Gods and Goddesses: "all the people in the two lands of Kemet (Ancient Egypt) are crying-out in joy for the god *Heru(Horus)*, the divine son of goddess *Aset(Isis)*!"

EGYPTIAN BOOK OF THE DEAD HIEROGLYPH TRANSLATIONS Volume 6: Featuring The Osirian Resurrection

The image above has been provided to give the reader a visual impression of the events and meaning at this stage in the text. The result of the spiritual journey of the myth of the Asarian Resurrection ends with a hawk trinity wherein the Hawk divinities (*Ra, Asar, Heru*) preside over all three realms of Creation. So, Asar presides over the *Duat*(Netherworld), *Ra* presides over the *Pet, the Heavenly Realm*, and Heru(Horus) presides over the *Ta* or earth realm. Thus, any person filling the position of a Royal Person (kings and queens or Initiates) is considered as an incarnation of Heru on earth. Heru is of course the incarnation of Asar, so every human is potentially a Royal Person and a Heru/Horus and an Asar/Osiris. And of course, since *Asar* is essentially *Neberdjer*, the Supreme Being, then humans are also able to realize their Royal Personhood which is also the realization of their transcendental Supreme Being (*Neberdjer*) nature.

Above: The Ancient Egyptian Hawk Trinity (Asar, Ra and Heru)

HERE BEGIN THE FINAL INVOCATIONS OF THE SCRIPTURE (Chester Beaty) -UTTERED BY GODDESS ASET (ISIS)

Verse 368.

368.1. un   in Aset{net}   her djed   Heru{net} aha im (heqa{net}) Ankh-Udja-Senab

368.2. presence of goddess Isis person saying Horus{div} rises-forward form (sovereign{div}) Life-Vitality-Health

368.3. Now the presence of goddess *Aset(Isis)* is felt as she begins the final invocations celebrating the victory of her son, the god *Heru(Horus)*. She starts by saying: "Oh, witness that the divine *Heru(Horus)* rises to the position of divine sovereign, Life, Vitality and Health to him!

Verse 369.

369.1. ta Pesedjetu {net} im heb   pet   im reshut   {mdj}

369.2. this Company{div} in festival   heaven in rejoicing {fig}

369.3. This Company of Gods and Goddesses is in festival mode now and heaven, the astral abode of gods and goddesses, is rejoicing, pleased and satisfied.

Verse 370.

370.1. tjay   senu mahu   im di   petra   senu Heru{net} sa{net} Aset{net}

370.2. man   they garland diadem through giving sight they Horus{div} son{div} Isis{div}

370.3. Now, by the simple act of giving a peek, looking at this man, the god *Heru(Horus)*, the divine son of goddess *Aset(Isis)*, they become garlanded with a diadem!

Verse 371.

371.1. *iu   F   aha   im   (heqa{net})   Ankh-Udja-Senab aah{mdj} Kemet*

371.2. it is he rising-forward form (sovereign{div}) Life-Vitality-Health greatness{fig} Egypt

371.3. It is he, the god *Heru(Horus),* who now rises forward to his position as divine sovereign, Life, Vitality and Health to him. Greatness has occurred in Egypt.

Verse 372.

372.1. *ta   Pesedjetu {net} ab senu hautu*

372.2. this Company{div} heart theirs exultation

372.3. The Company of Gods and Goddesses, the children of *Ra,* the cosmic forces that emerged with him in the first time of Creation and who, at his direction sustain the Creation, look at them, their hearts, and therefore, all Creation, are in a state of exultation over the ascension of the god *Heru(Horus).*

Verse 373.

373.1. *ta   er   djer   F   im   haaut   {mdj}*

373.2. land as-to entirety he in rejoicings{fig}

373.3. Now look over the entirety of the earth commanded by him. Everyone is, as if, raising arms to heaven, joyous, pleased and satisfied...

Verse 374.

374.1. *im   di   petra   senu   Heru{net}sa{net}   Aset{net}*

374.2. as give look   they   Horus{div}son{div}   Isis{div}

374.3. ...as they give a look at the god *Heru(Horus),* the divine son of goddess *Aset(Isis).*

EGYPTIAN BOOK OF THE DEAD HIEROGLYPH TRANSLATIONS Volume 6: Featuring The Osirian Resurrection

Verse 375.

375.1. iu   se-wadj en-F ta   aautet   {mdj} en atef{net} Asar{net} neb djeddu {net}

375.2.   it is caused-commanded to he that office{fig} of father{div} Osiris{div} Lord Busiris{div}

375.3.   All of these glories have been caused by the command that *Heru(Horus)*, the divine son of goddess *Aset(Isis)*, should assume the office that was held by his divine father, the sovereign rulership over all the land. He, the god *Heru(Horus)*, rules in the hearts of people now instead of unrighteousness and untruth that leads to suffering. The divine good god *Asar(Osiris)* previously ruled over all the land; he was the divine benevolent soul that brought the nourishment of greenery that sustains the life of the body and he also created religion to protect and elevate the souls on earth, to the heights of heaven, to join with his mother goddess *Nut*, as if, to reside in the heavens like a star, a Shining Spirit in the sky. That divine god, *Asar(Osiris)*, is the lord of *Busiris*, the city of the Djed Pillar on earth and the Djed Pillar in the netherworld (*Duat*).

Verse 376.

376.1. iu   sepu nefer   im   khanu   Waset{net} ta aset-per tebu[duat]

376.2.   comes time good   in   interior   Thebes{div} that abode astral

376.3.   The struggle between the god *Set(Seth)* and the god *Heru(Horus)* has come to this time now wherein everything is good in the interior of the divine city, Waset (Thebes), the final abode of souls in *Waset*, the Beautiful West. The disturbance that occurred for a temporary, fleeting time, in the land and in heaven, wherein the souls suffered due to unrighteousness, greed and anger, is now over. That time of untoward rulership that disturbed souls in the interior of Waset (Thebes), the heart of Kemet (Ancient Egypt), the body of Creation and the souls of the people, that were experiencing Shining Spirit Being in the interior of the West, has now ended and the soul of the god *Asar(Osiris)* and the souls of all, on earth and in the interior of the West, are at peace and satisfied.

EGYPTIAN BOOK OF THE DEAD HIEROGLYPH TRANSLATIONS Volume 6: Featuring The Osirian Resurrection

WINGED DISK & CONTENDINGS OF

HERU (HORUS) AND SET (SETH)

Version of the Conflict between Heru and Set based on the text of the Temple of Horus at Edfu

THE TREE OF MYTHIC SCRIPTURES OF THE ASARIAN RESURRECTION MYTH RENDERED IN ANCIENT EGYPTIAN HIEROGLYPHIC TEXT:

THE LEGEND OF HERU-BEHUDET AND THE WINGED DISK FROM THE WESTERN RETAINING WALL OF THE ANCIENT EGYPTIAN TEMPLE OF HERU(HORUS) AT EDFU, KEMET (EGYPT)

Trilinear Hieroglyph Translations by Dr. Muata Ashby ©2020

Now we will discuss the wisdom and symbolism of *Heru Behudet* as the quintessential example of a "Spiritual Warrior." A "spiritual warrior" is someone who fights for the redemption and elevation of Spirit as the central and highest facet of life by living and upholding spiritual principles. Heru-Behudet is the aspect of Heru/Ra/Ra-Herakty that appears in the boat of Ra at midday when the sun is at its peak of heat power and highest in the sky. So he is the most powerful aspect of Heru. This aspect, Heru-Behudet, may be translated as: *Heru/Horus-the-HighPower, The Warrior.*

The weapons of these principles are used for their energetic and psycho-iconographical significance. Specifically speaking of Heru, he is the highest example of a spiritual warrior example for humans, and he has three principal weapons that he uses: 1) a cutlass (a short sword with a slightly curved blade); 2) a mace; 3) a sword. These are principal weapons and these are weapons

that are used for dealing with gross enemies and gross targets; this means gross egoism, gross, thick expressions of anger and hatred, etc. A weapon for dealing with subtler impurities is the lance/harpoon/spear/staff, and an example of this is when Heru was battling with the god Set who symbolizes egoism, when Set was in the form of a hippopotamus. Heru used a lance/harpoon/spear/staff to strike the raging beast. This weapon is more pointed and directed as opposed to a weapon for something gross. It is directed at a substantial but definable target such as egoism (diseased ego due to ignorance of knowledge of Self). The bow and arrow is for something even finer, and it represents thoughts that strike at the heart of ignorant ideas and feelings. Now, the goddess *Net* actually also has a bow and arrow, which has a more pinpoint accuracy. This is a kind of weaponry for more subtle enemies. An example of that might be a confrontation with a person who is a dissembler, a liar. For catching the subtleties of a lie it is necessary to have sharpness and pin-point accuracy to point to and shoot down a statement of untruth. Each principle has its different representative objects that are important. These objects signify or are conduits for the way in which the energy operates through that principle.[14] Note: Going forth, we will only use the Kemetic (Ancient Egyptian) names instead of the Greek names or both names. So for Horus, we will use Heru, and for Osiris, Asar, and for Isis, Aset, and for Seth, Set, and for Thoth/Hermes, Djehuty, etc.

---

[14] For more details on the weapons of the divinities see the book *Egyptian Mysteries Vol. 2 Encyclopedic Dictionary of the Ancient Egyptian Gods and Goddesses* by Muata Ashby

EGYPTIAN BOOK OF THE DEAD HIEROGLYPH TRANSLATIONS Volume 6: Featuring The Osirian Resurrection

In this section of the book we will look at specific parts of panels of the temple that recount a version of the battle between Heru and Set. The sections are outlined in color.

PANEL 12

EGYPTIAN BOOK OF THE DEAD HIEROGLYPH TRANSLATIONS Volume 6: Featuring The Osirian Resurrection

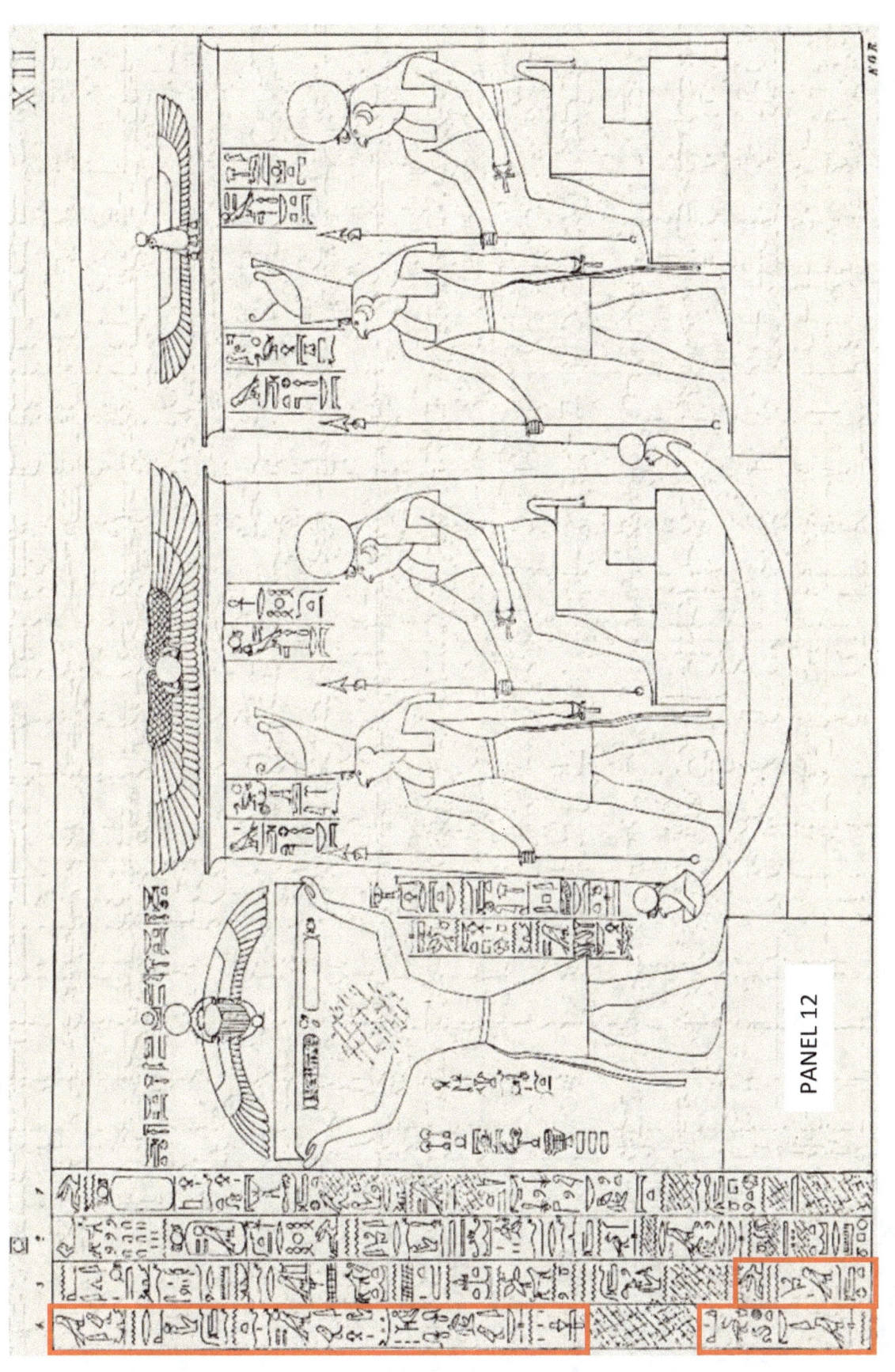

PANEL 12

Above: The gods Heru-the-HighPower, the-Warrior and Ra-of-two-Horizons(Creator Spirit) in two shrines; the firs is the divine boat and the second is a shrine on land. Both shrines are surmounted by two versions of the divine Winged Disk of Heru.

237

EGYPTIAN BOOK OF THE DEAD HIEROGLYPH TRANSLATIONS Volume 6: Featuring The Osirian Resurrection

PANEL 12 - Verses A, B, C

Transliteration	Translation	Contextual Translation
A		This is occurring to Heru-Behudet, Heru(Horus)-the-HighPower The-Warrior, whose dwelling place is in the town of Edfu. He is in the boat of his father, Ra, and says to him: "Oh Divine Father, in your form as the sun that stretches from horizon to horizon, I myself see your enemies that are blaspheming against you, saying that you are weak and Set(Seth) is strong. They are those fiends who are in confederacy with Set(Seth) and they are strengthening. Oh, Divine Father Ra, will you give of your own soul-power, your might, through the object you have on your forehead, the powerful cobra serpent goddess, to go into them and destroy them?
Unen	Happening	
En	to	
Heru Behudet	Horus-the-Warrior	
B		
Im	within	
ua	boat	
en	of	
Ra	Ra (Creator Spirit)	
Djed F	Says he	
En	to	
Tef	Father	
Ra-Herakty	Ra-of-The-Two-Horizons	
iu	It is	
A – her	I face	
maa	seeing	
cheftu	enemies	
uaua	blaspheming	
iu	it is	
neb	all	
zenu	them	
sekhem	strength	
C		
di	give	
ba	soul-power	
chet-arat	thing-serpent	
K	thine	
Im	in	
zen	them	

EGYPTIAN BOOK OF THE DEAD HIEROGLYPH TRANSLATIONS Volume 6: Featuring The Osirian Resurrection

PANEL 14 [right to left]

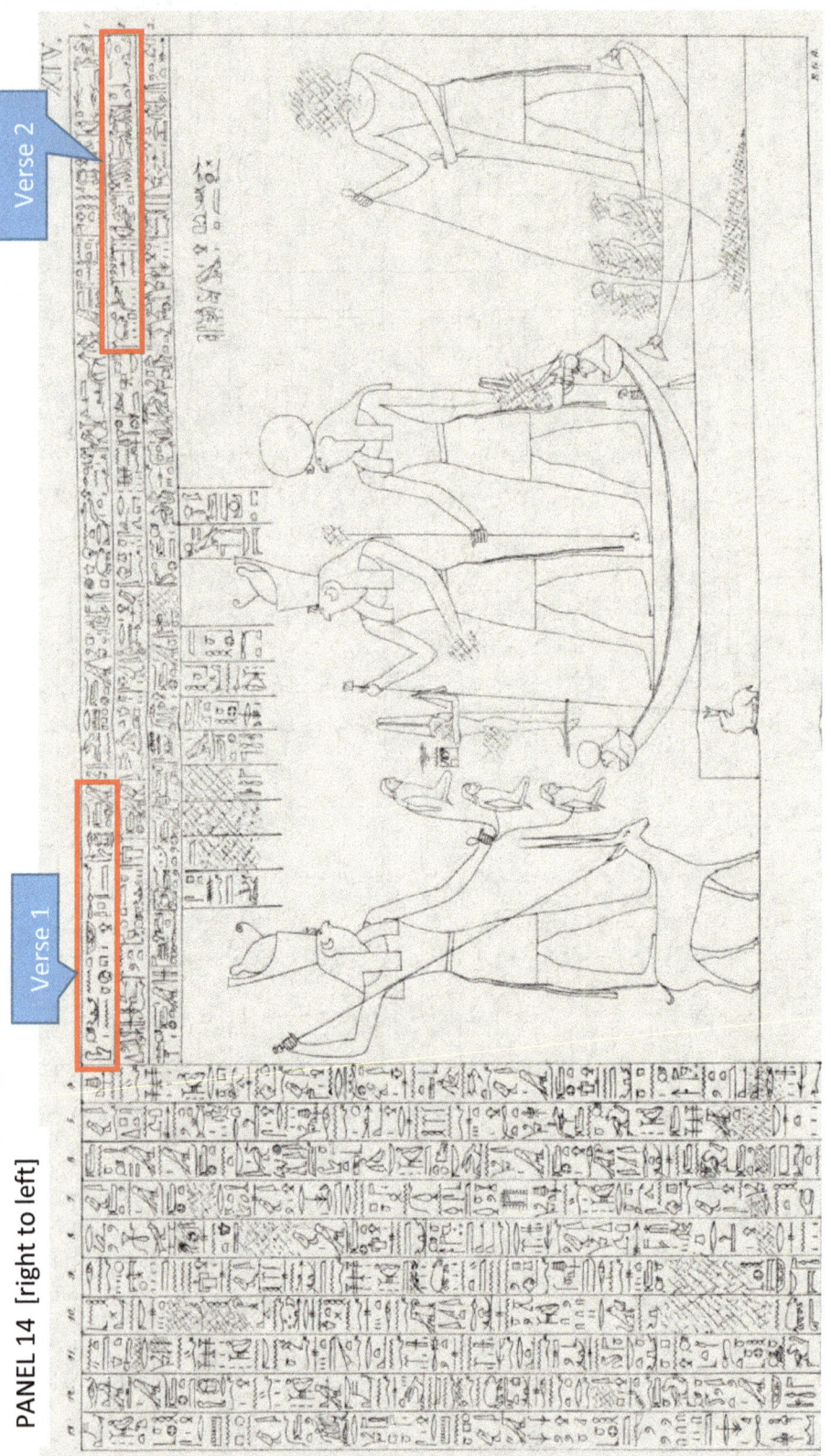

Above: The gods Heru-the-HighPower, the-Warrior, and Ra-of-two-Horizons (Creator Spirit) in the shrines while Heru spears the Hippo fiend and the second Heru (presumably Heru-Sa-Aset [glyphs damaged]), standing on a gazelle, are both rounding up and dispatching the minions of the God Set. This is done with their followers, the blacksmiths (one who is on the boat at far right capturing a fiend in the form of a crocodile).

EGYPTIAN BOOK OF THE DEAD HIEROGLYPH TRANSLATIONS Volume 6: Featuring The Osirian Resurrection

Verse 1   Verse 2

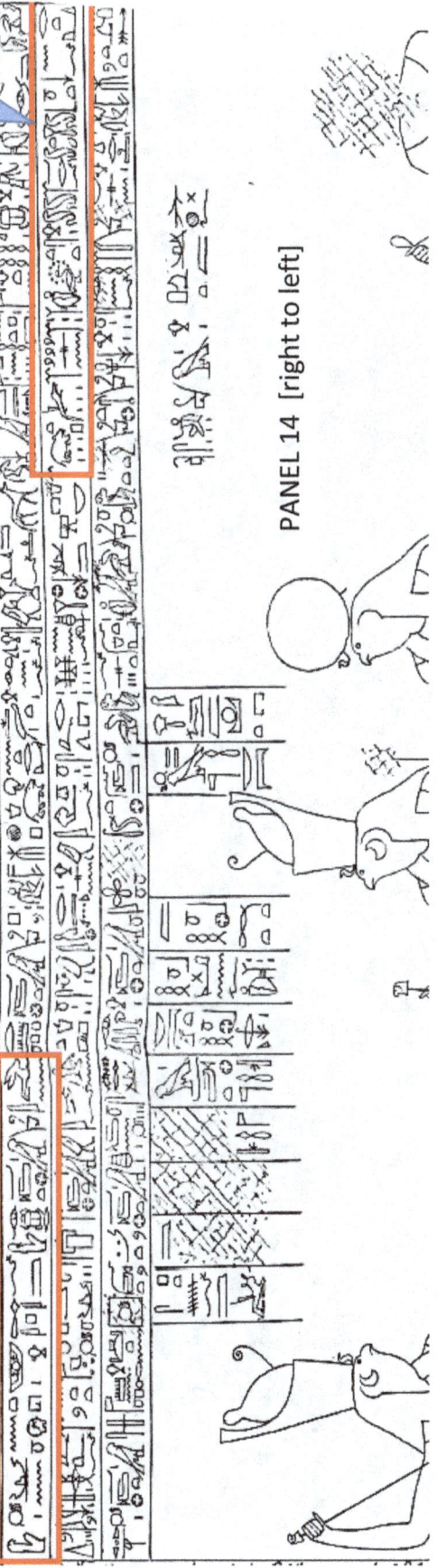

PANEL 14 [right to left]

PANEL 14.

14.1.

14.1.1. **Un in Heru Behudet   ary kheper F im aapa her   teh en tep nu uia en Ra**

14.1.2. Happening by Horus-the-Warrior does transformation he into-form Winged disk goes to board the boat of Ra

14.1.3. It is occurring that *Heru/Horus-the-HighPower* transformed himself into the form of a winged-disk and he flew up to the boat of *Ra*, the Creator Spirit, high up in the sky; he surveyed the land and saw where the enemies of *Ra* were.

14.2.

14.3. **erdit   en-F   Sunuteb Wadjit   sebh er F im Wadjty her setet sebau im aufu zen im afau tepu**

14.4. give to he   south serpent goddess & north flavor for he form both personalities tremble enemies form flesh theirs as crocodiles and hip

14.5. Give to him the Serpent Goddesses of creative and destructive life-force of the south and north so that together they will cause terror among my enemies who have taken the forms of crocodiles and hippopotami.

EGYPTIAN BOOK OF THE DEAD HIEROGLYPH TRANSLATIONS Volume 6: Featuring The Osirian Resurrection

PANEL 16 – Dr. Muata Ashby on site.

EGYPTIAN BOOK OF THE DEAD HIEROGLYPH TRANSLATIONS Volume 6: Featuring The Osirian Resurrection

PANEL 16

Above: The gods Heru-the-HighPower, the-Warrior and Heru-the-son-of-Aset both spearing a minion, a follower of Set. One spears the leg (controlling locomotion) while the other spears the lower back (controlling vital life-force). This occurs while Ra-of-two-Horizons (Creator Spirit) in the boat shrine, and Aset and Asar look on.

EGYPTIAN BOOK OF THE DEAD HIEROGLYPH TRANSLATIONS Volume 6: Featuring The Osirian Resurrection

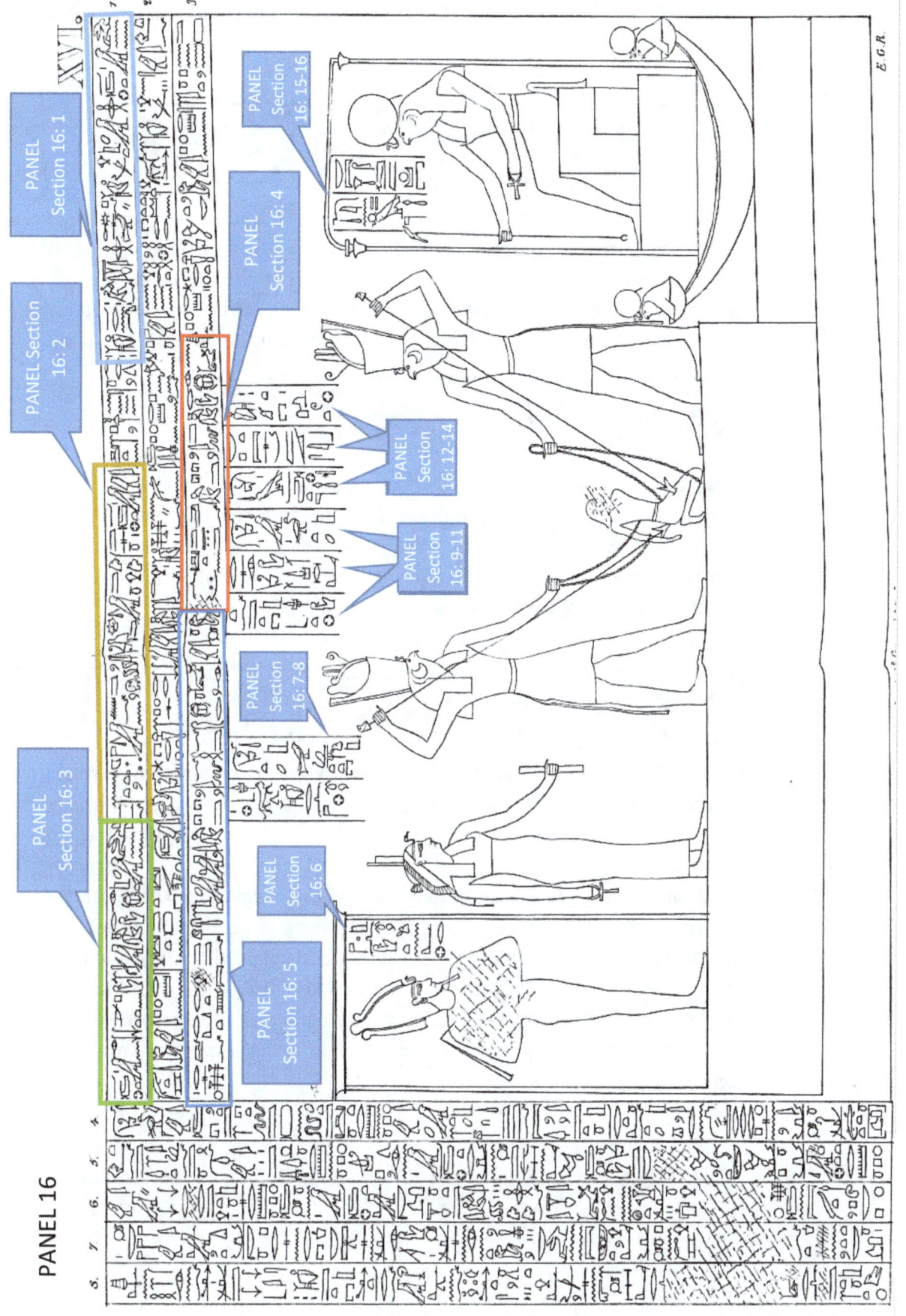

245

PANEL 16.

16.1.
- **16.1.1.** ***unen   Heru-Behudet   rehui Heru-sa-Aset her sma seba pefy***
- 16.1.2. <u>happening to Horus-the-Warrior together Horus son Isis personality slaying enemy/rebel they</u>
- 16.1.3. This is happening to *Heru-Behudet, Heru(Horus)-the-HighPower The-Warrior*, together with *Heru(Horus) Sa Aset(Isis), Heru(Horus) the Son* of *Aset (Isis)*, they joined forces and are slaughtering the enemies of *Ra* as…

- 16.1.4.
- 16.1.5. ***chat ze-ur rehui   smayu   F hur en setep sebau***
- 16.1.6. <u>body cause greatness together fiends his together cut up enemies</u>
- 16.1.7. …their bodies became greater being together, by facing the enemies head on and being in the mix of the fighting with the fiends of *Set(Seth)*; these enemies are being cut to pieces by the duo.

16.2.
- **16.2.1.** ***iu   Heru-Behudet imz nu   pehty im her nu Heru cha im hedg deshert shuty nu Wadjty***
- 16.2.2. <u>It is Horus-the-Warrior as that double strength form person Horus crown form white red plumes of serpent goddesses</u>
- 16.2.3. This is what it is; *Heru-Behudet, Heru(Horus)-the-HighPower The-Warrior* is a being of double (superhuman) strength as a form of personality reflecting *Heru(Horus)*, and even wearing his crown that displays the white and red crowns, meaning master of upper and lower Kemet(Egypt), metaphorically, the Higher Self and lower self, along with two plumes and the two Wadjty Serpent Goddesses both of which contain *Aset and Nebthet(Isis and Nephthys)*…

16.2.4.

16.2.5. ***im tep {auf} aat F en Heru neter banpi abeb entetu im auy F***

16.2.6. <u>in top   spine his of Horus divine iron   harpoon are   in   hands his</u>

16.2.7. ...being at the top of his head which is on top of the spine of *Heru(Horus)*, son of *Aset(Isis)*, that is in *Heru-Behudet, Heru(Horus)-the-HighPower* the *Warrior* aspect of Heru. *Heru-Behudet, Heru(Horus)-the-HighPower The-Warrior*, also holds a spear made of iron in both his hands; this aspect of *Heru(Horus)*, is an imposing figure to behold.

16.3.

16.3.1. *unen   Heru sa Aset ary kheper A kat im ds im neter pen mertet nent ary en Heru Behudet*

16.3.2. <u>happening to Horus-son-Isis does transformation self work through divine that likeness this action of Horus-the-HighPower</u>

16.3.3. This is happening to *Heru Sa Aset(Isis), Heru (Horus) the Son* of *Aset (Isis)*. He does a transformation of himself through a divine likeness of and adopting the actions of *Heru-Behudet, Heru(Horus)-the-HighPower The-Warrior*.

16.4.

16.4.1. *En Set   ary kheper A kat im hefau   hehem   aq F   im ta im iat en an maa*

16.4.2. <u>Of Set   does transform self work into snake cry-out   goes-in he into land into mound to not seen</u>

16.4.3. As for the god *Set(Seth)*, the leader of the blasphemers and fiends that opposed *Ra*, the Creator Spirit, he does his own transformation into the form of a snake. As he does so he cries out lamenting the slaughtering of his (Set's/Seth's) followers by *Heru(Horus) Sa Aset(Isis), Heru (Horus) the Son* of *Aset (Isis)* and *Heru(Horus)* the Warrior. Having transformed into the form of a snake, *Set(Seth)* then slithered underground and into a mound of earth so as not to be seen, to hide from the two *Heru(Horus)* gods and from *Ra*.

16.5.

16.5.1. Gaf nu Ra iu Be-Set ary {auf} nu kheper{tut} F im hefau auf hehem

16.5.2. statement of Ra it is Set doing of body transform {image} his into snake crying-out

16.5.3. This is a statement from *Ra*, the Creator Spirit: "It is *Set(Seth)*, who represents the unrighteousness of blasphemy, the disrespect of *Ra* and the exaltation of himself as he rouses dissent and the egoism in his followers; it is he who is acting on his body transformed into the form of a snake. He is crying out in protest against what has been done against him for his wrongdoing.

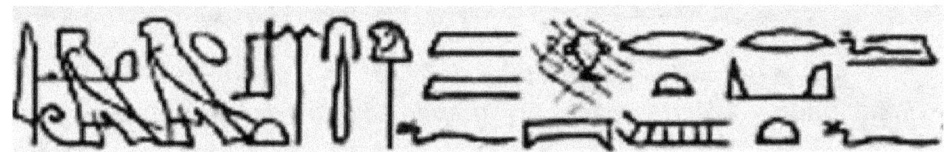

16.5.4. iu   ma   Heru-sa-Aset im ames mem F her pet er tem   erdit   pert F

16.5.5. it is behold Horus, transforming into staff together person heaven as-to end giving coming
-son-of-Isis   head hawk   out his

16.5.6. Behold *Heru(Horus)-the-son-of-Aset(Isis)*. He is transforming into a staff with the head of a hawk with his personality being in heaven. He has placed the staff on the mound so as to end *Set(Seth)*'s capacity of coming out from the place he is hiding, as *Heru(Horus)* reigns supreme from above.

16.6.

    ***16.6.1.** Asar   Neter   an-rudtef auf   khent   en ar {nut}*

    16.6.2. <u>Osiris Divinity nothing-grows body foremost of locale{location}</u>

    16.6.3. This is *Asar(Osiris)*, the divinity of the place where nothing grows, no plants, no thoughts, no movement; he is foremost in the locale of *Ar*.

16.7.

    ***16.7.1.** Medu dje   en Aset ur   Atef-peh   khent   aset-per*

    16.7.2. <u>Words spoken by Isis great Upper-Egypt foremost abode</u>

    16.7.3. These words are spoken by *Aset(Isis)*, the Great Goddess in Upper-Egypt, the foremost abode.

16.8.

    ***16.8.1.** abtet mai iu   sebau   er   an-rudtef   auf   neter*

    16.8.2. <u>east lioness coming enemies as-to nothing-grows   body divine</u>

    16.8.3. In the east a lioness is coming and she will deal with the enemies who are threatening the place where nothing grows, where the Divine body of *Asar*(Osiris) is located.

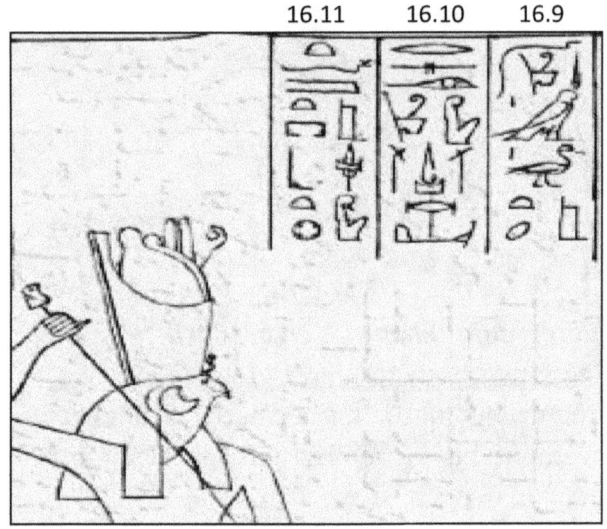

16.9.
- **16.9.1.** Medu   dje   en Heru-sa-Aset
- 16.9.2. <u>Words spoken by Horus-son-Isis</u>
- 16.9.3. These words are spoken by *Heru(Horus) the son* of *Goddess Aset(Isis)*…

16.10.
- **16.10.1.** er   z-ary   Neter en was-udja-was   netedj   necht
- 16.10.2. <u>as-to cause-action divinity of power-vitality-power redeemer strength</u>
- **16.10.3.** …he causes an action of double power to vitality, as a strong redeemer and protector…

16.11.
- **16.11.1.** Tef   im aset-per abtet
- 16.11.2. <u>Father in abode   east</u>
- **16.11.3.** …on behalf of his father (Ra) who is in the east.

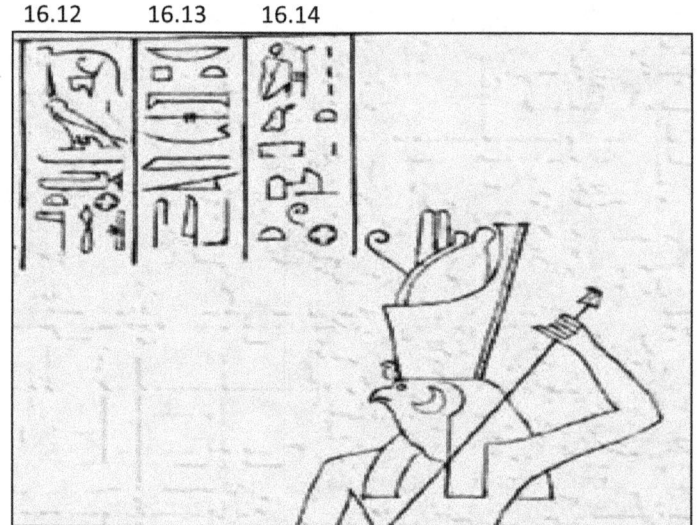

16.12.

16.12.1. **Medu dje   en Heru-Behudet   neter aah {mdj}**

16.12.2. <u>Words spoken by Horus-the-Warrior   great divinity{fig}</u>

16.12.3. These words are being spoken by *Heru(Horus)* in the aspect of the *Heru-Behudet, Heru(Horus)-the-HighPower The-Warrior*. He is a great divinity{fig}.

16.13.

16.13.1. **Neb pet   ze-mam   sebau**

16.13.2. <u>Lord heaven causing-slaughtering enemies</u>

16.13.3. He is the Lord of Heaven who causes the slaughtering of the enemies of the divine.

16.14.

16.14.1. **Khent   per   ahaut**

16.14.2. <u>Foremost place fighting</u>

16.14.3. This aspect of *Heru(Horus)*, the *Heru-Behudet, Heru(Horus)-the-HighPower* the fighter, the Warrior, is the foremost version of *Heru(Horus)*, which operates in the locale where the fighting occurs.

EGYPTIAN BOOK OF THE DEAD HIEROGLYPH TRANSLATIONS Volume 6: Featuring The Osirian Resurrection

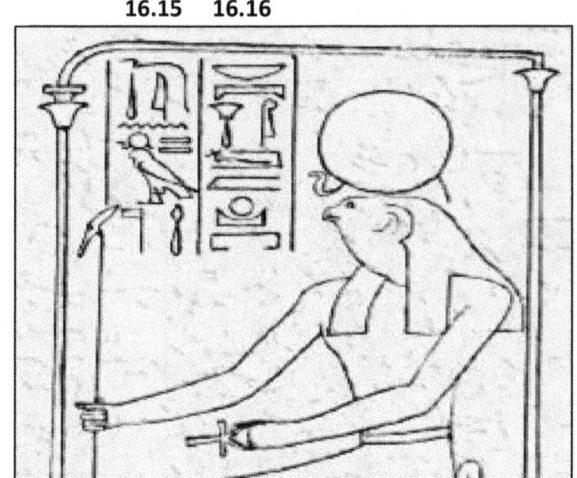

16.15   16.16

16.15.
 16.15.1. *Medu dje   in Ra-Herakty   Neter-aah*
 16.15.2. Words spoken by Creator-Spirit-two-Horizons great divinity
 16.15.3. These words are being spoken by *Ra, the Creator-Spirit* in his aspect as the Great Divinity of the two horizons, *Ra-Herakty,* east and west and all in between, from beginning to end.

16.16.
 16.16.1. *Neb pet   auf maat pert   im   akhet {per}*
 16.16.2. Lord heaven body truth coming-out through horizon
 16.17. He is the lord of heaven, the very embodiment of truth, truth incarnate, who is coming forth through the horizon.

Contextual wisdom in the translated text about the term "auf maat"

The text is a row that goes from left to right. It says, "*sab shut*" (also can be translated as *auf Maat*).

This text is a similar formula as the one presented in the temple of Asar (Osiris) at Abdu (Abydos), and other places. It means: "This is the symbol of the Great Hawk Divinity, the winged sundisk, Horus, whose dwelling place is the city of Edfu. He is the one with variegated (multicolor) feathers and the very one who is the embodiment of spiritual truth for eternity."

This is the divinity that is presiding over the message of this panel; he is the winged sun disk that is enfolding the whole scene if you will.

The iconography of the hawk and the presence of part of the remaining text, after the damage, indicate the name "Behudet" which is the name of the hawk god Heru when he defeated Set at the location commemorated by the temple at Edfu (Behudet). So, what is left, at the bottom, in the undamaged area, indicates the place name "Behudet", the city of the solar hawk god Heru/Horus.

This particular symbol (below) is the one that can be read as "sab (body) or auf" (flesh). The glyph **shut,** the feather, is also used to represent **maat** or truth. So, it can also mean, in this context, **sab shut** variegated, meaning multicolored feathers, hence, "body" of the hawk god or **auf maat** *"embodiment of truth"*.

Thus, we can think of this term as having a double meaning. The idea here is that *Neter Aah* (The Great Divinity) is presiding over this panel. This gives the idea that Amun-Ra is the chief but then we also have an idea that there's an overarching Divinity that is presiding over this whole scene. That is the Behudet, who is actually an aspect, a manifestation of the god Ra, who is also Amun-Ra. So we are dealing with aspects of the same Divinity.

EGYPTIAN BOOK OF THE DEAD HIEROGLYPH TRANSLATIONS Volume 6: Featuring The Osirian Resurrection

PANEL XVII.

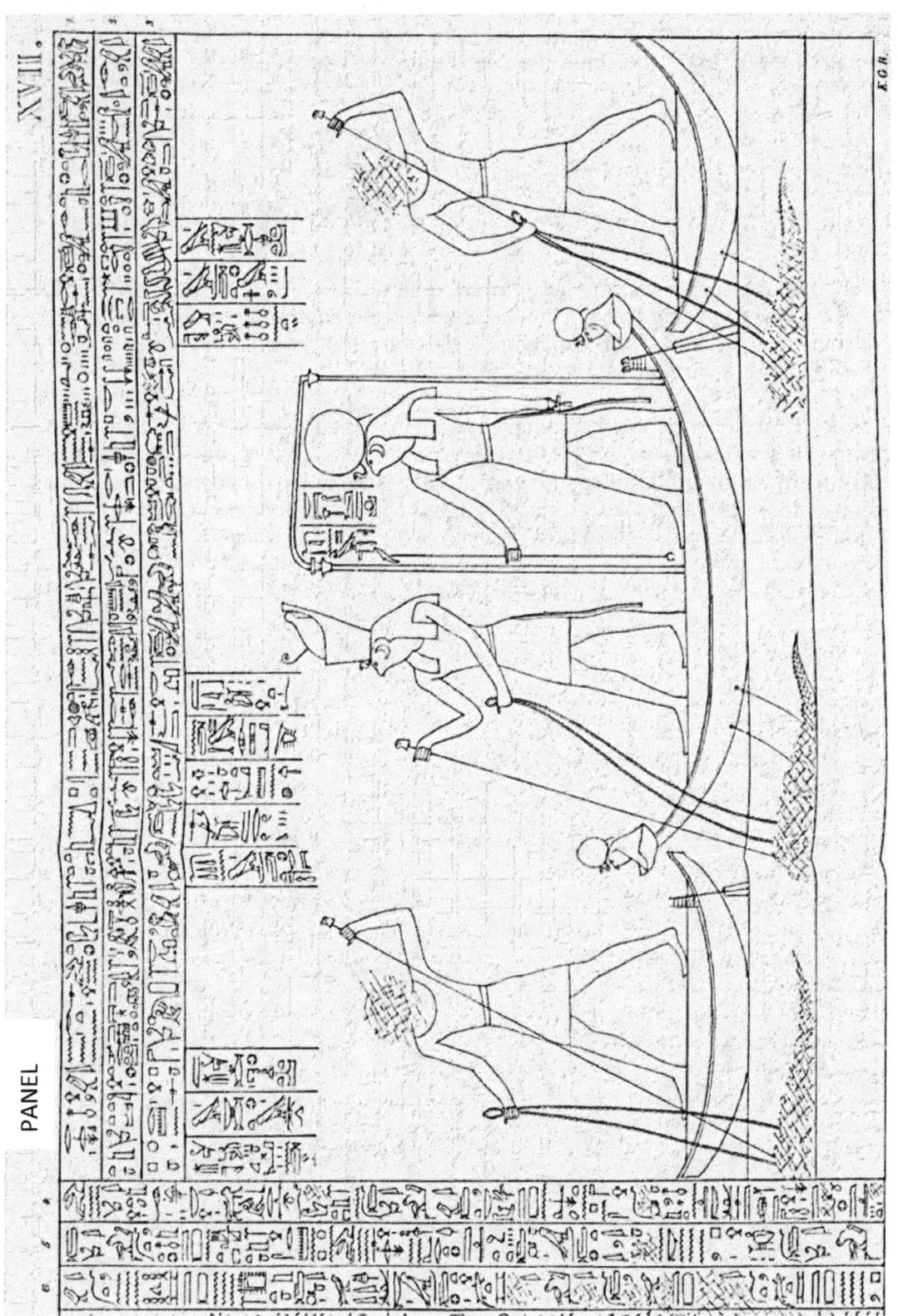

Above: The god Heru-the-HighPower, the-Warrior spearing a minion, a follower of Set, in the form of a crocodile. He is assisted by two blacksmiths. This occurs while Ra-of-two-Horizons (Creator Spirit), in his shrine looks on.

Panel 17

EGYPTIAN BOOK OF THE DEAD HIEROGLYPH TRANSLATIONS Volume 6: Featuring The Osirian Resurrection

PANEL 17

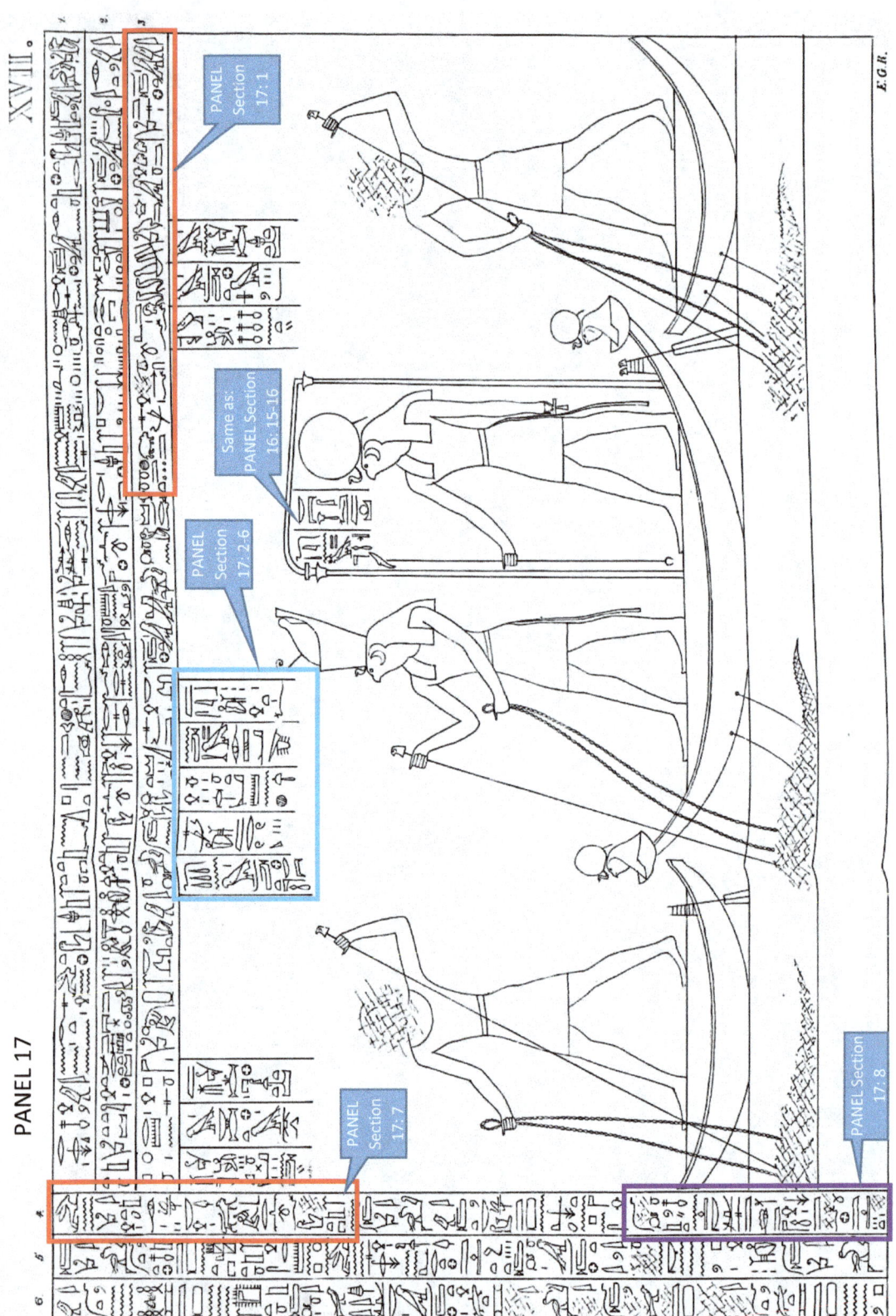

256

PANEL 17.

17.1.

17.1.1. *iu Heru-Behudet imz nu   pehty im her nu Heru cha im hedg deshert shuty urreret   Wadjty*

17.1.2. It is Horus-the-Warrior as that double strength form person Horus crown form white red plumes great-crown of serpent goddesses

17.1.3. This is what it is; *Heru-Behudet, Heru(Horus)-the-HighPower The-Warrior,* is a being of double (superhuman) strength as a form of personality reflecting *Heru(Horus)*, and even wearing his double crown that displays the white and red crowns meaning master of Upper and Lower Kemet/Ancient Egypt, along with two plumes combined signifying possession of the crown of greatness. He also has the two serpent goddesses, both of which contain *Aset(Isis)* and *Nebthet(Nephthys)*.

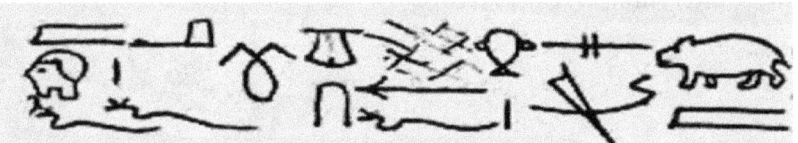

17.1.4. *im tep F a-F   rud   gatja [dmg] medju ua F her zma tepu im*

17.1.5. in top-head his arm-his succeeding violence [dmg] ten harpoon his person cause-slay hippo in

17.1.6. These goddesses are in the top of his head. His arms forge ahead successfully, acting violently on the transgressors with the use of 10 harpoons[15] which he uses to slay the fiends who are in the form of hippopotamuses.

---

[15] NOTE: 10 is the number of the god Heru. Notice that he is the tenth divinity in the tree of gods and goddesses of Anunian Theology –presented earlier. Thus ten is the number of spearings in which Heru plants the spear of Heru oneness in all 10 levels of Creation as represented by all the gods and goddesses of Creation. We are told in this very text that Heru is the divinity operating through all divinities and is so honored by the placement of a winged disk above the entrances of all the temples of the north and south.

17.2.

17.2.1. ***meduu djeu   en Heru-Behudet   Neter   aah   neb pet***

17.2.2. multiple words spoken by Horus-the-Warrior Divinity great lord heaven

17.2.3. These next columns of text are by *Heru(Horus)* as the HighPower, the Warrior, a great divinity who is also the lord of heaven...

17.3.

17.3.1. ***zma seba   meruu***

17.3.2. slayer fiends driving-out {region}

17.3.3. ..and who slays and drives out fiends from the region.

17.4.

17.4.1. ***her   abu   nedj-nut {necht} mench***

17.4.2. person-innermost hearts redeemer {strong} chiseler/sculpter

17.4.3. He is also the entity that is innermost in the hearts, their redeemer, protector as well as molder/sculptor, fashioner so as to chisel out and remove the rough, unrighteous parts...

17.5.

17.5.1. *en dit   hem   Ra-Herakty   ary sha*

17.5.2. to hand majesty Ra-Two-Horizons do cut-{vertebrae}

17.5.3. ...in order to be able to hand them over to The Creator Spirit of the Two Horizons, who will then cut their vertebrae...

17.6.

17.6.1. *im sebau her   tef*

17.6.2. in fiends person father

17.6.3. …in those fiends, thereby incapacitating them. This will be done by the person who is their father (Ra-Herakty).

	Transliteration 17.7.1	Translation 17.7.2	Contextual Translation 17.7.3
17.7.	Unen In Aset-her ary hekau neb nehat- her mai be/chefty er anrutef Neter[dmg] im aset-per	Happening to by Isis-person doing words-of-power all Sycamore person lioness Set/enemy concerning place-no-growth Divinity [damaged] within abode	This is happening to and the actions taken by *Aset(Isis)*. While *Ra-of-Two-Horizons* and *Heru-Behudet, Heru(Horus)-the-HighPower*, the *Warrior* are concerned with pursuing the fiends of *Set(Seth)* and stifling *Set's(Seth's)* movements, *Aset(Isis)* is taking action throughout all the lands of the south of *Kemet(Egypt)*. She uttered words of power to infuse the environment with protective energies. She acted as the sycamore goddess, provisioner and nurse for all who suffered due to the war. Then she felt the need to access her lioness power because *Set(Seth)* was able to threaten the specific location called "the place where nothing grows"; the sacred abode where *Asar(Osiris)*, in his resurrected form, dwelt. Hence, *Aset(Isis)* took the form of a lioness to thwart all the nefarious plans from any threat that might arise. One of her lioness aspects mentioned is *Aztjardet(Astarte)*, depicted in PANEL 13.

EGYPTIAN BOOK OF THE DEAD HIEROGLYPH TRANSLATIONS Volume 6: Featuring The Osirian Resurrection

Another image of goddess Aset/Isis, as a lioness, is presented in the temple of Khom Ombo

Façade of Khom Ombo Temple of Ancient Egypt

Panel containing an image of goddess Aset as a lioness.

Close up of panel containing an image of goddess Aset as a lioness.

A=words spoken by Aset

B=goddess lioness

EGYPTIAN BOOK OF THE DEAD HIEROGLYPH TRANSLATIONS Volume 6: Featuring The Osirian Resurrection

Ancient Egyptian Temple Khom Ombo presentation of Goddess Isis as lioness	Transliteration	Translation	Contextual Translation
	Khnum ka ushen k ankh was	unification maleness femaleness thine life flow	(placing instrument of life essence to the nostrils of the Royal Person[temple initiate]) Unify the duality within yourself by means of the life essence that I, as the goddess of wisdom and controller of the leonine life-force, am causing to flow through your nostrils to promote your spiritual enlightenment.

EGYPTIAN BOOK OF THE DEAD HIEROGLYPH TRANSLATIONS Volume 6: Featuring The Osirian Resurrection

Returning to the Temple of Heru at Edfu

	Transliteration 17.8.1	Translation 17.8.2	Contextual Translation 17.8.3
17.8.	*Medu dje Nu Ra* *Neferuy* *Aset* *en* *Hetep* *K* *uia* *ze* *im* *[ankh] maa* *im* *su-her Neter-aah* *im* *anrutef* *im* *heteput*	Words spoken of Ra, the Creator-Spirit beautiful! beautiful! Isis to peace thine boat cause manner living eye (watch) form royal-person Divinity great in place-no-growth in peacefulness	Now, these following words are from the god *Ra, the Creator-Spirit*. "Beautiful! Beautiful! *Aset(Isis)* has brought peace to the boat of *Asar(Osiris)*, the abode of the soul, which is anchored in the sacred region deep at the source of the personality, in the south. Beautiful! *Aset(Isis)* took up a watchful form watching over the royal person, the great Divinity who resides in the specific location called "the place where nothing grows" so that that great Divinity may remain in a peaceful state.

Note #1 on verse 17.8: The following image shows Asar in his abode in the center of the Anrutef/Yanrutf region of the Duat/Netherworld. He sits on a boat with 7 steps. (Image of the boat taken from papyrus Any.) The other regions of existence, according to the Ancient Egyptian Book of Coming Forth By Day, are included for geographical reference.

Ta= physical earth realm

Pet= heavenly realm

Duat= Netherworld

Sekhet Hetep= realm of seeking peace within oneself.

Sekhet Yaaru= abode of blessed souls.

Yanrutef= place beyond thoughts, feelings, desires and egoism.

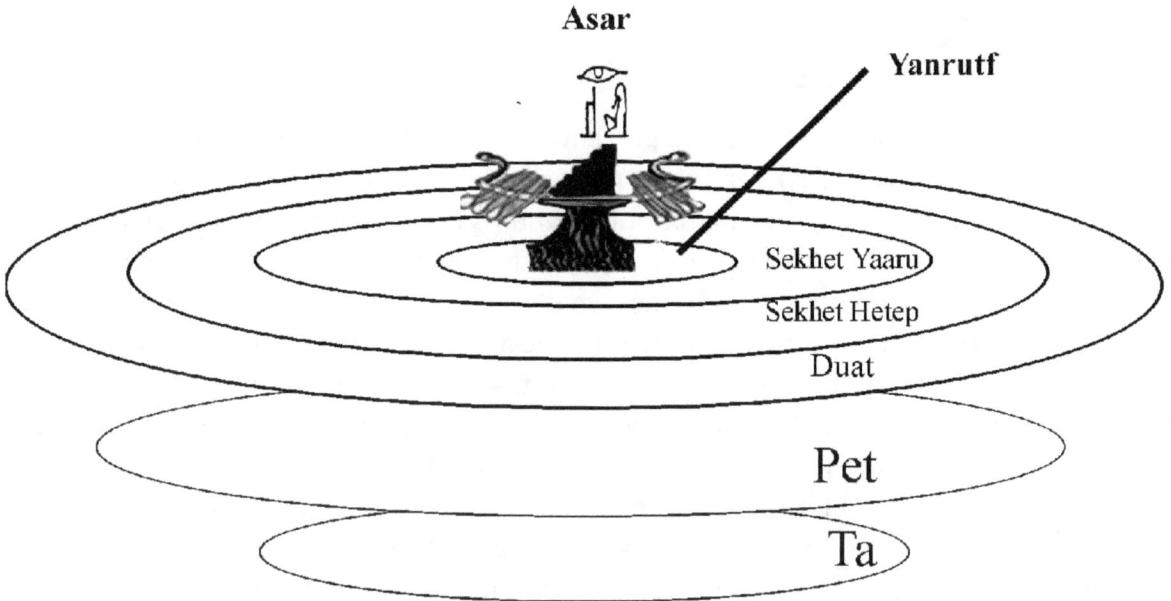

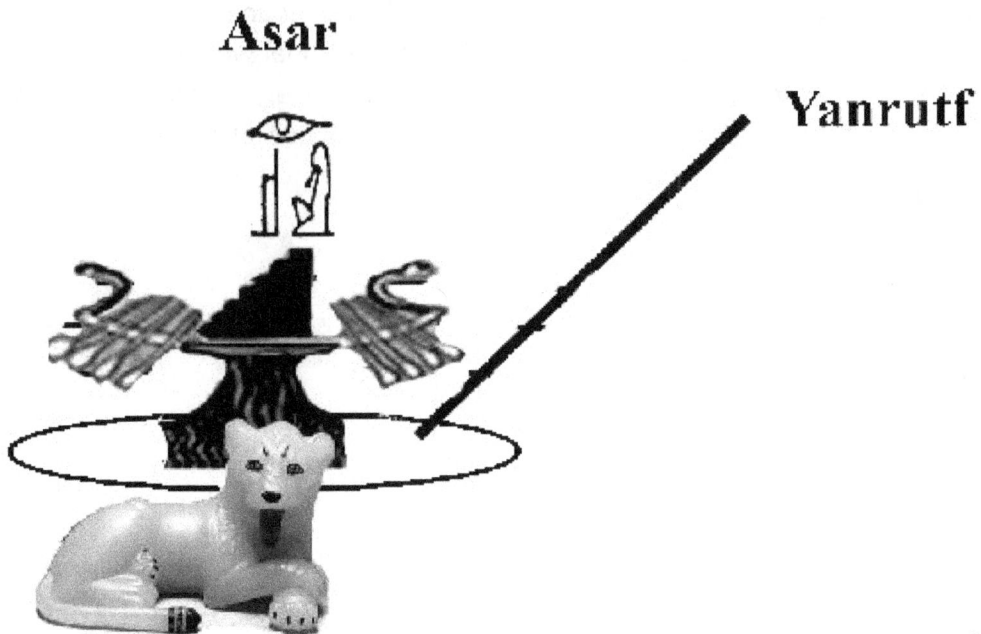

Note #2 on verse 17.8: The image above is presented to help the visualization of what the previous section of scripture was describing. It placed goddess Aset/Isis as being recumbent and watchful, after vanquishing the enemies of Ra and Asar/Osiris, around the area of the Duat/Netherworld called "yanrutef/anrutef" where the consciousness of Asar/Osiris (as Zokar) resides in peace (non-dual nature). Thus, what the goddess represents, i.e. intuitional wisdom, destroys the iniquitous forces, thoughts, feelings, the fiends/minions of the god *Set/Seth* that relentlessly try to disturb and dislodge the soul from its place of supremacy and rest in the center of the Duat/Netherworld – the unconscious. Thus, the goddess represents that aspect of the personality that destroys unrighteous thoughts, feelings and desires that prevent the Soul from being primary in conscious awareness and supreme as the notion of self-identity. In terms of meditation, where one is trying to experience the undifferentiated consciousness (anrutef) state, it is Intuitional Wisdom (goddess Aset/Isis) that keeps out the egoistic thoughts to allow one to experience the anrutef state of undifferentiated consciousness, and the undisturbed experience of Asar (her husband and brother), the Universal Soul-Ra-Neberdjer.

Another aspect of this concept is that the goddess vanquishes the subtle, inner challenges of the personality, the ignorance, the delusions and forces of negativity and inner psychological traumas, and protects the inner personality, the Soul, while her offspring (Heru) vanquishes external enemies and protects the external self, the subconscious and conscious mind and body, while putting the ego (Set) in its place.

EGYPTIAN BOOK OF THE DEAD HIEROGLYPH TRANSLATIONS Volume 6: Featuring The Osirian Resurrection

PANEL 13: [Focus on Goddess Isis as *Aztjardet* (Astarte)]

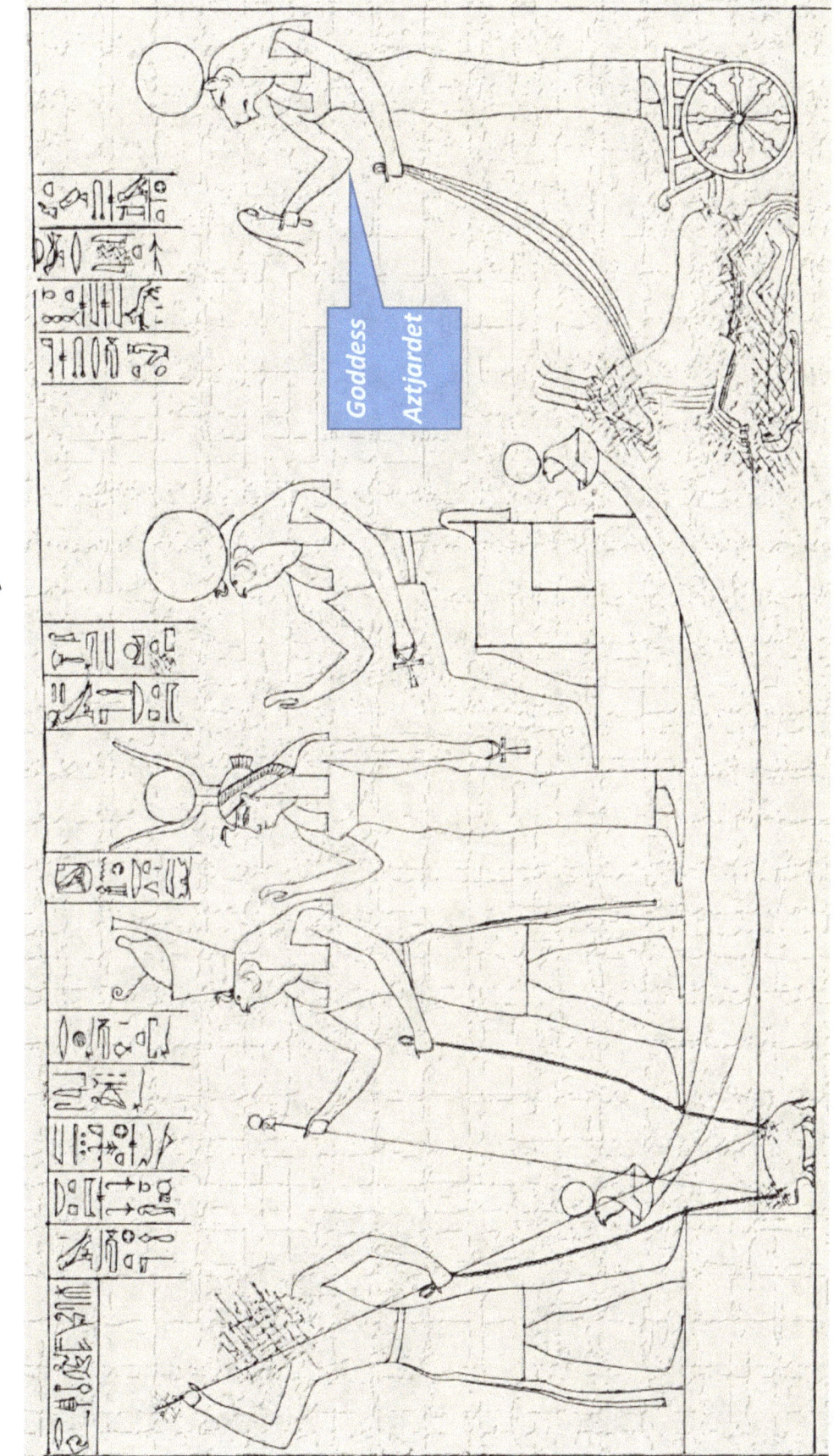

Above: The god Heru-the-HighPower, the-Warrior spearing a minion, a follower of Set, in the form of a hippo. He is assisted by one blacksmith. Goddess Aset and the god Ra-of-two-Horizons look on. To the right goddess Aztjardet, in her chariot, assists by trampling one of the minions of Set with her horses.

267

Above: Dr. Ashby studying the panels including PANEL 13.

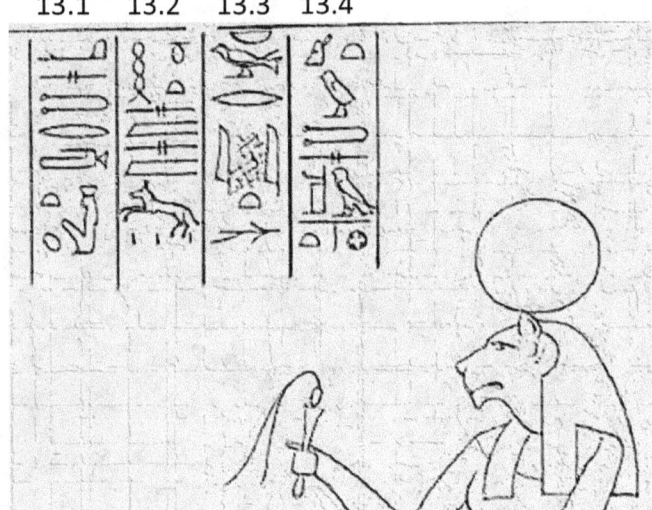

PANEL 13.

13.1.

13.1.1. Aztjardet

13.1.2. Astarte/Ishtar

13.1.3. This is *Ishtar*, a Syrian name for the lioness goddess identified as *Aset-Hetheru(Isis-Hathor)*; known as a moon goddess and war goddess…

13.2.

13.2.1. Henut- zemzemu

13.2.2. queen-mother horses

13.2.3. …and queen-mother and controller of the raging horses that rampage against the enemy.

13.3.

13.3.1. Neb   urrit {chet}

13.3.2. mistress chariot {wood}

13.3.3. She is the mistress of the chariot.

13.4.

13.4.1. Khent   utjez-Her

13.4.2. Foremost nome Horus

13.4.3. She is foremost in the nome (district) of Upper Kemet(Egypt) wherein Edfu(Behudt), the town and religious center of *Heru(Horus) Behudet(The HighPower, The-Warrior)*, is located.

EGYPTIAN BOOK OF THE DEAD HIEROGLYPH TRANSLATIONS Volume 6: Featuring The Osirian Resurrection

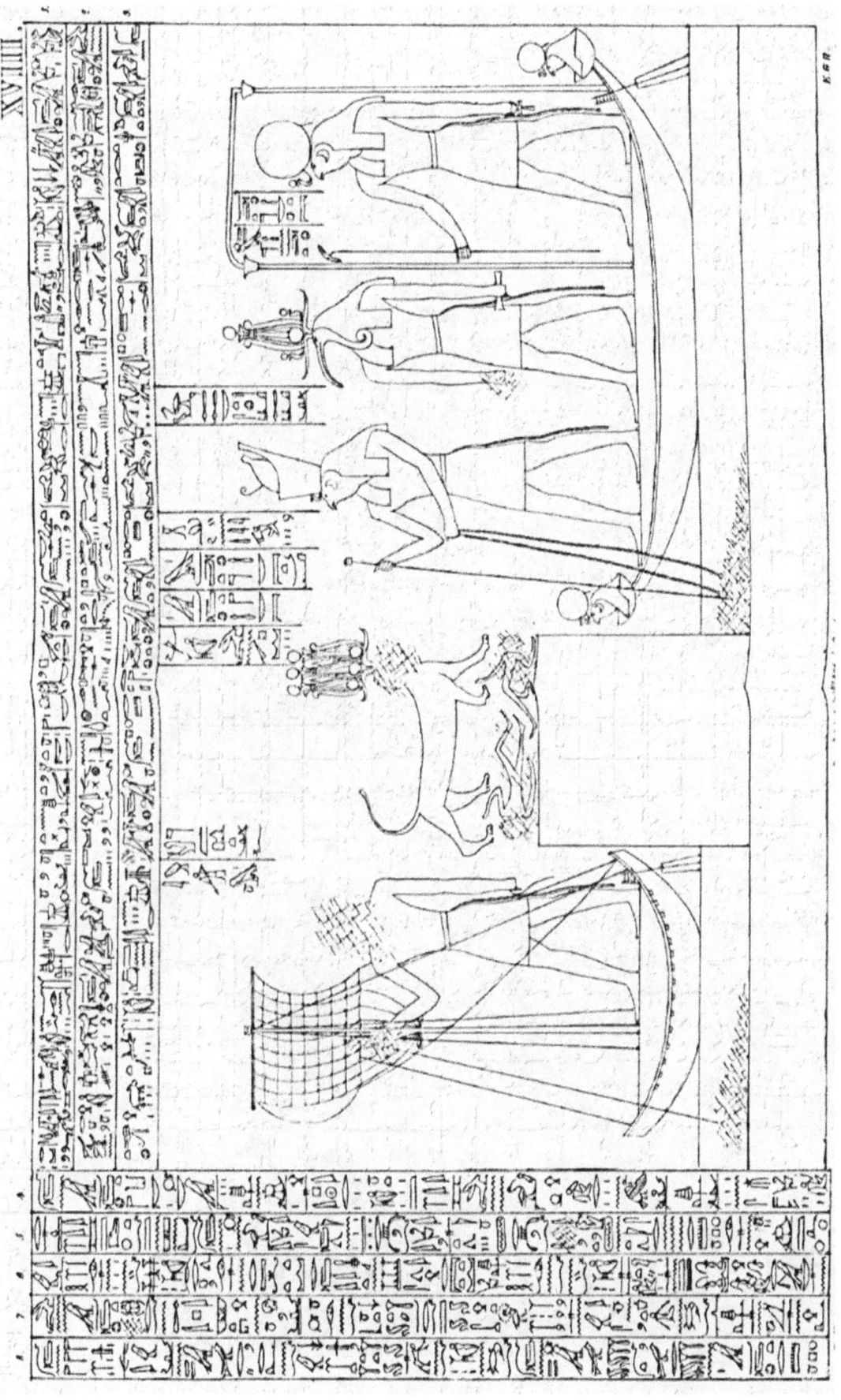

Panel 18- Above: The god Heru-the-HighPower, the-Warrior is in his boat spearing a minion, a follower of *Set*, in the form of a crocodile. He is assisted by one of his blacksmith followers and also by himself in the form of a lion, who is trampling the minions of *Set*. This occurs while the gods (both in the boat) *Djehuty*(Thoth) and *Ra-of-two-Horizons*(Creator Spirit), in his shrine look on.

EGYPTIAN BOOK OF THE DEAD HIEROGLYPH TRANSLATIONS Volume 6: Featuring The Osirian Resurrection

PANEL 18

PANEL 18. TRANSLITERATION – TRANSLATION – CONTEXTUAL TRANSLATION

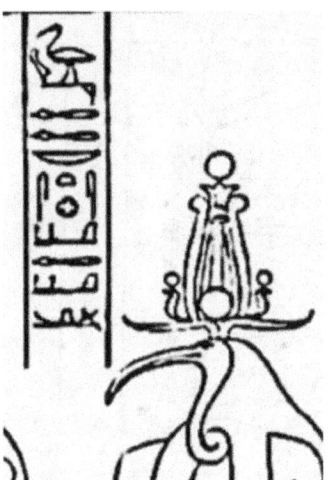

18.1.
- **18.1.1.** *Djehuty aay   neb setes mak   aah dpt*
- 18.1.2. Thoth twice-great lord city support great boat
- 18.1.3. The god *Djehuty(Thoth)*, the twice-great is the lord of the city of *Setes* and he is the support of the Great Boat (of *Ra*).

18.2.
- **18.2.1.** *Heru Behudet   Neter aah neb pet   ma*
- 18.2.2. Horus-The-HighPower Divinity great lord heaven coming
- 18.2.3. This is *Heru-Behudet, Heru(Horus)-the-HighPower The-Warrior*, the great divinity, the lord of heaven, is oncoming.

18.3.
- 18.3.1. *an   pehuy en tyu   {aufu}*
- 18.3.2. bringing towing of enemy {bodies}
- 18.3.3. He is dragging along the bodies of the enemies.

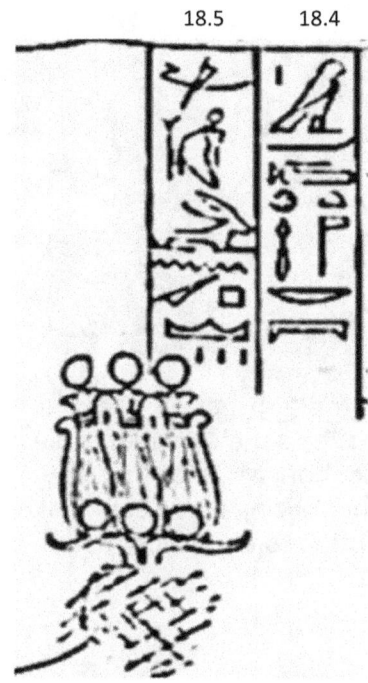

18.4.
    18.4.1. Heru Behudet   Neter aah neb pet
    18.4.2. <u>Horus-The-HighPower Divinity great lord heaven</u>

    18.4.3. This is *Heru-Behudet, Heru(Horus)-the-HighPower The-Warrior*, the great divinity, the lord of heaven.

18.5.
    18.5.1. sma   seba   un   pehedu
    18.5.2. <u>slaying enemy existing cutting hills</u>

    18.5.3. He is slaying the enemies, the followers of the god *Set(Seth)*, cutting them up, particularly, those in the hill country.

18.6.
    18.6.1. Unen Heru-Behudet   ary   kheper {tut}   f en mai en
    18.6.2. <u>Happening to Horus-the-HighPower-Warrior makes transformation{form} he of person of</u>

    18.6.3. This is happening to *Heru-Behudet, Heru(Horus)-the-HighPower The-Warrior*. He makes himself transform into the form of a lion of...

18.6.4. *her nu {offer} khauy im hemhem*
18.6.5. {person that makes offerings} crowned with triple rushes
18.6.6. … a personality of a benevolent person who wears the crown of triple rushes, with SunDisk, plumes, and cobra serpents and ram horns.[16] With this crown *Heru(Horus)* is the sound of the battle cry announcing fierce action. In this aspect of lion *Heru(Horus)* offers purity and redemption to *Ra* by destruction of his enemies.

18.7.

18.7.1. *Medu   dje   en Ra nu Djehuty   mak   Heru-Behudet   mit mai her*
18.7.2. Words spoken of Ra to Thoth   behold Horus-the-Warrior like lion person
18.7.3. These are the words of *Ra*, the Creator Spirit, to *Djehuty(Thoth)*, the god of intellect and the scribe of the gods and goddesses: "Look over there; *Heru(Horus)* the-HighPower, the-warrior is in his lion form,…

18.7.4. *ba F her sa seba her ra aab nu auf atebu zen*
18.7.5. load he person back enemy person mouth container of part tongues theirs
18.7.6. …and his being and dynamic presence is a load weighing down, oppressing overwhelming, crushing the enemies, so much so that their tongues are coming out of their mouths and they cannot utter blasphemies against me any longer!"

---

[16] Triple Rushes

1. a. Any of various grass-like wetland plants of the genus *Juncus*, having stiff hollow or pithy stems and small usually clustered brownish flowers.
b. Any of various similar plants, such as a bulrush.
2. The stem of one of these plants, used in making baskets, mats, and chair seats.

EGYPTIAN BOOK OF THE DEAD HIEROGLYPH TRANSLATIONS Volume 6: Featuring The Osirian Resurrection

Section 18.8	Transliteration 18.8.1	Translation 18.8.2	Contextual Translation 18.8.3
18.8.	*Unen Heru-Behudet* *Kheper F en aapa* *her th en tep nu uia nu Ra ary en F* *Sunuteb Wadjit hur F im Wadjty her set* *sett imuim aufu zen iu* *ab en s hut urdu en send F an aha zen*	Happening to Horus-the-HighPowerWarrior transforming himself to Winged-Disk Person traverse to top of boat of Ra doing to himself south goddess north goddess joining he with serpent goddesses personality move against shudder in within body parts theirs it is heart of it terror / fear weak / faint of fright his not stand they	Now this is happening to *Heru* (Horus) Behudet -the-HighPower, the-Warrior. He transformed himself into the form of a Sundisk with wings. As the son of *Ra*, whose dynamic manifestation is the Sundisk, *Heru(Horus)-The-HighPowerWarrior* took that form and added wings to it, now not only having the Sundisk symbol of power but also the capacity to expand and encompass and overwhelm the enemies with it. But the transformation did not stop there. *Heru(Horus)* went up to the boat of *Ra* and stood on the deck of the boat which was flying along the sky, above, in the heavens. There he joined to himself the goddesses of the south and the north, the power of source(south) from where Creation is sustained and fruition(north) where that power reaches its height in the dynamic expression of control over all Creation itself. From the heights of the heavens, shining with the power of the sun, joined with the goddesses he shined down on the enemies of *Ra* and their body parts shuddered in terror at the sight of the Winged-Disk form. Their fear was so great that they froze in terror, fell unconscious and could not get up; all that happened just at the mere sight of this special form of Heru.

EGYPTIAN BOOK OF THE DEAD HIEROGLYPH TRANSLATIONS Volume 6: Featuring The Osirian Resurrection

Section 18.9	Transliteration 18.9.1	Translation 18.9.2	Contextual Translation 18.9.3
18.9.	*Djed en Ra-Herakty* *Ur Wadjty Dje ut ur* *Wadjty en Heru-Behudet* *er menu*	Speech of Creator-Spirit-of-two-Horizons Great Two serpent goddesses Spoken decree Great Two serpent goddesses of Horus-the-Warrior As-to monuments	*These are the words of Ra, the Creator-Spirit in the form of the Great Divinity of the two horizons,* Ra-Herakty, *east and west and all in between, from beginning to end.* "*This is a great thing; I declare that this form of Heru-Behudet, Heru(Horus)-the-HighPower -The-Warrior with the two serpent goddesses should be on every monument.*

278

EGYPTIAN BOOK OF THE DEAD HIEROGLYPH TRANSLATIONS Volume 6: Featuring The Osirian Resurrection

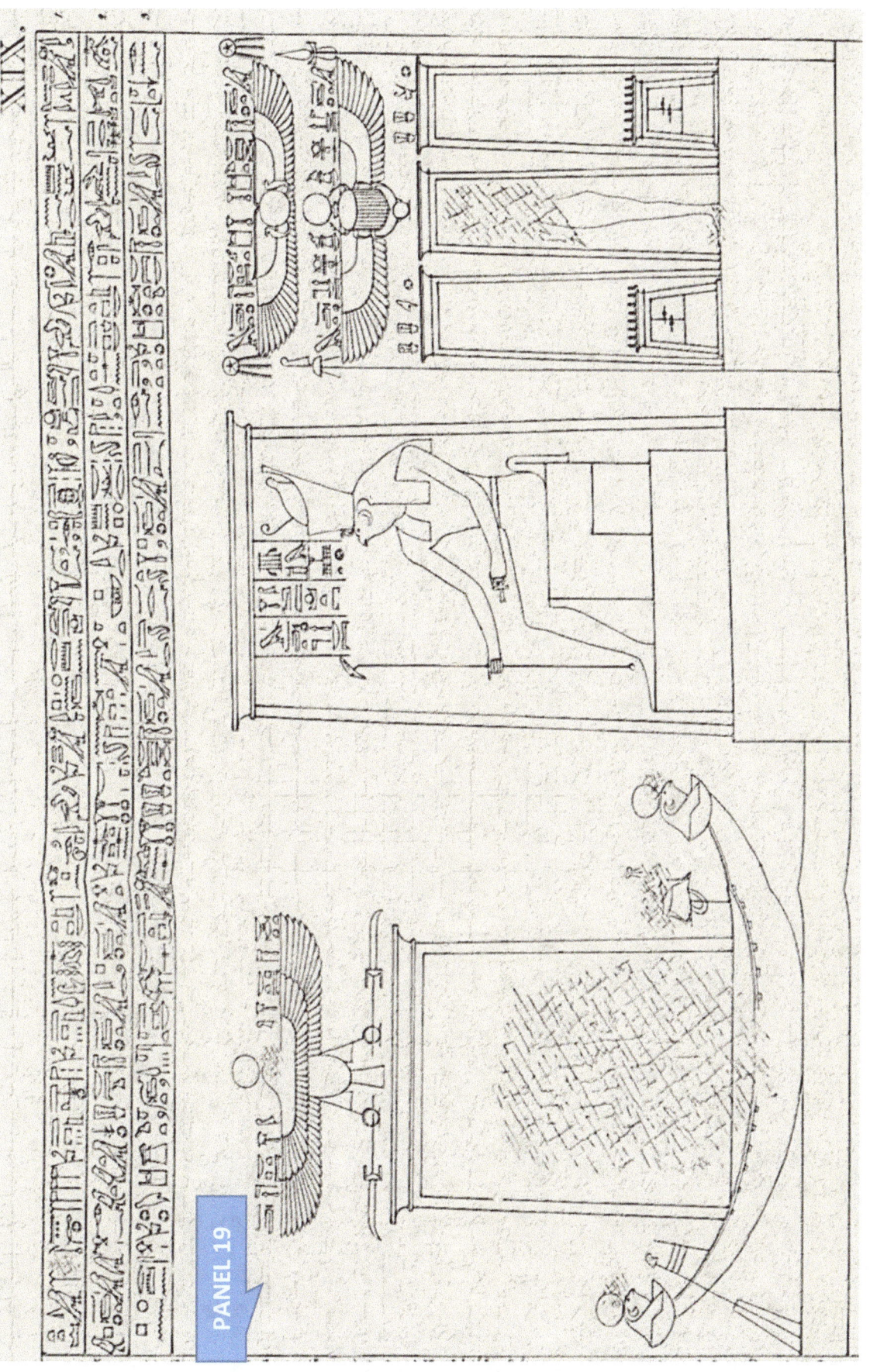

Above: The god Heru-the-HighPower, the-Warrior is in his shrine looking at the divine boat. Behind him there is a double shrine, one with the Hedjet crown of the south and the other of the deshert crown of the north (with two forms of the winged disk commemorating that Heru is now presiding over the shrines of all the gods and goddesses of all directions).

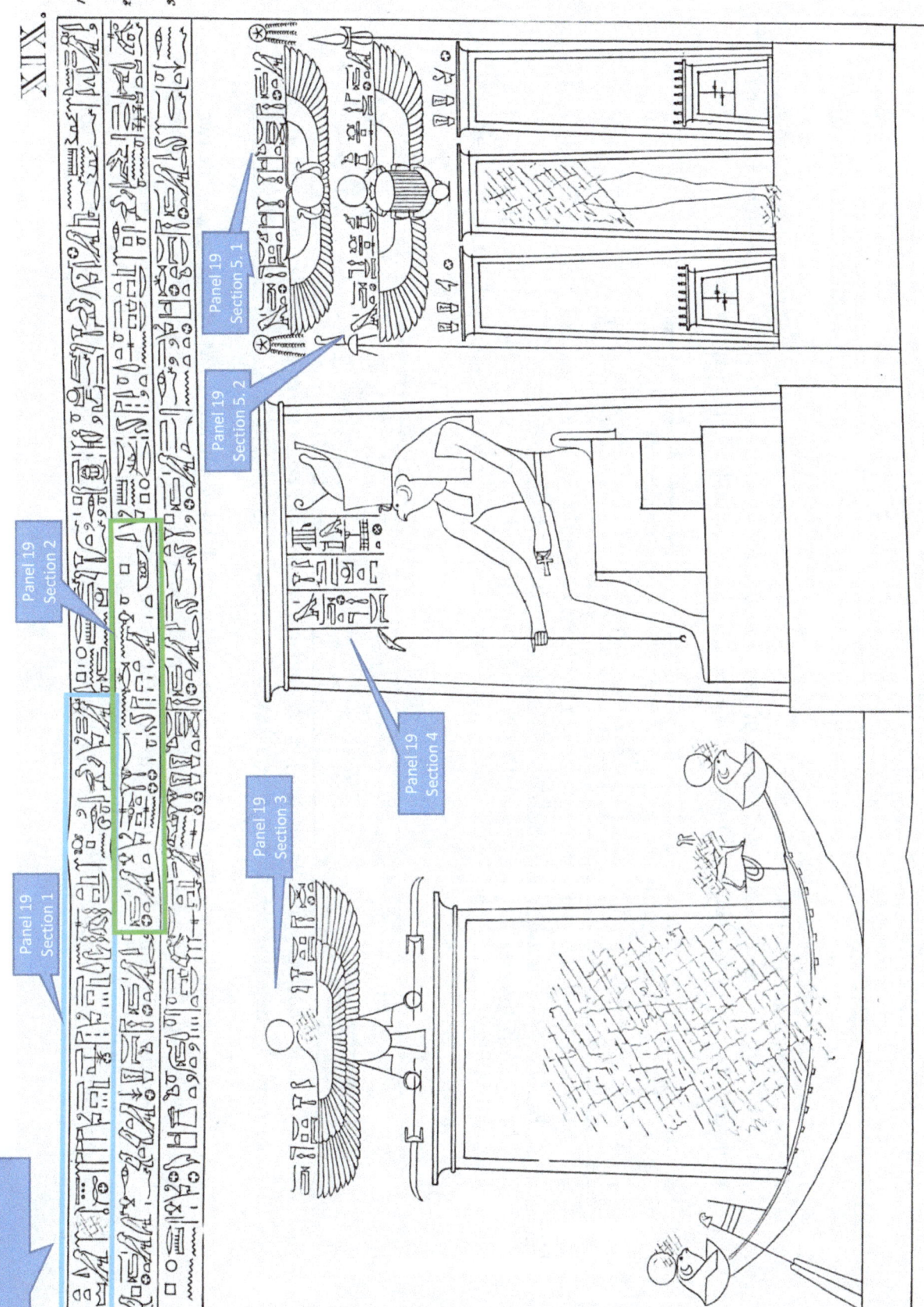

EGYPTIAN BOOK OF THE DEAD HIEROGLYPH TRANSLATIONS Volume 6: Featuring The Osirian Resurrection

19.1.

- 19.1.1. **Ra-Herakty   en   Djehuty   iu ary nu {k}   aapi pen im aset-per neb z-nedjmy-urd en Neter im aset-peru**
- 19.1.2. Creator-Spirit to Thoth   it is doing of crowning Winged-Disk that in abodes all cause sweet-rest to divinity in abodes
- 19.1.3. *Ra, the Creator-Spirit* spoke to *Djehuty(Thoth)*. It is an action I want you to undertake, which I will explain to you now. I want you to place the *Winged Sundisk*, of *Heru-Behudet, Heru(Horus)-the-HighPower The-Warrior*, in such a placement so that it will serve the function, as a crown, on all the abodes (temples, shrines)...

- 19.1.4. **en   neteru im shema im aset-peru en neteru im ta meh was {dmg}im Heru   Amentet**
- 19.1.5. of god/goddesses in south in abodes   of god/goddesses in land north power {dmg} in Horus west
- 19.1.6. ... of all the gods and goddesses in the south region of Kemet(Egypt) as well as the abodes, the temples of all the gods and goddesses in the lands of the north part of Kemet(Egypt)... as well as the abode of Heru in the west (Amentet).

19.2.

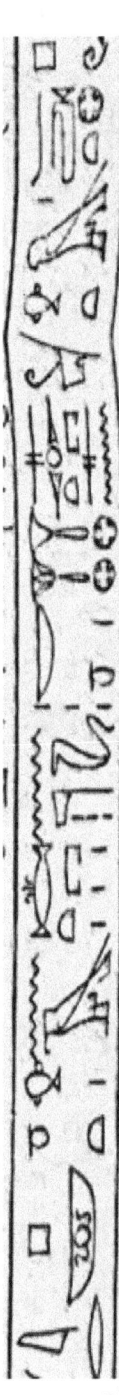

- 19.2.1. **ar   aapi   nut her   n-a   gautu en neteru netertu neb nu tawy ze-chem zen en hert Heru-Behudet pu**
- 19.2.2. about Winged-Disk that symbol of-I coffers of gods goddesses all that two-lands causing-shrines theirs to personality Horus-the-Warrior this
- 19.2.3. ...so as to be presided over with the *Winged Disk*. That symbol is to be placed over the buildings, shrines, chapels, etc. of all gods and goddesses alike, throughout the two lands, of upper and lower KMT/Egypt, where the two goddesses preside, *Wadjit* of the North and *Sunuteb* of the South; thereby this act hereby causes their shrines to be consecrated to *Heru-Behudet, Heru(Horus)-the-HighPower The-Warrior*. Thus, anyone worshiping any of the gods and goddesses will be protected by the victorious winged disk and they will also realize that when they are worshipping any god or goddess they are worshipping *Heru-Behudet, Heru(Horus)-the-HighPower The-Warrior*,

EGYPTIAN BOOK OF THE DEAD HIEROGLYPH TRANSLATIONS Volume 6: Featuring The Osirian Resurrection

who is an aspect, a manifestation of me; so in fact as they are worshipping any god or goddess they are worshiping me and in this realization there is to be the understanding that there is One Ultimate Dvinity above and encompassing all the lesser gods and goddesses. This is my decree and my order to you, *Djehuty(Thoth)* to be carried out immediately.

Above: Example of a temple doorway where the winged disk has been placed.

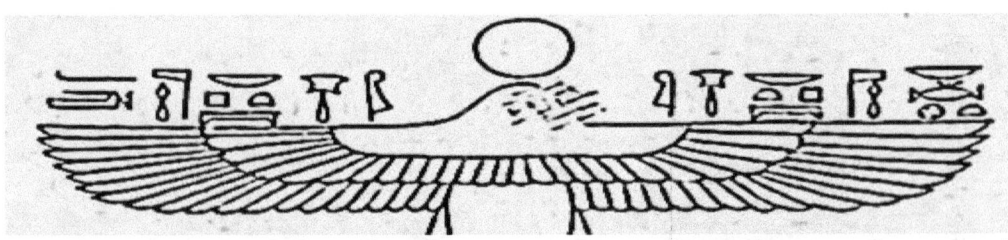

19.3.

19.3.1. *Behudet aah-Neter Neb pet auf Maat*	19.3.1A *Maat auf pet Neb Neter aah mesen neb*
19.3.2. <u>*Horus-the-HighPower, the-Warrior,* Great-Divinity Lord heaven embodiment truth</u>	19.3.2A <u>Lord of Mesen town Great-Divinity Lord heaven embodiment truth</u>
19.3.3. *Heru(Horus)-the-HighPower, the-Warrior*, This is THE Great Divinity and the Lord of heaven and none other than the embodiment of Maat, absolute truth!	19.3.3A This is the Lord of Mesen town in the north. THE Great Divinity and the Lord of heaven and none other than the embodiment of Maat, absolute truth!

19.4.   19.4.1   19.4.2   19.4.3

19.4.1.
    19.4.1.1. ***Heru-Behudet   Neter   Aah neb pet***
    19.4.1.2. <u>Horus-the-HighPower, divinity great lord heaven</u>
    19.4.1.3. This is *Heru-Behudet, Heru(Horus)-the-HighPower The-Warrior*, the great divinity, the lord of heaven.

19.4.2.
    19.4.2.1. *auf   maat   pert   im   akhet {per}*
    19.4.2.2. <u>body truth coming-out through   horizon</u>
    19.4.2.3. … He is the very embodiment of truth, truth incarnate, who is coming forth through the horizon.

EGYPTIAN BOOK OF THE DEAD HIEROGLYPH TRANSLATIONS Volume 6: Featuring The Osirian Resurrection

19.4.3.
    19.4.3.1. **Khent   utjez-Her**
    19.4.3.2. <u>Foremost nome-Horus</u>
    19.4.3.3. ...the foremost in the nome(district) of Upper Egypt wherein *Edfu(Behudt)*, the town of *Heru(Horus)* Behudet(The-HighPower, The-Warrior), is located.

TEXT of the Winged Disk:

Panel 19

19.4.4. *LtoR*
19.4.4.1.   **akhu Behudet-Heru neter aah neb pet khent atert wadj**
19.4.4.2.   <u>shining-spirit Horus-the-HighPower great divinity lord heaven foremost shrines north</u>
19.4.4.3.   This is the manifestation of the Divine Shining Spirit of the Supreme Being. In the manifestation under the name *Heru-Behudet, Heru(Horus)-the-HighPower The-Warrior*, this is the great divinity, the lord of heaven and the chief, the principal being in the shrines of the north.

19.4.5.   *RtoL*

19.4.5.1.   *wadj atert khent pet neb aah neter Behudet-Heru akhu*
19.4.5.2. northern - shrines foremost town Mesen Lord heaven Lord great divinity Horus Spirit-Shining
                                                                                                    the-High
                                                                                                    Power   *RtoL*

19.4.5.3. This is the manifestation of the Divine Shining Spirit of the Supreme Being. In the manifestation under the name *Heru-Behudet, Heru(Horus)-the-HighPower The-Warrior;* this is the great divinity, the lord of heaven, the lord of Mesen town in Lower (northern) Kemet(Egypt) and the chief, the principal being in the shrines of the north.

TEXT of the Winged Scarab:

19.4.6.
   19.4.6.1. ***Heru-Behudet neter aah neb pet aapa sheps khent atert neb***
   19.4.6.2. Horus-the-HighPower-Warrior divinity great lord heaven Winged-Disk holy foremost shrines all

19.4.6.3. In the manifestation under the name *Heru-Behudet, Heru(Horus)-the-HighPower The-Warrior*, this is the great divinity, the lord of heaven, manifesting as the Winged-Disk, the holy image above the temples and shrines of Kemet(Egypt) and the chief, the principal being in all shrines.

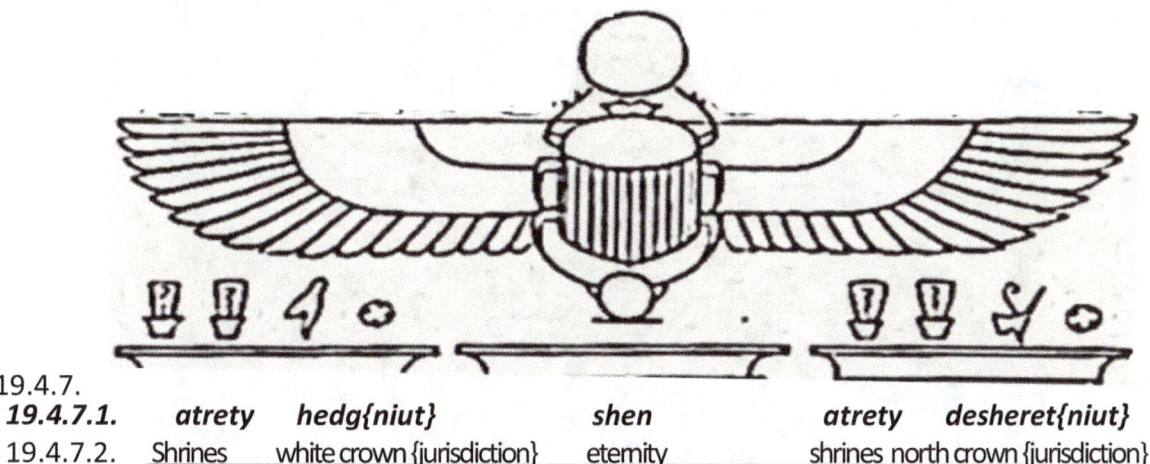

19.4.7.
19.4.7.1.   *atrety   hedg{niut}*   *shen*   *atrety   desheret{niut}*
19.4.7.2.   Shrines   white crown {jurisdiction}   eternity   shrines   north crown {jurisdiction}

19.4.7.3.   The Winged-Disk with the form of the scarab flies over the shrines of the south jurisdiction (all Upper Kemet/Egypt) and the shrines of the north (all Lower Kemet/Egypt). It brings eternity to them and with eternity also immortality, holiness and enlightenment. Even more, it brings eternity that is ever creating, moving, and shining for eternity.

Samples of the hieroglyph *atrety* – "shrines"

19.4.8.

19.4.8.1. ***waset***	***abtet***
19.4.8.2. west	east
19.4.8.3. The western abode of God and noble souls.	The east, source of the sun and sustenance of Creation.

Directional Matrix of the Winged Disks on Panel 19

The Winged-Disk section of panel 19 contains within it the Directional Matrix of the Winged Disk wisdom. It expresses that the winged disk form of the Divine spans all directions of existence and therefore the Supreme Divine is all encompassing and thus also all pervading.

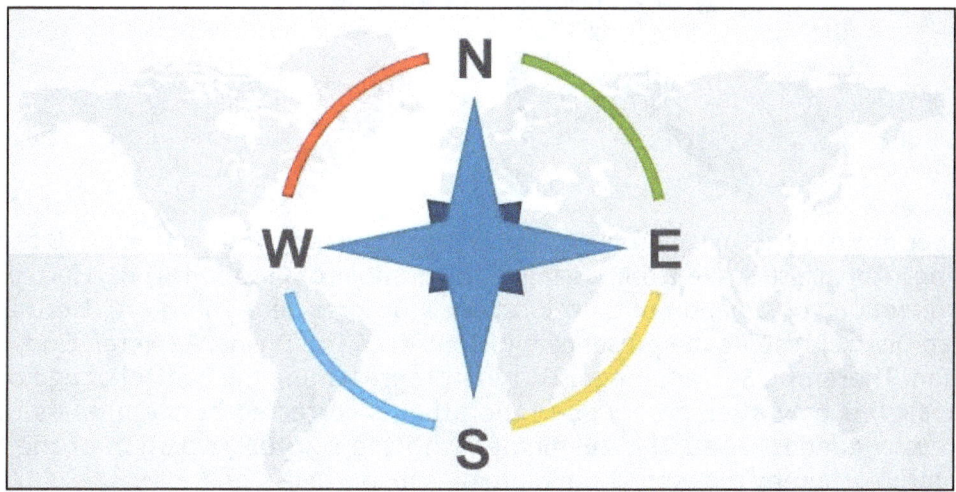

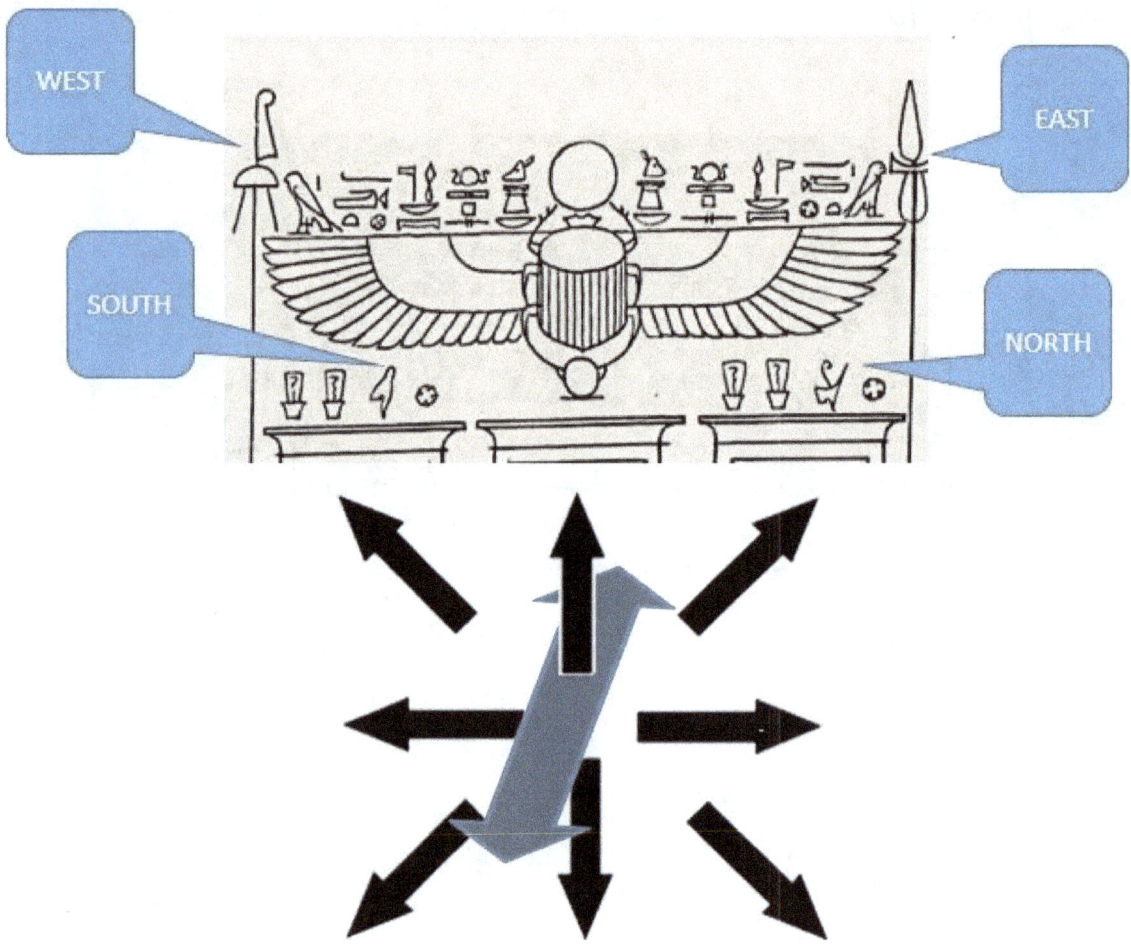

Ten is the number of Heru (Horus). Illustrated above is the concept of the number 10 as arrows pointing in all directions, encompassing 9, the number of Creation. Thus, Heru presides in all directions of Creation and no location is un-presided. Therefore, Heru and the Winged Disk represents the presence and control of The Divine/Pa Neter/God, over all Creation. Therefore, Set, as an egoistic tyrant representing the control of ego over the personality, is only a temporary aberration that is corrected by the process of being initiated by goddess Aset. This culminates with the spiritual evolution of the human Heru nature, thereby redeeming the human Asar soul self.

Considering the arrangement of the two solar winged expresions of divinity, the placement of the winged disk of Heru above the winged scarab signals an intentional display of relative expansion of divinity. The winged solar disk with dual cobras, being above the winges scarab, relates to transcendental expansiveness of Divinity. In other words, the winged disk of Heru Behudet relates to Divinity as encompassing all. The winged scarab relates to Divinity that permeates, pervades and interpenetrates all of Creation. Thus, divinity pervades all of Creation while the winged solar disc encompasses all Creation.

EGYPTIAN BOOK OF THE DEAD HIEROGLYPH TRANSLATIONS Volume 6: Featuring The Osirian Resurrection

STELE OF AMEMNOSE Part 4

BACK TO AMENMOSE-Epilog for the End of the Contendings of Heru and Set and the Joy in every Heart that sees Heru and the Splendor of Heru's Spiritual Victory for and Spiritual Redemption of Every Soul

===

Verse 31.
- 31.1. *pautyu {Net} her reshresh iuy Asar sa Heru men-ab maa-kheru*
- 31.2. <u>Company divine person rejoicings Osiris son Horus firm hearted spiritually-Gods/Goddesses victorious…</u>

31.3. The Company of Gods and Goddesses, to a person, are all rejoicing repeatedly because *Asar(Osiris)*' son, *Heru(Horus)* has been found to be firm of heart and spiritually victorious over *Set(Seth)*, the brother of *Asar(Osiris)* and egoistic personality that had tried to kill *Asar(Osiris)* and steal his rightful throne. The Gods and Goddesses know that *Heru(Horus)* redeemed his father, the soul of all, and now order and truth will reign throughout the land and human beings will have a true guide towards righteousness in life and the path to discover the ultimate truth of existence, the nature of and oneness with, the Divine.

31.4.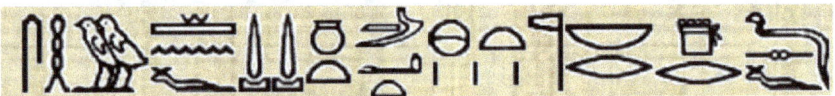
31.5. ***Sa   Aset   au   au   Asar***
31.6. Son   Isis   child   heir   Osiris

31.7. …he is the son of *Aset(Isis)*, and the child and heir of *Asar(Osiris)*.

Verse 32.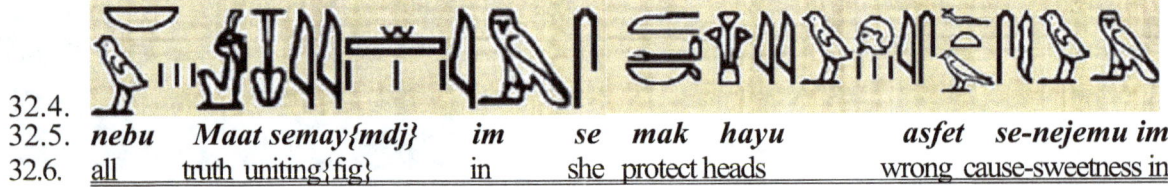
32.1. ***sehuu {mdj} en F udjaynut Maat pautyu {Net} Neberdjer djezef***
32.2. assembly{fig} to he judges settlement truth Company divine All-Encompassing-Divine
                                                                  Gods/Goddesses   himself

32.3. The Company of Gods and Goddesses, who are also the judges between truth and falsehood, they assemble themselves as the Divine *Lord-of-All,* the one who transcends and encompasses all, he* himself is present for the proceedings.[17]

32.4.
32.5. ***nebu   Maat semay{mdj}   im   se   mak   hayu   asfet   se-nejemu im***
32.6. all   truth uniting{fig}   in   she   protect heads   wrong cause-sweetness in

32.7. They are all righteous and they unite in her, goddess Ma'at, the goddess of truth, to protect the heads from wrongdoing and unrighteousness; instead she causes them to be the fount of sweetness harmony and agreeableness within…

---

[17] [Although the masculine is being used as it is being related to the divinity Ra, Neberdjer, the transcendental all encompassing Divine (True) Absolute Self is neither male or female, but encompasses both male and female.]

32.8.
32.9. ushchet geb   rer at aaut en neb suata   en maat zen f
32.10. hall   Geb   roll rest office of all transport of truth they he

32.11. ....of the hall of his grandfather, the god Geb. All of them agree that *Heru(Horus)* should rest in the office previously occupied by his father and thus they become the vehicle for this truth to be actualized for him; so the gods and goddesses agree and install *Heru(Horus)* on the throne.

Verse 33.

33.1. gem   en tu   heru   kheru F maau   rau   en F   aaut   ent tef
33.2. finding   of he   Horus speaking he truthful words   of he   office   of father

33.3. Having found him, that is, *Heru(Horus)*, to be speaking truthful words about his father *Asar's(Osiris')* rightful rulership and about his office as the true sovereign having been usurped by *Set(Seth)*, and having acted in accord with his voice about these matters, challenging *Set(Seth)* and defeating untruth and unrighteousness,...

Verse 34.

34.1. pert   en F wahu   im   wadj en geb   seshep   en-F   heqa tawy
34.2. going forth of he wreathed through of command Geb   received   to-he rulership two-lands

34.3. The Company of Neteru (Gods and Goddesses) proceeded to place a wreath on *Heru's(Horus')* head upon the command of the god Geb. Thus, *Heru(Horus)* received the crook of the two lands, thus affirming that he is the rightful ruler, and shepherd for the two lands of Upper and Lower Egypt;

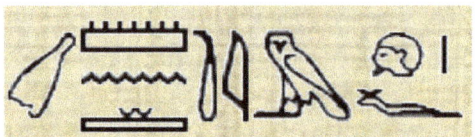

34.4.
34.5. ***hedg men{mdj} ti   im   tep F***
34.6. white-crown firmly   through head his

34.7. Now, having received the judgment in his favor, having received the wreath from Neteru (Gods and Goddesses) and the crook of rulership and shepherdhood, the Neteru (Gods and Goddesses) proceeded to place the white crown of his father, on the head of *Heru(Horus)* .

Verse 35.
35.1. ap n F   ta er   khert F pet ta kher aset her F
35.2. reckoned to he land as to under he heaven earth under throne personality he

35.3. A reckoning was done of the land and it was accordingly recognized as being under his rule. Additionally, the heaven, the astral plane, and the land/earth (the physical realm) all were found to be under the rulership of his throne.

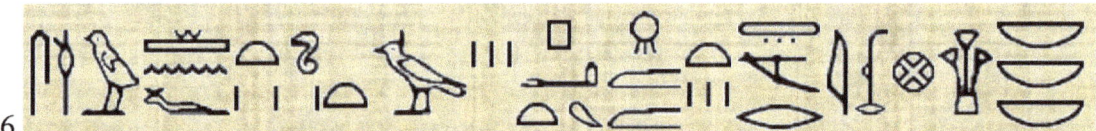

Verse 36.
36.1. Se-wadju{mdj} en F remteju rechytu   pat   hememtu   ta-meri   ha-nebu
36.2. cause-command{fig} for he folk common mortals sun-people land beloved   Aegean

36.3. Thus the dominion, by his domain, extends over the common folk, the people who are mortals living on earth within the borders of the beloved land, Kemet/Egypt, as well as to the people living in the islands of the Mediterranean, whose peoples include the inhabitants of the Aegean islands of the Ancient Greeks as well as the present day Greeks.[18]

---

[18] Note(.**** present here refers to an earlier time from the time of this writing which was done at the Ancient Egyptian historical period of the 18th Dynasty***)

Verse 38.

38.1. Nepra   di   F   sechtet   F   neb   djefau   bes   F
38.2. Nepra   gives he   greenery   he   lord   food-provisions initiates he

38.3. *Asar(Osiris)* gives greenery, including fields of vegetables gardens and herbs; and therefore, he is the lord of food that sustains life; this he does in his name of **Nepra**. He is the one who leads spiritual aspirants (initiates into)…

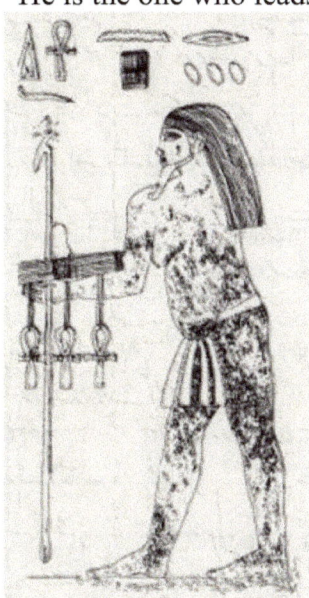

> **Nepr** means corn and grains in general
>
> The god Neper is identified as an aspect of Osiris

Verse 39.

39.1. sesau   di   F   su   im   taiu   bu   neb   chent {mdj}
39.2. copiousness gives he person throughout lands place every joyfulness{fig}

39.3. …copious abundance. He gives to every person throughout the lands, not just in Kemet/Egypt, but in all lands; the greenery and abundance of food substances in the form of greens and herbs. So, those greens and herbs everywhere come from him. Consequently, everywhere there is joyousness at the prospect of being sustained by the Divine, wherever one may be.

Verse 40.
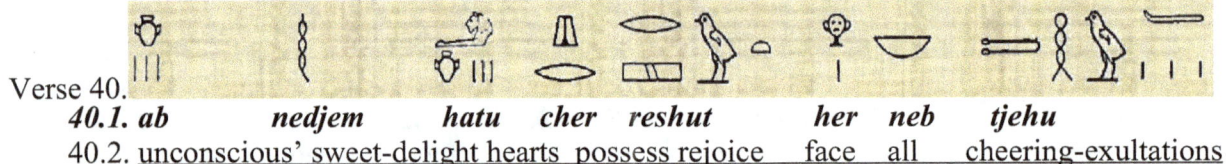
40.1. ab   nedjem   hatu   cher   reshut   her   neb   tjehu
40.2. unconscious' sweet-delight hearts possess rejoice face all cheering-exultations

40.3. There is sweet-delight in the unconscious minds of people; their conscious hearts (minds) rejoice; all the faces cheer exultations to the Lord.

Verse 41.
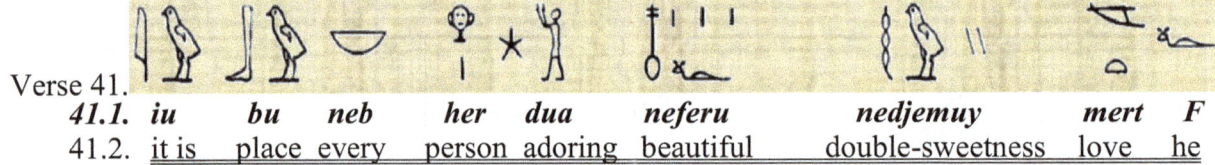
41.1. iu   bu   neb   her   dua   neferu   nedjemuy   mert   F
41.2. it is place every person adoring beautiful double-sweetness love he

41.3. Everywhere there are people adoring his beautiful person, which is double sweet. His love…

Verse 42.
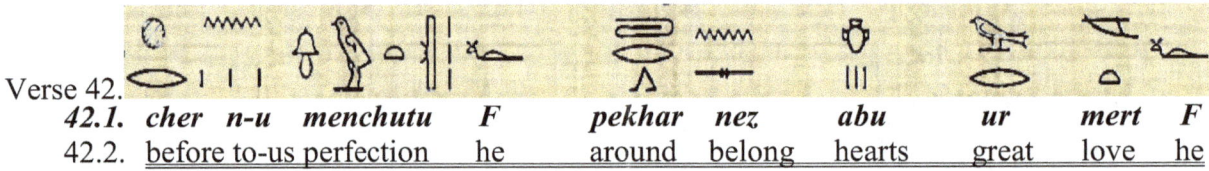
42.1. cher   n-u   menchutu   F   pekhar   nez   abu   ur   mert   F
42.2. before to-us perfection he around belong hearts great love he

42.3. …which is in front of us and obvious to be seen and felt, is perfection itself as he goes around each of us and our hearts can feel his great love …

Verse 43.
43.1. im   khat   nebt   maa   en   senu   en   sa   Aset
43.2. within body every truth of they to son Isis

43.3. …which is within every person. The majesty and caring of *Heru(Horus)* has inspired them to decree their truth, their judgment for the son of *Aset(Isis)*.

Verse 44.
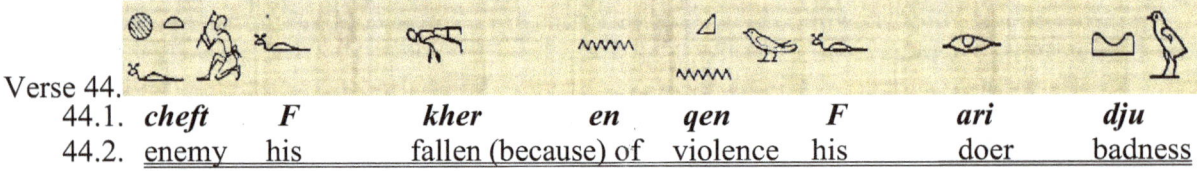
44.1. cheft   F   kher   en   qen   F   ari   dju
44.2. enemy his fallen (because) of violence his doer badness

44.3. His enemy, the god *Set(Seth)*, has been defeated because of the violence and bad behavior that he perpetrated.

EGYPTIAN BOOK OF THE DEAD HIEROGLYPH TRANSLATIONS Volume 6: Featuring The Osirian Resurrection

Verse 45.

45.1.	ra	shed	kheru	ud	qen	zep	F
45.2.	mouth	assessor god	speaks	violent person	offender	time	his

45.3. One of the 42 assessors of *Asar(Osiris)* has announced that the person who is a violent offender that has opposed *Heru(Horus)*, of exacerbated egoism has come to his time of reckoning.

Verse 46.

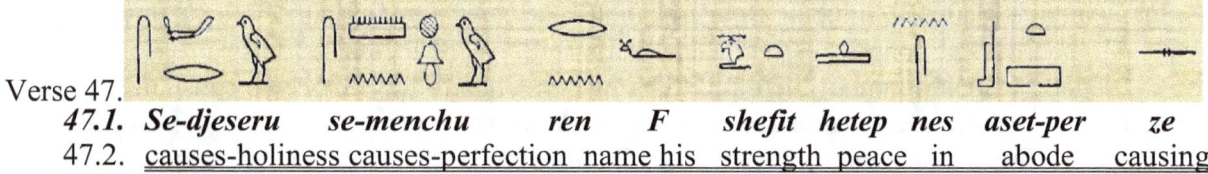

46.1.	sper	er	F	sa	Aset	netedjnut	en- F	atef
46.2.	comes	as	to he	son	Isis	redeemer	to-his	father

46.3. The son of *Aset(Isis)*, the redeemer of the soul, comes to his father…

Verse 47.

47.1.	Se-djeseru	se-menchu	ren	F	shefit	hetep	nes	aset-per	ze
47.2.	causes-holiness	causes-perfection	name	his	strength	peace	in	abode	causing

47.3. …the coming closer, of *Heru(Horus)* to his father, is the coming closer of our spiritual redemptive aspiration (what *Heru{Horus}* symbolizes), to our Soul. This occurrence, when spiritual life awakens and allows spiritual aspiration to redeem our Soul, through success on the spiritual path, that comes from the strength of his name, this causes inner peace and holiness to the personality. Additionally it causes the personality to reach a perfected state of being such as when *Heru(Horus)* is installed in the throne-room, which is his abode, as King. When *Heru(Horus)*, our spiritually redemptive movement in life, reaches his abode, it is the redemption of our Soul (Asar/Osiris) and our reaching the goal of life, to be installed on our throne which is the abode of the redeemed and resurrected Spirit Self (Asar/Osiris) and the defeat of egoism (Set). These wonders cause…

EGYPTIAN BOOK OF THE DEAD HIEROGLYPH TRANSLATIONS Volume 6: Featuring The Osirian Resurrection

Verse 48.
48.1. *fau*   *men {mdj} er*   *hepu {mdj} F*   *wat*   *zeshti*
48.2. expansive establishment {fig} as to regulations{fig} his path opened

48.3. …expansiveness of the personality, beyond the little ego identity, leading to our firm establishment in the rules and regulations of the virtues that *Heru(Horus)* (our spiritually redemptive capacity) stands for, beyond obstructions due to egoism. Now the spiritual path of life is open and unobstructed…

Verse 49.
49.1. *matjenu*   *un*   *se-heruy*   *{tawy}*   *auyt*
49.2. roads/paths open causes-contentment {two lands} unrighteous

49.3. …and the roads are all open. Since unrighteousness of egoism with its fears, desires and pettiness no longer obstruct life, all possibilities are accessible and there is no longer the constriction of the mind to being benevolent; thus this is the cause of instead experiencing contentment in the two lands of Upper and Lower Egypt, which are a symbol of the duality experienced by most people to whom Heru has not yet been able to approach. The contentment in the two lands is the contentment from ending the conflict between the lower self and Higher Self, such that the ego has been sublimated and the Higher Self rules the personality unobstructed. Heru brings unity to duality. Thus the previous separation of the Heru nature from the Soul, its father, due to the interruption by egoism that disintegrates the integrated consciousness of Transcendental Spirit, which caused unrest, strife and pain (Set) in the personality has ended. Now the unrighteous…

Verse 50.
50.1. *shems*   *auyu*   *ruu*   *ta*   *im-hetepu*   *cher*
50.2. shrinks-away unrighteousness driven-away land in-peacefullness under

50.3. …shrinks-away, powerless and diminutive. It is driven away from the land which is now in peace being under…

EGYPTIAN BOOK OF THE DEAD HIEROGLYPH TRANSLATIONS Volume 6: Featuring The Osirian Resurrection

Verse 51.
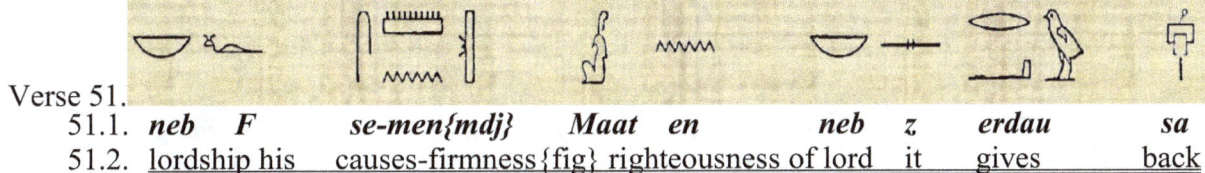
51.1. **neb   F   se-men{mdj}   Maat   en   neb   z   erdau   sa**
51.2. lordship his   causes-firmness{fig} righteousness of lord   it   gives   back

51.3. …his lordship. His lordship causes firmness in his righteousness. This is the spiritual strength and fortitude to vanquish iniquity which obstructs the path of peace and expansiveness. His resolute nature as if gives its back, that is, turns its back…

Verse 52.
52.1. **er   asfet   nedjm   ab   k   Un-nefer   sa   Aset   seshep**
52.2. as to   wickedness   sweet   heart thine Existence-Beautiful son Isis received

52.3. …on wickedness, malice, evil. This makes your heart experience delight, oh *Asar(Osiris)*, Beautiful-Existence, finally seeing the son of *Aset(Isis)* has received…

Verse 53.

53.1. **en F   hedg   se-maatu {mdj} en F   autet   ent   tef**
53.2. to he   white-crown   causes-truth {fig} to him   office   of   father

53.3. …the white crown for himself. This is justice being done for him *(Heru{Horus})*, the receipt of the office previously held by his father…

Verse 54.
54.1. **im khenu   ushchet Geb   Ra   djed F   Djehuty**
54.2. within interior   Hall   Geb   Ra   speak he   Thoth

54.3. …in the interior of the Hall of Geb, the god of the earth, and when Ra, the Creator Spirit spoke, and when *Djehuty(Thoth/Hermes)*, the god of writing and scribal arts…

EGYPTIAN BOOK OF THE DEAD HIEROGLYPH TRANSLATIONS Volume 6: Featuring The Osirian Resurrection

Verse 55.
- **55.1.** seshu   F   udjaynutu   herta {mdj}   ud {mdj} en
- 55.2. writings his   judges   satisfied{fig}   decreed {fig} for

- 55.3. …wrote his writings. Additionally, the judges, the gods and goddesses who preside over the laws of right and wrong, are indeed satisfied with the outcome. They have decreed for…

Verse 56.
- **56.1.** en k   atef k   Geb   ari entu   chetf djedt en F
- 56.2. to thee   father thine   Geb   do for-thee   inasmuch as declared by him

- 56.3. …you that your (*Asar's{Osiris'}*) father Geb should do for you, what is in accord with his (Geb's) declaration that the throne should be given to him…

A Royal Offering of non-dualism for the Soul and Ritual of Communing with Pure-existence. {From the STELE OF AMEMNOSE}

Verse 57.
57.1. **su- di-hetep**   **Asar**   **khenty**   **Amenta**   **neb**   **abdu**
57.2. royal-offering   Osiris   foremost   west-abode   Lord   Abydos

57.3. …a royal offering to *Asar(Osiris)*, the Soul of all, the foremost being in the Beautiful West, who is the final abode of enlightened souls, he who is the Lord of Abydos, the sacred city.

Verse 58.
58.1. **di   F   per-kheru   ka   aped   menchet   sentjer   merhet**
58.2. give   him   sacred-offerings   maleness   femaleness   clothing   incense   unguent

58.3. Give to him the offering of peace (Hetep) for dissolution of duality and the sacred offerings of one who is spiritually mature, the principles of maleness and femaleness (mystic dissolution of gender identity), having achieved victory in the knowledge of the unity of opposites, the Unity of the Universal Soul, *Asar(Osiris)*, who has been redeemed. Give to him, *Asar(Osiris)*, the *Asar(Osiris)* Initiate, additionally, the ceremonial cloth of integrated/consolidated personality and spiritual victory, along with incense and unguent.

Verse 59.
59.1. *dereptu   renpet   neb   ari   Kheperu   sekhem*
59.2. giving   herbs   all   do   transformations   life-force

59.3. Additionally, give, to *Asar(Osiris)*, the *Asar(Osiris)* Initiate, who offers this hymn, all herbs and the capacity to transform from weak mortal existence to an existence with the power of…

The image above from Papyrus Any show an offering such as what is described at this point in the sctipture. Any, referred to as Asar/Osiris Any, has been led by *Heru(Horus)* to the inner shrine where he makes a non-dual Hotep/Hetep offering to Asar/Osiris, who is in his shrine. [A-aped, B-ka]

Verse 60.
60.1. ***Hapi   pert   im   ba   ankhy   maa   im   atjen***
60.2.   Nile   coming-forth   form   soul   living   seeing   form   Sundisk

60.3. …the Nile River as well as the capacity to come forth into enlightenment, to come out of mortal awareness to the status of a living Soul, that is, not as a temporary earthly mortal personality experiencing limited fleeting existence with limited time, but as a being that knows itself as an immortal Soul and has the ability to see the shining manifestation of Spirit Being within and without…

EGYPTIAN BOOK OF THE DEAD HIEROGLYPH TRANSLATIONS Volume 6: Featuring The Osirian Resurrection

Verse 61.
- 61.1. tep duayt   au   chetchet im rastau   an   shena
- 61.2. top morning go-in come-out through corridor not repulsed

- 61.3. …at first light of dawn as well as being able to go-in and come out of the corridor that leads between the after-death state to the netherworld wherein the abode of the Divine, my higher Self, is located. Furthermore, the one who has attained this victory of *Heru(Horus)* shall not be repulsed.

Verse 62.
- 62.1. hesyu   embah   Un-nefer   seshep zenu   pert
- 62.2. preferred ones in-front-of Existence-beautiful receive they   going forth

- 62.3. Those beings who have received the grace of *Asar(Osiris)*, the Beautiful Existence, and who enjoy the blessing of being in *Asar's(Osiris')* presence, realizing their oneness with *Asar(Osiris)*, they receive the capacity of going forth, of going from mortal awareness to enlightened realization …

Verse 63.
- 63.1. embah   her khaut   ent Neter   aah{mdj}   sesent   naf
- 63.2. in-front-of person altar   of   Divine Great{fig} smelling air

- 63.3. …while in the presence of "The Great Divinity", who is beyond form, name, gender, time or space. This is the smelling of the air…

Verse 64.
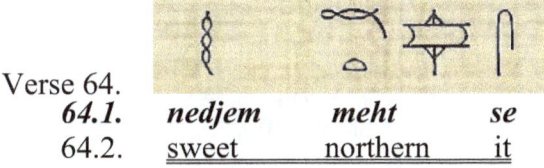
- 64.1. nedjem meht   se
- 64.2. sweet   northern it

- 64.3. …that is sweet, that contains the sweet fragrance of fullness of consciousness that enlivens every soul and all Creation.

INDEX

Abdu, 103, 252
Absolute, 212, 213, 311
Africa, 180, 317, 324, 326, 328, 329
African Proverbial Wisdom Teachings, 335
African Religion, 311, 318, 319, 323
Allopathic, 311
Amenta, 301, 317
Amentet, 282, 319
American Heritage Dictionary, Dictionary, 11, 235, 323
American Theocracy, 327
Amma, 227
Amun, 31, 76, 78, 79, 253
Anat, 143, 144
Ancient Egypt, 3, 4, 10, 11, 14, 15, 20, 21, 22, 33, 45, 49, 50, 53, 54, 57, 58, 64, 70, 71, 148, 150, 174, 175, 180, 200, 207, 212, 230, 235, 260, 263, 265, 294, 311, 312, 313, 314, 315, 316, 317, 318, 319, 320, 321, 322, 323, 324, 325, 326, 328, 329, 332, 333, 334, 335, 336, 337, 338, 339, 340, 342
Ancient Egyptian Book of the Dead, 22, 49
Ancient Egyptian Wisdom Texts, 334
Ancient Greeks, 294
anger, 94, 103, 137, 145, 171, 172, 179, 233, 235, 321
Ankh, 79, 225, 227, 231, 232
Anpu, 52, 53
Anu, 102, 103, 134, 152, 165, 219, 318
Anu (Greek Heliopolis), 102, 103, 134, 152, 165, 219, 318
Anunian Theology, 257, 318
Apep serpent, 51
Apophis, 51, 105
Architecture, 45, 57
Aryan, 312
Asar, 4, 22, 31, 32, 33, 34, 35, 36, 37, 39, 40, 41, 43, 44, 45, 46, 48, 49, 50, 51, 52, 53, 54, 56, 58, 59, 60, 62, 63, 64, 65, 66, 67, 68, 70, 71, 78, 83, 84, 93, 96, 102, 109, 110, 113, 114, 115, 118, 119, 124, 127, 130, 135, 137, 139, 142, 145, 146, 165, 166, 174, 208, 209, 211, 212, 213, 218, 219, 224, 229, 230, 233, 244, 249, 252, 259, 264, 265, 266, 290, 291, 292, 295, 297, 299, 300, 301, 302, 303, 317, 320, 321
Asar and Aset, 49, 317
Asarian Resurrection, 10, 22, 52, 53, 229, 317, 320, 321, 324
Aset, 4, 36, 39, 46, 48, 49, 50, 51, 52, 53, 54, 56, 58, 59, 62, 63, 64, 66, 69, 70, 71, 76, 78, 79, 81, 83, 91, 92, 93, 94, 95, 96, 97, 98, 100, 107, 109, 114, 115, 116, 117, 120, 121, 122, 123, 124, 125, 127, 135, 137, 151, 153, 155, 156, 158, 160, 161, 162, 163, 165, 166, 167, 169, 170, 171, 172, 175, 184, 185, 186, 187, 188, 207, 219, 223, 224, 225, 227, 228, 231, 232, 233, 240, 244, 246, 247, 248, 249, 250, 257, 259, 260, 261, 262, 264, 266, 267, 270, 292, 296, 297, 299, 313, 317, 319, 320, 321
Aset (Isis), 4, 36, 39, 46, 48, 49, 50, 51, 52, 53, 54, 56, 58, 59, 62, 63, 64, 66, 69, 70, 71, 76, 78, 79, 81, 83, 91, 92, 93, 94, 95, 96, 97, 98, 100, 107, 109, 114, 115, 116, 117, 120, 121, 122, 123, 124, 125, 127, 135, 137, 151, 153, 155, 156, 158, 160, 161, 162, 163, 165, 166, 167, 169, 170, 171, 172, 175, 184, 185, 186, 187, 188, 207, 219, 223, 224, 225, 227, 228, 231, 232, 233, 240, 244, 246, 247, 248, 249, 250, 257, 259, 260, 261, 262, 264, 266, 267, 270, 292, 296, 297, 299, 313, 317, 319, 320, 321
Ashanti, 335
Asia, 329
Asia Minor, 329
Asiatic, 326, 328, 329
Assyrians, 333
Astral, 50, 317
Astral Plane, 50, 317
Atlantis, 325
Aton, 126
Awakening, 219, 317, 341
Awareness, 123
Ba (also see Soul), 50
Baby, 109
Behudet, 235, 238, 241, 246, 247, 251, 257, 258, 259, 270, 274, 275, 276, 277, 278, 282, 284, 285, 286
Being, 48, 50, 56, 66, 229, 233, 302, 319
Bhagavad Gita, 333
Bible, 320
Black, 329
Black Africa, 329
Boat of Millions of Years, 123
Body, 45, 50, 340
Book of Coming Forth By Day, 265, 317, 318
Book of Enlightenment, 22
Book of the Dead, see also Rau Nu Prt M Hru, 3, 318, 334
Buddha, 324, 326, 344
Buddhism, 318, 326
Buddhist, 317, 326
Caduceus, 70, 71
Catholic, 320
Catholic Church, 320
Causal Plane, 50
Child, 31, 116, 320, 321
Christ, 318
Christianity, 310, 318, 320
Church, 320
Civilization, 313, 326, 327, 328, 329, 339, 340
coercion, 327
Collapse, 327, 339, 342
color, 45, 57, 236, 332, 335
Color, 332
Conception, 58, 59, 60, 63, 65, 72, 78
Conflict, 130, 234, 327, 336

Confusion, 130
Congress, 3
Conscious, 31, 123
Consciousness, 78, 79, 148, 180, 181, 317, 335
Consciousness, human, 311
contentment, 23, 298, 343
Coptic, 317
cosmic force, 33, 85, 98, 232, 319, 325
Creation, 12, 22, 33, 51, 70, 83, 98, 102, 103, 113, 122, 126, 134, 137, 141, 148, 149, 152, 165, 212, 216, 218, 219, 224, 229, 232, 233, 257, 277, 288, 290, 303, 317, 318, 335
Culture, 316, 325, 330, 341
Death, 69, 327, 339
December, 319
Delta, 89
delusion, 23, 71, 202
Denderah, 317
depression, 23
Desire, 336
Devotional Love, 314
Diet, 312
Divine Consciousness, 99, 219
Dollar, U.S. Dollar, 342
Duat, 168, 229, 233, 265, 266, 317
dullness, 103
Earth, 106
Edfu, 144, 234, 238, 252, 253, 264, 270, 285, 317
Egoism, 169
Egyptian Book of Coming Forth By Day, 317
Egyptian Mysteries, 20, 235, 312, 322, 323, 336, 337, 338
Egyptian Physics, 319
Egyptian Proverb, 314
EGYPTIAN PROVERBS, 314
Egyptian Yoga, 310, 312, 317, 318
Egyptian Yoga see also Kamitan Yoga, 310, 311, 312, 317, 318, 344
Egyptologists, 323, 332
Empire culture, 327
Enlightenment, 3, 123, 124, 169, 311, 312, 313, 315, 317, 318, 319, 321, 322, 325, 336, 338, 340

ETHICS, 312, 313, 326, 328, 329, 335
Ethiopia, 335
Eucharist, 318
evil, 92, 124, 126, 191, 299, 321, 323
Evil, 324
Exercise, 317
Existence, 48, 107, 119, 299, 303
Eye, 134, 147
Eye of Ra, 147
Faith, 329, 330
Fate, 156, 163
Fight, 167, 168, 175, 197
Finances, 340
Form, 15
frustration, 23
Fullness, 98, 180
Galla, 335
Galla culture, 335
Geb, 36, 74, 92, 94, 95, 106, 117, 118, 212, 293, 299, 300, 317
Ghana, 335
global economy, 327
Globalization, 327
God, 31, 33, 36, 46, 83, 106, 117, 118, 146, 210, 219, 240, 288, 290, 313, 314, 318, 319, 324, 331
Goddess, 41, 44, 49, 54, 62, 63, 66, 69, 78, 94, 98, 104, 109, 121, 124, 141, 142, 144, 147, 179, 181, 186, 210, 216, 249, 250, 263, 267, 319, 331
Goddesses, 12, 33, 34, 35, 46, 48, 50, 52, 70, 71, 76, 107, 113, 118, 134, 137, 138, 140, 141, 145, 149, 151, 155, 166, 167, 176, 182, 189, 190, 191, 192, 197, 202, 204, 205, 207, 208, 209, 210, 212, 219, 224, 228, 231, 232, 235, 241, 246, 291, 292, 293, 294, 317, 323
Gods, 12, 33, 34, 35, 76, 113, 118, 134, 137, 138, 140, 141, 145, 149, 151, 155, 166, 167, 176, 182, 189, 190, 191, 192, 197, 202, 204, 205, 207, 208, 209, 210, 212, 216, 219, 224, 228, 231, 232, 235, 291, 292, 293, 317, 323

gods and goddesses, 22, 31, 33, 94, 98, 99, 130, 135, 191, 196, 209, 210, 212, 214, 218, 231, 257, 276, 279, 282, 293, 300, 318, 323, 325
Good, 223, 225, 324
Gospels, 320
Great Pyramid, 200
Greece, 53, 312, 325
Greek mythology, 53
Greek philosophy, 310
Greeks, 294, 333
Hapi, 32, 302
Hate, 336
Hatha Yoga, 328
Hathor, 44, 147, 148, 179, 180, 181, 182, 270, 317, 319, 322, 344
Hatred, 336
Hawk, 229, 230, 252
Health, 190, 225, 227, 231, 232, 311, 319
Hearing, 100
Heart, 13, 291, 321, 330
Heart (also see Ab, mind, conscience), 13, 291, 321, 330
Heaven, 98, 251, 320
Heh, 123
Hekau, 39, 343
Heliopolis, 102, 103, 134, 152, 165, 219
Hermes, 33, 192, 193, 194, 195, 196, 197, 299, 338
Hermes (see also Djehuti, Thoth), 33, 192, 193, 194, 195, 196, 197, 299, 338
Hermetic, 337
Hermeticism, 338
Heru, 4, 22, 46, 48, 49, 50, 52, 53, 54, 58, 59, 60, 62, 63, 64, 65, 66, 69, 70, 71, 76, 78, 79, 83, 84, 89, 97, 99, 100, 101, 103, 106, 109, 110, 111, 112, 114, 115, 117, 119, 121, 122, 124, 125, 126, 127, 129, 130, 135, 137, 138, 139, 140, 142, 145, 146, 148, 163, 164, 165, 166, 167, 168, 170, 171, 172, 174, 175, 176, 179, 180, 181, 182, 183, 184, 185, 186, 188, 189, 190, 191, 192, 193, 195, 196, 197, 198, 199, 201, 202, 204, 205, 206, 207, 209, 210, 213, 219, 224,

225, 226, 227, 228, 229, 230, 231, 232, 234, 235, 236, 237, 238, 240, 241, 244, 246, 247, 248, 250, 251, 253, 254, 257, 258, 259, 264, 266, 267, 270, 271, 274, 275, 276, 277, 278, 279, 282, 284, 285, 286, 290, 291, 297, 298, 302, 303, 317, 318, 319, 320, 321, 324, 334

Heru (see Horus), 4, 22, 46, 48, 49, 50, 52, 53, 54, 58, 59, 60, 62, 63, 64, 65, 66, 69, 70, 71, 76, 78, 79, 83, 84, 89, 97, 99, 100, 101, 103, 106, 109, 110, 111, 112, 114, 115, 117, 119, 121, 122, 124, 125, 126, 127, 129, 130, 135, 137, 138, 139, 140, 142, 145, 146, 148, 163, 164, 165, 166, 167, 168, 170, 171, 172, 174, 175, 176, 179, 180, 181, 182, 183, 184, 185, 186, 188, 189, 190, 191, 192, 193, 195, 196, 197, 198, 199, 201, 202, 204, 205, 206, 207, 209, 210, 213, 219, 224, 225, 226, 227, 228, 229, 230, 231, 232, 234, 235, 236, 237, 238, 240, 241, 244, 246, 247, 248, 250, 251, 253, 254, 257, 258, 259, 264, 266, 267, 270, 271, 274, 275, 276, 277, 278, 279, 282, 284, 285, 286, 290, 291, 297, 298, 302, 303, 317, 318, 319, 320, 321, 324, 334

Hetep, 33, 84, 110, 168, 264, 265, 301

Hetheru, 49, 66, 144, 147, 148, 179, 180, 181, 182, 270, 322

Hetheru (Hetheru, Hathor), 49, 66, 144, 147, 148, 179, 180, 181, 182, 270, 322

Hieroglyphic, 15, 20, 21, 22, 69, 315, 332, 338

Hieroglyphic Writing, language, 15, 20, 21, 22, 69, 315, 332, 338

Hieroglyphs, 3, 21

High God, 137

Hinduism, 318

Hindus, 323

Holy of Holies, 58, 78

hope, 331, 332

Horus, 4, 22, 41, 45, 49, 54, 57, 58, 59, 76, 77, 78, 79, 84, 89, 97, 99, 100, 101, 103, 106, 109, 110, 111, 112, 114, 115, 117, 119, 121, 122, 124, 125, 126, 127, 129, 130, 135, 137, 138, 139, 140, 142, 145, 146, 163, 164, 165, 166, 167, 168, 170, 171, 172, 175, 176, 178, 179, 180, 181, 182, 183, 184, 185, 186, 188, 189, 190, 191, 192, 193, 195, 196, 197, 198, 199, 201, 202, 204, 205, 206, 207, 209, 210, 213, 219, 223, 224, 225, 226, 227, 228, 229, 231, 232, 233, 234, 235, 238, 241, 246, 247, 248, 250, 251, 252, 253, 257, 258, 259, 270, 274, 275, 276, 277, 278, 282, 284, 285, 286, 291, 293, 294, 296, 297, 298, 299, 302, 303

HUMANITY, 322

Iamblichus, 333

Ibis, 47

Identification, 10

Image, 32, 37, 43, 44, 51, 54, 72, 76, 77, 133, 142, 200, 265

India, 312, 313, 315, 317, 326, 328

Indian Yoga, 312

Indus, 312

Indus Valley, 312

Initiate, 312

Intellect, 33, 78

Intuitional Wisdom, 53, 91, 107

Isis, 4, 22, 36, 39, 40, 41, 44, 45, 46, 48, 49, 50, 52, 53, 54, 56, 58, 66, 70, 71, 74, 76, 77, 78, 79, 81, 83, 91, 92, 93, 94, 95, 96, 97, 98, 100, 107, 109, 114, 115, 116, 117, 120, 121, 122, 123, 124, 125, 127, 135, 137, 148, 151, 153, 155, 156, 158, 160, 161, 162, 163, 165, 166, 167, 169, 170, 171, 172, 173, 175, 184, 185, 186, 187, 188, 207, 219, 223, 224, 225, 227, 228, 231, 232, 233, 246, 247, 248, 249, 250, 257, 259, 260, 263, 264, 266, 267, 270, 292, 296, 297, 299, 313, 317, 319, 344

Isis, See also Aset, 4, 22, 36, 39, 40, 41, 44, 45, 46, 48, 49, 50, 52, 53, 54, 56, 58, 66, 70, 71, 74, 76, 77, 78, 79, 81, 83, 91, 92, 93, 94, 95, 96, 97, 98, 100, 107, 109, 114, 115, 116, 117, 120, 121, 122, 123, 124, 125, 127, 135, 137, 148, 151, 153, 155, 156, 158, 160, 161, 162, 163, 165, 166, 167, 169, 170, 171, 172, 173, 175, 184, 185, 186, 187, 188, 207, 219, 223, 224, 225, 227, 228, 231, 232, 233, 246, 247, 248, 249, 250, 257, 259, 260, 263, 264, 266, 267, 270, 292, 296, 297, 299, 313, 317, 319, 344

Islam, 310

Jesus, 318, 320, 344

Jesus Christ, 318

Joy, 291

Judaism, 310

judges, 292, 300

Ka, 110, 187

Kabbalah, 310

Kamit (Egypt), 323

Kamitan, 312, 325

Karma, 315

Kemetic, 4, 326, 330, 337, 340, 344

Khemn, see also ignorance, 323

Khnum, 263

King, 32, 37, 41, 48, 51, 88, 198, 225, 297, 320, 324

Kingdom, 320

Kingdom of Heaven, 320

KMT (Ancient Egypt). See also Kamit, 282

Krishna, 320

Kybalion, 337, 338

Life, 12, 79, 190, 225, 227, 231, 232, 316, 324, 329, 331, 335

Life Force, 316

Lord of Eternity, 33

Love, 314, 343

Lower Egypt, 34, 36, 70, 165, 257, 287, 293, 298

Maakheru, 4

Maat, 35, 48, 216, 218, 252, 284, 292, 299, 315, 319, 321, 325, 330, 334, 336, 337, 338, 339, 340

MAAT, 314

Maat Philosophy, 321, 325, 330, 338, 339

MAATI, 315
Malawi, 335
Matrix, 289
Matter, 79, 319
media, 327
Meditation, 3, 312, 314, 316
Mediterranean, 294
Medu Neter, 323, 343
Mehurt, 180
Memphis, 32
Memphite Theology, 319
Meskhenet, 315
Metaphor, 10
Metaphysics, 319, 335
Middle East, 310
Middle Kingdom, 64
Min, 317
Mind, 33, 340
Music, 332
Mut, 152
Mysteries, 20, 45, 57, 97, 123, 312, 322, 323, 333, 336, 337, 338
mystical philosophy, 326, 334
Mysticism, 4, 13, 312, 313, 318, 319, 322, 326, 328, 329
Mythology, 10
Nature, 172
Neberdjer, 130, 132, 133, 134, 135, 141, 145, 147, 153, 155, 208, 212, 229, 292, 311
Nebethet, see also Nebthet, 48, 51, 52, 53, 54, 70, 71, 107, 120
Nebthet, see also Nebethet, 107, 246, 257
Nefer, 48, 119
Nefertari, Queen, 30
Nefertem, See also Nefertum, 50
Nehast, 219, 323
neo-con, 327
Neolithic, 174
Nephthys, 52, 53, 54, 70, 71, 107, 120, 246, 257
Net, goddess, 56, 103, 104, 107, 141, 142, 152, 205, 235, 291, 292
Neter, 34, 35, 83, 106, 116, 141, 149, 152, 191, 192, 197, 205, 210, 216, 249, 250, 252, 253, 258, 259, 264, 274, 275, 282, 284, 303, 314, 317, 323, 324, 326, 332, 336, 341, 342, 343

Neterian, 323, 324, 326, 341, 342, 344
Neterianism, 338, 341
Neteru, 22, 323
Netherworld, 48, 168, 216, 217, 229, 265, 266
Nigeria, 335
Nile River, 39, 302
non-dualism, 301
Nu, 264
Nun (See also Nu primeval waters-unformed matter), 118, 134, 180
Nut, 137, 139, 149, 151, 175, 227, 233, 317
Ocean, 134, 180
Ontology, 10
Orion Star Constellation, 319
Orthodox, 323
Osiris, 4, 20, 22, 31, 32, 33, 34, 35, 36, 37, 39, 40, 41, 43, 44, 45, 46, 48, 49, 51, 54, 56, 57, 58, 59, 60, 64, 66, 69, 70, 71, 78, 83, 84, 96, 102, 109, 110, 113, 114, 115, 118, 119, 130, 135, 137, 139, 142, 145, 146, 166, 207, 208, 210, 211, 212, 213, 218, 219, 224, 229, 233, 249, 252, 259, 264, 266, 291, 292, 295, 297, 299, 300, 301, 302, 303, 317, 324
Passion, 81
Peace, 336, 338, 340
Peace (see also Hetep), 336, 338, 340
Persians, 333
PERT EM HERU, SEE ALSO BOOK OF THE DEAD, 318
phallus, 183, 185
Pharaoh, 340
Philae, 317
Philosophy, 3, 10, 20, 45, 57, 311, 312, 313, 314, 318, 319, 321, 325, 326, 328, 329, 330, 338, 339, 340
Phoenix, 102
Physical, 50, 107
Physical body, 50
physical realm, 50, 294
physical world, 48
Plutarch, 53
priests and priestesses, 20, 317, 324

Priests and Priestesses, 312, 324
Primeval Waters, 118
Proverbial Wisdom, 335
Psychology, 319, 337
Ptah, 32, 46, 48, 49, 51, 59, 63, 152, 319
Pyramid, 49, 53
Queen, 324
Ra, 32, 43, 48, 51, 69, 70, 97, 102, 103, 117, 118, 121, 122, 123, 124, 126, 127, 134, 135, 137, 139, 140, 146, 147, 148, 149, 152, 163, 164, 165, 178, 181, 182, 195, 196, 200, 207, 210, 212, 213, 216, 219, 226, 227, 228, 229, 230, 232, 235, 237, 238, 240, 241, 244, 246, 247, 248, 250, 252, 253, 254, 258, 259, 264, 266, 267, 271, 274, 276, 277, 278, 282, 299, 317
racism, 336
Racism, 336
Rameses II, 67
Realization, 313
Religion, 10, 13, 311, 313, 317, 318, 319, 320, 321, 323, 324, 325, 326, 328, 329, 341, 342, 344
Rest, 175
Resurrection, 41, 45, 49, 57, 317, 318, 319, 320, 321, 324
Righteousness, 35
Ritual, 13, 301, 322
Rituals, 319
Roman, 148, 333
Romans, 333
Rome, 325
Saa (spiritual understanding faculty), 76, 79
Sages, 4, 95, 311, 317, 318, 321, 325, 344
Sahu, 50
Saints, 318, 344
Sais, 205
Sebai, 4, 326, 331, 338, 341
See also Ra-Hrakti, 32, 43, 48, 51, 69, 70, 97, 102, 103, 117, 118, 121, 122, 123, 124, 126, 127, 134, 135, 137, 139, 140, 146, 147, 148, 149, 152, 163, 164, 165, 178, 181, 182, 195, 196, 200, 207, 210, 212, 213, 216, 219, 226, 227, 228, 229, 230,

232, 235, 237, 238, 240, 241, 244, 246, 247, 248, 250, 252, 253, 254, 258, 259, 264, 266, 267, 271, 274, 276, 277, 278, 282, 299, 317
See Nat, 56, 103, 104, 107, 141, 142, 152, 205, 235, 291, 292
Sekhem, 48, 49
Sekhemit, 49, 144
Sekhmet, 49
Self (see Ba, soul, Spirit, Universal, Ba, Neter, Heru)., 3, 48, 50, 71, 93, 94, 95, 97, 130, 246, 297, 298, 303, 312, 313, 315, 317, 322, 331
Sema, 3, 93, 324, 336, 339, 343
Semitic, 144
Serpent, 46, 48, 50, 70, 241, 246
Serpent Power, 48, 70
Serpent Power (see also Kundalini and Buto), 48, 70
Serpent Power see also Kundalini Yoga, 48, 70
Serqet, 107, 120, 121
Seshat, See Sesheta, 54
Sesheta, 54
Set, 4, 37, 39, 41, 49, 51, 71, 81, 83, 84, 88, 109, 113, 114, 130, 135, 137, 138, 139, 143, 149, 151, 153, 155, 156, 157, 158, 159, 160, 161, 162, 163, 164, 165, 167, 168, 169, 170, 171, 172, 175, 176, 181, 182, 183, 184, 187, 188, 190, 191, 192, 193, 194, 195, 196, 197, 198, 201, 202, 203, 204, 206, 219, 223, 227, 233, 234, 236, 238, 240, 244, 246, 247, 248, 253, 254, 259, 266, 267, 271, 275, 290, 291, 297, 298, 324
Seti I, 316
Setian, 50
Seven, 85
Sex, 317
sexism, 336
Sexism, 336
Shedy, 312
Shetaut Neter, 317, 323, 324, 326, 336, 341, 342, 343
Shetaut Neter See also Egyptian Religion, 317, 323, 324, 326, 336, 341, 342, 343

Shu (air and space), 117, 118, 134, 207
Signs, 3
Sirius, 319
slavery, 323
society, 11, 311, 323, 325, 330, 335, 336, 337, 339, 342
Society, 338, 339, 342
Soul, 45, 50, 56, 57, 66, 78, 79, 93, 291, 297, 298, 301, 324, 340
Spirit, 32, 38, 39, 48, 50, 56, 66, 69, 70, 79, 101, 102, 103, 117, 118, 121, 122, 123, 124, 126, 134, 137, 139, 140, 146, 148, 163, 164, 165, 181, 196, 210, 213, 219, 226, 227, 233, 235, 237, 238, 240, 241, 244, 247, 248, 252, 254, 258, 264, 271, 276, 278, 282, 285, 286, 297, 298, 299, 302
Spiritual discipline, 312
SPIRITUALITY, 312, 330, 341, 342, 344
Sublimation, 317
sun, 152, 219
Sun, 152, 219
Sundisk, 123, 126, 195, 196, 197, 200, 277, 282, 302
Superpower, 327
Superpower Syndrome, 327
Superpower Syndrome Mandatory Conflict Complex, 327
Supreme Being, 130, 135, 212, 213, 229, 285, 286, 319
TANTRA, 317
TANTRA YOGA, 317
Taoism, 310
Tawi, 34
Tem, 43, 113, 114, 116
Temple, 22, 40, 41, 44, 45, 46, 48, 57, 58, 62, 63, 64, 65, 66, 67, 69, 70, 71, 76, 77, 78, 103, 125, 234, 260, 263, 264, 317, 322, 341
Temple of Aset, 22, 125, 317
Temu, 152, 165, 219, 223
The Absolute, 311
The Black, 329
The God, 39, 46, 70, 71, 140, 146, 182, 291, 317
The Gods, 182, 291, 317
Theban Theology, 311
Thebes, 233, 311, 316

Themis, 216
Theocracy, 327
Theology, 311, 318, 319
Thoth, 33, 78, 83, 123, 124, 125, 134, 135, 138, 139, 141, 151, 192, 193, 194, 195, 196, 197, 207, 208, 218, 219, 271, 274, 276, 282, 283, 299
time and space, 48, 50, 53, 70, 94, 109, 122, 130, 135, 147, 148, 212, 213, 323
Tomb, 175, 316
Tomb of Seti I, 316
transcendental reality, 323
Tree, 175, 335
Tree of Life, 335
Triad, 311
Trinity, 230, 318
Truth, 156, 172, 216
Tutankhamun, 107
Tutankhamun, Pharaoh, 107
Understanding, 3, 10, 12, 323, 338
United States of America, 327
Universal Consciousness, 317
Upanishads, 318, 333
Upper Egypt, 224, 285, 287
Ur, 52, 278
Vedic, 312
Violence, 336
Vitality, 190, 225, 227, 231, 232
Was scepter (see also Ptah) -, 79
Waset, 233, 311
Water, 197
Wealth, Money, 340
Western, West, 59, 60, 62, 63, 64, 65, 66, 218, 233, 301
White, 166, 339
Will, 160
Wisdom, 10, 49, 88, 109, 314, 316, 333, 334, 335, 340
Wisdom (also see Djehuti, Aset), 10, 49, 88, 109, 314, 316, 333, 334, 335, 340
World War II, 327
Yoga, 3, 310, 311, 312, 313, 317, 318, 319, 321, 324, 326, 328, 329, 343, 344
Yoga of Devotion (see Yoga of Divine Love), 343
Yogic, 328, 336
Yoruba, 335

Other Books From C M Books

P.O.Box 570459

Miami, Florida, 33257

(305) 378-6253 Fax: (305) 378-6253

Prices subject to change.

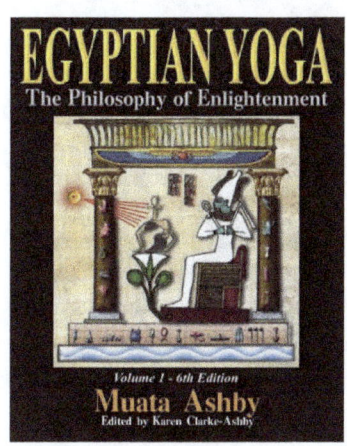

1. *EGYPTIAN YOGA: THE PHILOSOPHY OF ENLIGHTENMENT* An original, fully illustrated work, including hieroglyphs, detailing the meaning of the Egyptian mysteries, tantric yoga, psycho-spiritual and physical exercises. Egyptian Yoga is a guide to the practice of the highest spiritual philosophy which leads to absolute freedom from human misery and to immortality. It is well known by scholars that Egyptian philosophy is the basis of Western and Middle Eastern religious philosophies such as *Christianity, Islam, Judaism,* the *Kabala,* and Greek philosophy, but what about Indian philosophy, Yoga and Taoism? What were the original teachings? How can they be practiced today? What is the source of pain and suffering in the world and what is the solution? Discover the deepest mysteries of the mind and universe within and outside of your self. 8.5" X 11" ISBN: 1-884564-01-1 Soft $19.95

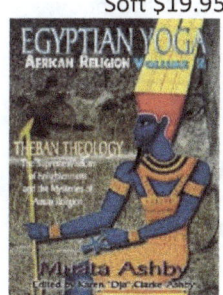

2. *EGYPTIAN YOGA: African Religion Volume 2-* Theban Theology U.S. In this long awaited sequel to *Egyptian Yoga: The Philosophy of Enlightenment* you will take a fascinating and enlightening journey back in time and discover the teachings which constituted the epitome of Ancient Egyptian spiritual wisdom. What are the disciplines which lead to the fulfillment of all desires? Delve into the three states of consciousness (waking, dream and deep sleep) and the fourth state which transcends them all, Neberdjer, "The Absolute." These teachings of the city of Waset (Thebes) were the crowning achievement of the Sages of Ancient Egypt. They establish the standard mystical keys for understanding the profound mystical symbolism of the Triad of human consciousness. ISBN 1-884564-39-9 $23.95

3. *THE KEMETIC DIET: GUIDE TO HEALTH, DIET AND FASTING* Health issues have always been important to human beings since the beginning of time. The earliest records of history show that the art of healing was held in high esteem since the time of Ancient Egypt. In the early 20th century, medical doctors had almost attained the status of sainthood by the promotion of the idea that they alone were "scientists" while other healing modalities and traditional healers who did not follow the "scientific method' were nothing but superstitious, ignorant charlatans who at best would take the money of their clients and at worst kill them with the unscientific "snake oils" and "irrational theories". In the late 20th century, the failure of the modern medical establishment's ability to lead the general public to good health, promoted the move by many in society towards "alternative medicine". Alternative medicine disciplines are those healing modalities which do not adhere to the philosophy of allopathic medicine. Allopathic medicine is what medical doctors practice by an large. It is the theory that disease is caused by agencies outside the body such as bacteria, viruses or physical means which affect the body. These can therefore be treated by medicines and therapies The natural healing method began in the absence of extensive technologies with the idea that all the answers for health may be found in nature or rather, the deviation from nature. Therefore, the health of the body can be restored by correcting the aberration and thereby restoring balance. This is the area that will be covered in this volume. Allopathic techniques have their place in the art of healing. However, we should not forget that the body is a grand achievement of the spirit and built into it is the capacity to maintain itself and heal itself. Ashby, Muata ISBN: 1-884564-49-6 $28.95

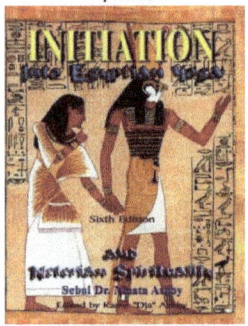

4. INITIATION INTO EGYPTIAN YOGA Shedy: Spiritual discipline or program, to go deeply into the mysteries, to study the mystery teachings and literature profoundly, to penetrate the mysteries. You will learn about the mysteries of initiation into the teachings and practice of Yoga and how to become an Initiate of the mystical sciences. This insightful manual is the first in a series which introduces you to the goals of daily spiritual and yoga practices: Meditation, Diet, Words of Power and the ancient wisdom teachings. 8.5" X 11" ISBN 1-884564-02-X Soft Cover $24.95 U.S.

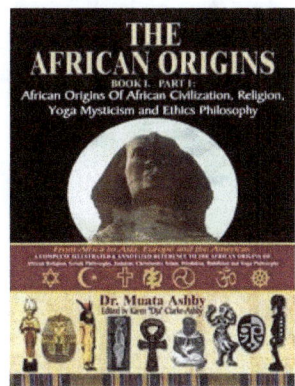

5. *THE AFRICAN ORIGINS OF CIVILIZATION, RELIGION AND YOGA SPIRITUALITY AND ETHICS PHILOSOPHY* HARD COVER EDITION Part 1, Part 2, Part 3 in one volume 683 Pages Hard Cover First Edition Three volumes in one. Over the past several years I have been asked to put together in one volume the most important evidences showing the correlations and common teachings between Kamitan (Ancient Egyptian) culture and religion and that of India. The questions of the history of Ancient Egypt, and the latest archeological evidences showing civilization and culture in Ancient Egypt and its spread to other countries, has intrigued many scholars as well as mystics over the years. Also, the possibility that Ancient Egyptian Priests and Priestesses migrated to Greece, India and other countries to carry on the traditions of the Ancient Egyptian Mysteries, has been speculated over the years as well. In chapter 1 of the book *Egyptian Yoga The Philosophy of Enlightenment,* 1995, I first introduced the deepest comparison between Ancient Egypt and India that had been brought forth up to that time. Now, in the year 2001 this new book, *THE AFRICAN ORIGINS OF CIVILIZATION, MYSTICAL RELIGION AND YOGA PHILOSOPHY,* more fully explores the motifs, symbols and philosophical correlations between Ancient Egyptian and Indian mysticism and clearly shows not only that Ancient Egypt and India were connected culturally but also spiritually. How does this knowledge help the spiritual aspirant? This discovery has great importance for the Yogis and mystics who follow the philosophy of Ancient Egypt and the mysticism of India. It means that India has a longer history and heritage than was previously understood. It shows that the mysteries of Ancient Egypt were essentially a yoga tradition which did not die but rather developed into the modern day systems of Yoga technology of India. It further shows that African culture developed Yoga Mysticism earlier than any other civilization in history. All of this expands our understanding of the unity of culture and the deep legacy of Yoga, which stretches into the distant past, beyond the Indus Valley civilization, the earliest known high culture in India as well as the Vedic tradition of Aryan culture. Therefore, Yoga culture and mysticism is the oldest known tradition of spiritual development and Indian mysticism is an extension of the Ancient Egyptian mysticism. By understanding the legacy which Ancient Egypt gave to India the mysticism of India is better understood and by comprehending the heritage of Indian Yoga, which is rooted in Ancient Egypt the Mysticism of Ancient Egypt is also better understood. This expanded

understanding allows us to prove the underlying kinship of humanity, through the common symbols, motifs and philosophies which are not disparate and confusing teachings but in reality expressions of the same study of truth through metaphysics and mystical realization of Self. (HARD COVER) ISBN: 1-884564-50-X $45.00 U.S. 8 1/2" X 11"

6. *AFRICAN ORIGINS BOOK 1 PART 1* African Origins of African Civilization, Religion, Yoga Mysticism and Ethics Philosophy-<u>Soft Cover</u> $24.95 ISBN: 1-884564-55-0

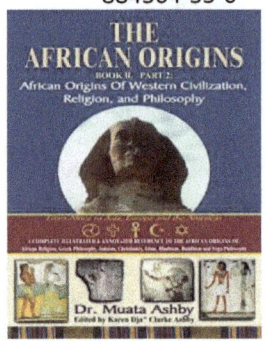

7. *AFRICAN ORIGINS BOOK 2 PART 2* African Origins of Western Civilization, Religion and Philosophy (Soft) - <u>Soft Cover</u> $24.95 ISBN: 1-884564-56-9

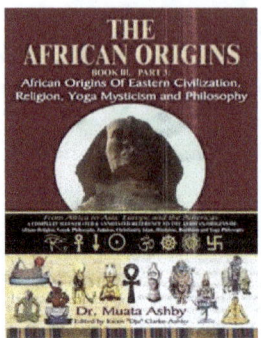

8. *EGYPT AND INDIA AFRICAN ORIGINS OF Eastern Civilization, Religion, Yoga Mysticism and Philosophy*-<u>Soft Cover</u> $29.95 (Soft) ISBN: 1-884564-57-7

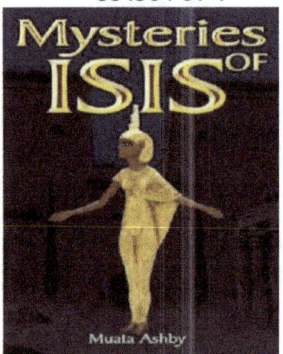

9. *THE MYSTERIES OF ISIS: **The Ancient Egyptian Philosophy of Self-Realization*** - There are several paths to discover the Divine and the mysteries of the higher Self. This volume details the mystery teachings of the goddess Aset (Isis) from Ancient Egypt- the path of wisdom. It includes the teachings of her temple and the disciplines that are enjoined for the initiates of the temple of Aset as they were given in ancient times. Also, this book includes the teachings of the main myths of Aset that lead a human being to spiritual enlightenment and immortality. Through the study of ancient myth and the illumination of initiatic understanding the idea of God is expanded from the mythological comprehension to the metaphysical. Then this metaphysical understanding is related to you, the student, so as to begin understanding your true divine nature. ISBN 1-884564-24-0 $22.99

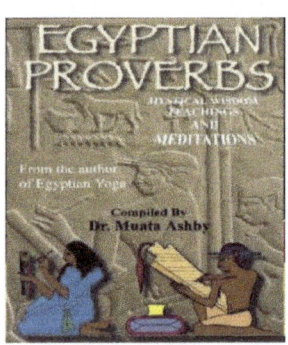

10. *EGYPTIAN PROVERBS:* collection of ―Ancient Egyptian Proverbs and Wisdom Teachings - How to live according to MAAT Philosophy. Beginning Meditation. All proverbs are indexed for easy

searches. For the first time in one volume, — —Ancient Egyptian Proverbs, wisdom teachings and meditations, fully illustrated with hieroglyphic text and symbols. EGYPTIAN PROVERBS is a unique collection of knowledge and wisdom which you can put into practice today and transform your life. $14.95 U.S ISBN: 1-884564-00-3

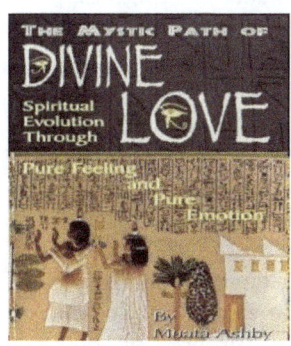

11. *GOD OF LOVE: THE PATH OF DIVINE LOVE The Process of Mystical Transformation and The Path of Divine Love* This Volume focuses on the ancient wisdom teachings of "Neter Merri" –the Ancient Egyptian philosophy of Divine Love and how to use them in a scientific process for self-transformation. Love is one of the most powerful human emotions. It is also the source of Divine feeling that unifies God and the individual human being. When love is fragmented and diminished by egoism the Divine connection is lost. The Ancient tradition of Neter Merri leads human beings back to their Divine connection, allowing them to discover their innate glorious self that is actually Divine and immortal. This volume will detail the process of transformation from ordinary consciousness to cosmic consciousness through the integrated practice of the teachings and the path of Devotional Love toward the Divine. 5.5"x 8.5" ISBN 1-884564-11-9 $22.95

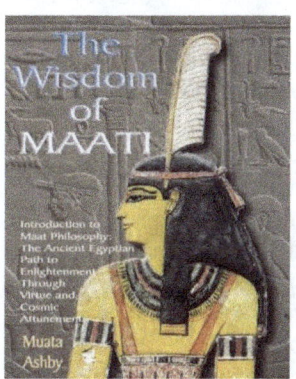

12. *INTRODUCTION TO MAAT PHILOSOPHY: Spiritual Enlightenment Through the Path of Virtue* Known commonly as Karma in India, the teachings of MAAT contain an extensive philosophy based on ariu (deeds) and their fructification in the form of shai and renenet (fortune and destiny, leading to Meskhenet (fate in a future birth) for living virtuously and with orderly wisdom are explained and the student is to begin practicing the precepts of Maat in daily life so as to promote the process of purification of the heart in preparation for the judgment of the soul. This judgment will be understood not as an event that will occur at the time of death but as an event that occurs continuously, at every moment in the life of the individual. The student will learn how to become allied with the forces of the Higher Self and to thereby begin cleansing the mind (heart) of impurities so as to attain a higher vision of reality. ISBN 1-884564-20-8 $22.99

13. **MEDITATION The Ancient Egyptian Path to Enlightenment** Many people do not know about the rich history of meditation practice in Ancient Egypt. This volume outlines the theory of meditation and presents the Ancient Egyptian Hieroglyphic text which give instruction as to the nature of the mind and its three modes of expression. It also presents the texts which give instruction on the practice of meditation for spiritual Enlightenment and unity with the Divine. This volume allows the reader to begin practicing meditation by explaining, in easy to understand terms, the simplest form of meditation and working up to the most advanced form which was practiced in ancient times and which is still practiced by yogis around the world in modern times. ISBN 1-884564-27-7 $22.99

14. *THE GLORIOUS LIGHT MEDITATION* TECHNIQUE OF ANCIENT EGYPT New for the year 2000. This volume is based on the earliest known instruction in history given for the practice of formal meditation. Discovered by Dr. Muata Ashby, it is inscribed on the walls of the Tomb of Seti I in Thebes Egypt. This volume details the philosophy and practice of this unique system of meditation originated in Ancient Egypt and the earliest practice of meditation known in the world which occurred in the most advanced African Culture. ISBN: 1-884564-15-1 $16.95 (PB)

15. *THE SERPENT POWER: The Ancient Egyptian Mystical Wisdom of the Inner Life Force.* This Volume specifically deals with the latent life Force energy of the universe and in the human body, its control and sublimation. How to develop the Life Force energy of the subtle body. This Volume will introduce the esoteric wisdom of the science of how virtuous living acts in a subtle and mysterious way to cleanse the latent psychic energy conduits and vortices of the spiritual body. ISBN 1-884564-19-4 $22.95

16. *EGYPTIAN YOGA The Postures of The Gods and Goddesses* Discover the physical postures and exercises practiced thousands of years ago in Ancient Egypt which are today known as Yoga exercises. Discover the history of the postures and how they were transferred from Ancient Egypt in Africa to India through Buddhist Tantrism. Then practice the postures as you discover the mythic teaching that originally gave birth to the postures and was practiced by the Ancient Egyptian priests and priestesses. This work is based on the pictures and teachings from the Creation story of Ra, The Asarian Resurrection Myth and the carvings and reliefs from various Temples in Ancient Egypt 8.5" X 11" ISBN 1-884564-10-0 Soft Cover $21.95 Exercise video $20

17. *SACRED SEXUALITY: ANCIENT EGYPTIAN TANTRA YOGA: The Art of Sex* Sublimation and Universal Consciousness This Volume will expand on the male and female principles within the human body and in the universe and further detail the sublimation of sexual energy into spiritual energy. The student will study the deities Min and Hathor, Asar and Aset, Geb and Nut and discover the mystical implications for a practical spiritual discipline. This Volume will also focus on the Tantric aspects of Ancient Egyptian and Indian mysticism, the purpose of sex and the mystical teachings of sexual sublimation which lead to self-knowledge and Enlightenment. ISBN 1-884564-03-8 $24.95

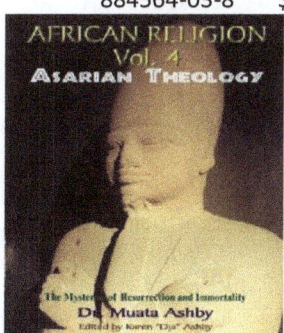

18. *AFRICAN RELIGION Volume 4: ASARIAN THEOLOGY: RESURRECTING OSIRIS* The path of Mystical Awakening and the Keys to Immortality NEW REVISED AND EXPANDED EDITION! The Ancient Sages created stories based on human and superhuman beings whose struggles, aspirations, needs and desires ultimately lead them to discover their true Self. The myth of Aset, Asar and Heru is no exception in this area. While there is no one source where the entire story may be found, pieces of it are inscribed in various ancient Temples walls, tombs, steles and papyri. For the first time available, the complete myth of Asar, Aset and Heru has been compiled from original Ancient Egyptian, Greek and Coptic Texts. This epic myth has been richly illustrated with reliefs from the Temple of Heru at Edfu, the Temple of Aset at Philae, the Temple of Asar at Abydos, the Temple of Hathor at Denderah and various papyri, inscriptions and reliefs. Discover the myth which inspired the teachings of the *Shetaut Neter* (Egyptian Mystery System - Egyptian Yoga) and the Egyptian Book of

EGYPTIAN BOOK OF THE DEAD HIEROGLYPH TRANSLATIONS Volume 6: Featuring The Osirian Resurrection

Coming Forth By Day. Also, discover the three levels of Ancient Egyptian Religion, how to understand the mysteries of the Duat or Astral World and how to discover the abode of the Supreme in the Amenta, *The Other World* The ancient religion of Asar, Aset and Heru, if properly understood, contains all of the elements necessary to lead the sincere aspirant to attain immortality through inner self-discovery. This volume presents the entire myth and explores the main mystical themes and rituals associated with the myth for understating human existence, creation and the way to achieve spiritual emancipation - *Resurrection*. The Asarian myth is so powerful that it influenced and is still having an effect on the major world religions. Discover the origins and mystical meaning of the Christian Trinity, the Eucharist ritual and the ancient origin of the birthday of Jesus Christ. Soft Cover ISBN: 1-884564-27-5 $24.95

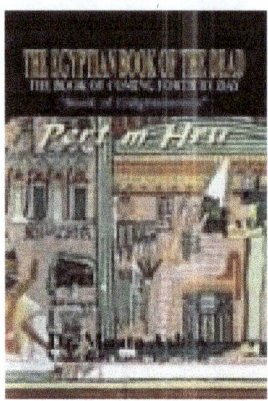

19. **THE EGYPTIAN BOOK OF THE DEAD MYSTICISM OF THE PERT EM HERU** " I Know myself, I know myself, I am One With God!– From the Pert Em Heru "The Ru Pert em Heru" or "Ancient Egyptian Book of The Dead," or "Book of Coming Forth By Day" as it is more popularly known, has fascinated the world since the successful translation of Ancient Egyptian hieroglyphic scripture over 150 years ago. The astonishing writings in it reveal that the Ancient Egyptians believed in life after death and in an ultimate destiny to discover the Divine. The elegance and aesthetic beauty of the hieroglyphic text itself has inspired many see it as an art form in and of itself. But is there more to it than that? Did the Ancient Egyptian wisdom contain more than just aphorisms and hopes of eternal life beyond death? In this volume Dr. Muata Ashby, the author of over 25 books on Ancient Egyptian Yoga Philosophy has produced a new translation of the original texts which uncovers a mystical teaching underlying the sayings and rituals instituted by the Ancient Egyptian Sages and Saints. "Once the philosophy of Ancient Egypt is understood as a mystical tradition instead of as a religion or primitive mythology, it reveals its secrets which if practiced today will lead anyone to discover the glory of spiritual self-discovery. The Pert em Heru is in every way comparable to the Indian Upanishads or the Tibetan Book of the Dead." ⁂ $28.95 ISBN# 1-884564-28-3 Size: 8½" X 11

20. *African Religion VOL. 1- ANUNIAN THEOLOGY THE MYSTERIES OF RA* The Philosophy of Anu and The Mystical Teachings of The Ancient Egyptian Creation Myth Discover the mystical teachings contained in the Creation Myth and the gods and goddesses who brought creation and human beings into existence. The Creation myth of Anu is the source of Anunian Theology but also of the other main theological systems of Ancient Egypt that also influenced other world religions including Christianity, Hinduism and Buddhism. The Creation Myth holds the key to understanding the universe and for attaining spiritual Enlightenment. ISBN: 1-884564-38-0 $19.95

21. *African Religion VOL 3: Memphite Theology: MYSTERIES OF MIND* Mystical Psychology & Mental Health for Enlightenment and Immortality based on the Ancient Egyptian Philosophy of Menefer -Mysticism of Ptah, Egyptian Physics and Yoga Metaphysics and the Hidden properties of Matter. This volume uncovers the mystical psychology of the Ancient Egyptian wisdom teachings centering on the philosophy of the Ancient Egyptian city of Menefer (Memphite Theology). How to understand the mind and how to control the senses and lead the mind to health, clarity and mystical self-discovery. This Volume will also go deeper into the philosophy of God as creation and will explore the concepts of modern science and how they correlate with ancient teachings. This Volume will lay the ground work for the understanding of the philosophy of universal consciousness and the initiatic/yogic insight into who or what is God? ISBN 1-884564-07-0 $22.95

22. *AFRICAN RELIGION VOLUME 5: THE GODDESS AND THE EGYPTIAN MYSTERIESTHE PATH OF THE GODDESS THE GODDESS PATH* The Secret Forms of the Goddess and the Rituals of Resurrection The Supreme Being may be worshipped as father or as mother. *Ushet Rekhat* or *Mother Worship*, is the spiritual process of worshipping the Divine in the form of the Divine Goddess. It celebrates the most important forms of the Goddess including *Nathor, Maat, Aset, Arat, Amentet and Hathor* and explores

their mystical meaning as well as the rising of *Sirius,* the star of Aset (Aset) and the new birth of Hor (Heru). The end of the year is a time of reckoning, reflection and engendering a new or renewed positive movement toward attaining spiritual Enlightenment. The Mother Worship devotional meditation ritual, performed on five days during the month of December and on New Year's Eve, is based on the Ushet Rekhit. During the ceremony, the cosmic forces, symbolized by Sirius - and the constellation of Orion --, are harnessed through the understanding and devotional attitude of the participant. This propitiation draws the light of wisdom and health to all those who share in the ritual, leading to prosperity and wisdom. $14.95 ISBN 1-884564-18-6

23. *THE MYSTICAL JOURNEY FROM JESUS TO CHRIST* Discover the ancient Egyptian origins of Christianity before the Catholic Church and learn the mystical teachings given by Jesus to assist all humanity in becoming Christlike. Discover the secret meaning of the Gospels that were discovered in Egypt. Also discover how and why so many Christian churches came into being. Discover that the Bible still holds the keys to mystical realization even though its original writings were changed by the church. Discover how to practice the original teachings of Christianity which leads to the Kingdom of Heaven. $24.95 ISBN# 1-884564-05-4 size: 8½" X 11"

24. *THE STORY OF ASAR, ASET AND HERU:* An Ancient Egyptian Legend (For Children) Now for the first time, the most ancient myth of Ancient Egypt comes alive for children. Inspired by the books *The Asarian Resurrection: The Ancient Egyptian Bible* and *The Mystical Teachings of The Asarian Resurrection, The Story of Asar, Aset and Heru* is an easy to understand and thrilling tale which inspired the children of Ancient Egypt to aspire to greatness and righteousness. If you and your child have enjoyed stories like *The Lion King* and *Star Wars* you will love *The Story of Asar, Aset and Heru.* Also, if you know the story of Jesus and Krishna you will discover than Ancient Egypt had a similar myth and that this myth carries important spiritual teachings for living a fruitful and fulfilling life. This book may be used along with *The Parents Guide To The Asarian Resurrection Myth: How to Teach Yourself and Your Child the Principles of Universal Mystical Religion.* The guide provides some background to the Asarian Resurrection myth and it also gives insight into the mystical teachings contained in

it which you may introduce to your child. It is designed for parents who wish to grow spiritually with their children and it serves as an introduction for those who would like to study the Asarian Resurrection Myth in depth and to practice its teachings. 8.5" X 11" ISBN: 1-884564-31-3 $12.95

25. THE PARENTS GUIDE TO THE AUSARIAN RESURRECTION MYTH: How to Teach Yourself and Your Child the Principles of Universal Mystical Religion. This insightful manual brings for the timeless wisdom of the ancient through the Ancient Egyptian myth of Asar, Aset and Heru and the mystical teachings contained in it for parents who want to guide their children to understand and practice the teachings of mystical spirituality. This manual may be used with the children's storybook *The Story of Asar, Aset and Heru* by Dr. Muata Abhaya Ashby. ISBN: 1-884564-30-5 $16.95

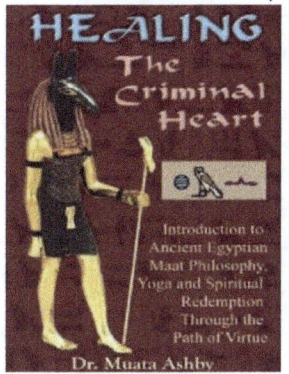

26. HEALING THE CRIMINAL HEART. Introduction to Maat Philosophy, Yoga and Spiritual Redemption Through the Path of Virtue Who is a criminal? Is there such a thing as a criminal heart? What is the source of evil and sinfulness and is there any way to rise above it? Is there redemption for those who have committed sins, even the worst crimes? Ancient Egyptian mystical psychology holds important answers to these questions. Over ten thousand years ago mystical psychologists, the Sages of Ancient Egypt, studied and charted the human mind and spirit and laid out a path which will lead to spiritual redemption, prosperity and Enlightenment. This introductory volume brings forth the teachings of the Asarian Resurrection, the most important myth of Ancient Egypt, with relation to the faults of human existence: anger, hatred, greed, lust, animosity, discontent, ignorance, egoism jealousy, bitterness, and a myriad of psycho-spiritual ailments which keep a human being in a state of negativity and adversity ISBN: 1-884564-17-8 $15.95

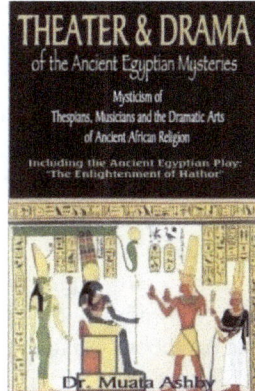

27. TEMPLE RITUAL OF THE ANCIENT EGYPTIAN MYSTERIES--THEATER & DRAMA OF THE ANCIENT EGYPTIAN MYSTERIES: Details the practice of the mysteries and ritual program of the temple

and the philosophy an practice of the ritual of the mysteries, its purpose and execution. Featuring the Ancient Egyptian stage play- "The Enlightenment of Hathor' Based on an Ancient Egyptian Drama, The original Theater -Mysticism of the Temple of Hetheru 1-884564-14-3 $19.95 By Dr. Muata Ashby

28. GUIDE TO PRINT ON DEMAND: SELF-PUBLISH FOR PROFIT, SPIRITUAL FULFILLMENT AND SERVICE TO HUMANITY Everyone asks us how we produced so many books in such a short time. Here are the secrets to writing and producing books that uplift humanity and how to get them printed for a fraction of the regular cost. Anyone can become an author even if they have limited funds. All that is necessary is the willingness to learn how the printing and book business work and the desire to follow the special instructions given here for preparing your manuscript format. Then you take your work directly to the non-traditional companies who can produce your books for less than the traditional book printer can. ISBN: 1-884564-40-2 $16.95 U.S.

29. *Egyptian Mysteries: Vol. 1,* Shetaut Neter What are the Mysteries? For thousands of years the spiritual tradition of Ancient Egypt, *Shetaut Neter,* "The Egyptian Mysteries," "The Secret Teachings," have fascinated, tantalized and amazed the world. At one time exalted and recognized as the highest culture of the world, by Africans, Europeans, Asiatics, Hindus, Buddhists and other cultures of the ancient world, in time it was shunned by the emerging orthodox world religions. Its temples desecrated, its philosophy maligned, its tradition spurned, its philosophy dormant in the mystical *Medu Neter,* the mysterious hieroglyphic texts which hold the secret symbolic meaning that has scarcely been discerned up to now. What are the secrets of *Nehast* {spiritual awakening and emancipation, resurrection}. More than just a literal translation, this volume is for awakening to the secret code *Shetitu* of the teaching which was not deciphered by Egyptologists, nor could be understood by ordinary spiritualists. This book is a reinstatement of the original science made available for our times, to the reincarnated followers of Ancient Egyptian culture and the prospect of spiritual freedom to break the bonds of *Khemn,* "ignorance," and slavery to evil forces: *Såaa* . ISBN: 1-884564-41-0 $19.99

30. *EGYPTIAN MYSTERIES VOL 2:* Dictionary of Gods and Goddesses This book is about the mystery of neteru, the gods and goddesses of Ancient Egypt (Kamit, Kemet). Neteru means "Gods and Goddesses." But the Neterian teaching of Neteru represents more than the usual limited modern day concept of "divinities" or "spirits." The Neteru of Kamit are also metaphors, cosmic principles and vehicles for the enlightening teachings of Shetaut Neter (Ancient Egyptian-African Religion). Actually they are the elements for one of the most advanced systems of spirituality ever conceived in human history. Understanding the concept of neteru provides a firm basis for spiritual evolution and the pathway for viable culture, peace on earth and a healthy human society. Why is it important to have gods and goddesses in our lives? In order for spiritual evolution to be possible, once a human being has accepted that there is existence after death and there is a transcendental being who exists beyond time and space knowledge, human beings need a connection to that which transcends the ordinary experience of human life in time and space and a means to understand the transcendental reality beyond the mundane reality. ISBN: 1-884564-23-2 $21.95

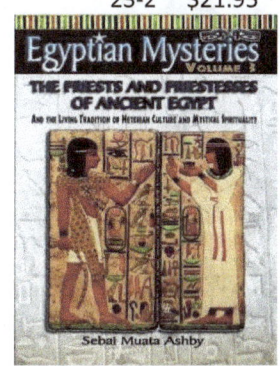

31. *EGYPTIAN MYSTERIES VOL. 3* The Priests and Priestesses of Ancient Egypt This volume details the path of Neterian priesthood, the joys, challenges and rewards of advanced Neterian life, the teachings that allowed the priests and priestesses to manage the most long lived civilization in human history and how that path can be adopted today; for those who want to tread the path of the Clergy of Shetaut Neter. ISBN: 1-884564-53-4 $24.95

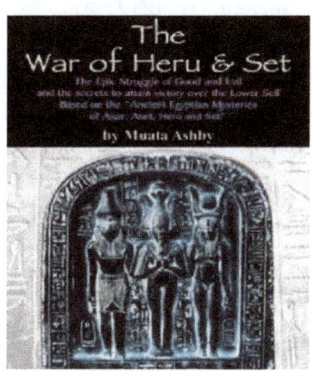

32. *The War of Heru and Set:* The Struggle of Good and Evil for Control of the World and The Human Soul This volume contains a novelized version of the Asarian Resurrection myth that is based on the actual scriptures presented in the Book Asarian Religion (old name –Resurrecting Osiris). This volume is prepared in the form of a screenplay and can be easily adapted to be used as a stage play. Spiritual seeking is a mythic journey that has many emotional highs and lows, ecstasies and depressions, victories and frustrations. This is

the War of Life that is played out in the myth as the struggle of Heru and Set and those are mythic characters that represent the human Higher and Lower self. How to understand the war and emerge victorious in the journey o life? The ultimate victory and fulfillment can be experienced, which is not changeable or lost in time. The purpose of myth is to convey the wisdom of life through the story of divinities who show the way to overcome the challenges and foibles of life. In this volume the feelings and emotions of the characters of the myth have been highlighted to show the deeply rich texture of the Ancient Egyptian myth. This myth contains deep spiritual teachings and insights into the nature of self, of God and the mysteries of life and the means to discover the true meaning of life and thereby achieve the true purpose of life. To become victorious in the battle of life means to become the King (or Queen) of Egypt.Have you seen movies like The Lion King, Hamlet, The Odyssey, or The Little Buddha? These have been some of the most popular movies in modern times. The Sema Institute of Yoga is dedicated to researching and presenting the wisdom and culture of ancient Africa. The Script is designed to be produced as a motion picture but may be addapted for the theater as well. $21.95 copyright 1998 By Dr. Muata Ashby ISBN 1-8840564-44-5

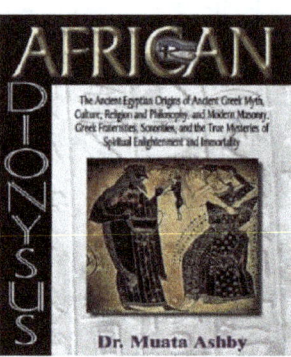

33. AFRICAN DIONYSUS: FROM EGYPT TO GREECE: The Kamitan Origins of Greek Culture and Religion ISBN: 1-884564-47-X FROM EGYPT TO GREECE This insightful manual is a reference to Ancient Egyptian mythology and philosophy and its correlation to what later became known as Greek and Rome mythology and philosophy. It outlines the basic tenets of the mythologies and shoes the ancient origins of Greek culture in Ancient Egypt. This volume also documents the origins of the Greek alphabet in Egypt as well as Greek religion, myth and philosophy of the gods and goddesses from Egypt from the myth of Atlantis and archaic period with the Minoans to the Classical period. This volume also acts as a resource for Colleges students who would like to set up fraternities and sororities based on the original Ancient Egyptian principles of Sheti and Maat philosophy. ISBN: 1-884564-47-X $22.95 U.S.

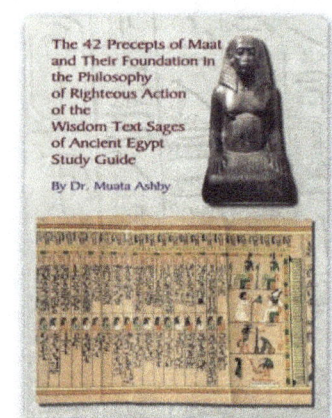

34. THE FORTY TWO PRECEPTS OF MAAT, THE PHILOSOPHY OF RIGHTEOUS ACTION

AND THE ANCIENT EGYPTIAN WISDOM TEXTS ADVANCED STUDIES This manual is designed for use with the 1998 Maat Philosophy Class conducted by Dr. Muata Ashby. This is a detailed study of Maat Philosophy. It contains a compilation of the 42 laws or precepts of Maat and the corresponding principles which they represent along with the teachings of the ancient Egyptian Sages relating to each. Maat philosophy was the basis of Ancient Egyptian society and government as well as the heart of Ancient Egyptian myth and spirituality. Maat is at once a goddess, a cosmic force and a living social doctrine, which promotes social harmony and thereby paves the way for spiritual evolution in all levels of society. ISBN: 1-884564-48-8 $16.95 U.S.

35. THE SECRET LOTUS: Poetry of Enlightenment

Discover the mystical sentiment of the Kemetic teaching as expressed through the poetry of Sebai Muata Ashby. The teaching of spiritual awakening is uniquely experienced when the poetic sensibility is present. This first volume contains the poems written between 1996 and 2003. **1-884564--16 -X $16.99**

36. The Ancient Egyptian Buddha: The Ancient Egyptian Origins of Buddhism

This book is a compilation of several sections of a larger work, a book by the name of African Origins of Civilization, Religion, Yoga Mysticism and Ethics Philosophy. It also contains some additional evidences not contained in the larger work that demonstrate the correlation between Ancient Egyptian Religion and Buddhism. This book is one of several compiled short volumes that has been compiled so as to facilitate access to specific subjects contained in the larger work which is over 680 pages long. These short and small volumes have been specifically designed to cover one subject in a brief and low cost format. This present volume, The Ancient Egyptian Buddha: The Ancient Egyptian Origins of Buddhism, formed one subject in the larger work; actually it was one chapter of the larger work. However, this volume has some new additional evidences and comparisons of Buddhist and Neterian (Ancient Egyptian) philosophies not previously discussed. It was felt that this subject needed to be discussed because even in the early 21st century, the idea persists that Buddhism originated only in India independently. Yet there is ample evidence from ancient writings and perhaps more importantly, iconographical evidences from the Ancient Egyptians and early Buddhists themselves that prove otherwise. This handy volume has been designed to be accessible to young adults and all others who would like to have an easy reference with documentation on this important subject. This is an important subject because the frame of reference with which we look at a culture depends strongly on our conceptions about its origins. in this case, if we look at the Buddhism as an Asiatic religion we would treat it and it's culture in one way. If we id as African [Ancient Egyptian] we not only would see it in a different light but we also must ascribe Africa with a glorious legacy that matches any other culture in human history and gave rise to one of the present day most important religious philosophies. We would also look at the culture and philosophies of the Ancient Egyptians as having African insights that offer us greater depth into the Buddhist philosophies. Those insights inform our knowledge about other African traditions and we can also begin to understand in a deeper way the effect of Ancient Egyptian culture on African culture and also on the Asiatic as well. We would also be able to discover the glorious and wondrous teaching of mystical philosophy that Ancient Egyptian Shetaut Neter religion offers, that is as powerful as any other mystic system of spiritual philosophy in the world today. ISBN: 1-884564-61-5 $28.95

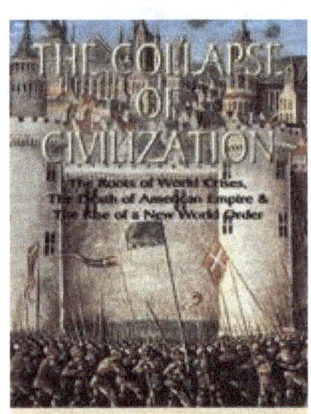

37. **The Death of American Empire: Neo-conservatism, Theocracy, Economic Imperialism, Environmental Disaster and the Collapse of Civilization**

This work is a collection of essays relating to social and economic, leadership, and ethics, ecological and religious issues that are facing the world today in order to understand the course of history that has led humanity to its present condition and then arrive at positive solutions that will lead to better outcomes for all humanity. It surveys the development and decline of major empires throughout history and focuses on the creation of American Empire along with the social, political and economic policies that led to the prominence of the United States of America as a Superpower including the rise of the political control of the neo-con political philosophy including militarism and the military industrial complex in American politics and the rise of the religious right into and American Theocracy movement. This volume details, through historical and current events, the psychology behind the dominance of western culture in world politics through the "Superpower Syndrome Mandatory Conflict Complex" that drives the Superpower culture to establish itself above all others and then act hubristically to dominate world culture through legitimate influences as well as coercion, media censorship and misinformation leading to international hegemony and world conflict. This volume also details the financial policies that gave rise to American prominence in the global economy, especially after World War II, and promoted American preeminence over the world economy through Globalization as well as the environmental policies, including the oil economy, that are promoting degradation of the world ecology and contribute to the decline of America as an Empire culture. This volume finally explores the factors pointing to the decline of the American Empire economy and imperial power and what to expect in the aftermath of American prominence and how to survive the decline while at the same time promoting policies and social-economic-religious-political changes that are needed in order to promote the emergence of a beneficial and sustainable culture. **$25.95soft** 1-884564-25-9, Hard Cover **$29.95** 1-884564-45-3

38. The African Origins of Hatha Yoga: And its Ancient Mystical Teaching

The subject of this present volume, The Ancient Egyptian Origins of Yoga Postures, formed one subject in the larger works, African Origins of Civilization Religion, Yoga Mysticism and Ethics Philosophy and the Book Egypt and India is the section of the book African Origins of Civilization. Those works contain the collection of all correlations between Ancient Egypt and India. This volume also contains some additional information not contained in the previous work. It was felt that this subject needed to be discussed more directly, being treated in one volume, as opposed to being contained in the larger work along with other subjects, because even in the early 21st century, the idea persists that the Yoga and specifically, Yoga Postures, were invented and developed only in India. The Ancient Egyptians were peoples originally from Africa who were, in ancient times, colonists in India. Therefore it is no surprise that many Indian traditions including religious and Yogic, would be found earlier in Ancient Egypt. Yet there is ample evidence from ancient writings and perhaps more importantly, iconographical evidences from the Ancient Egyptians themselves and the Indians themselves that prove the connection between Ancient Egypt and India as well as the existence of a discipline of Yoga Postures in Ancient Egypt long before its practice in India. This handy volume has been designed to be accessible to young adults and all others who would like to have an easy reference with documentation on this important subject. This is an important subject because the frame of reference with which we look at a culture depends strongly on our conceptions about its origins. In this case, if we look at the Ancient Egyptians as Asiatic peoples we would treat them and their culture in one way. If we see them as Africans we not only see them in a different light but we also must ascribe Africa with a glorious legacy that matches any other culture in human history. We would also look at the culture and philosophies of the Ancient Egyptians as having African insights instead of Asiatic ones. Those insights inform our knowledge bout other African traditions and we can also begin to understand in a deeper way the effect of Ancient Egyptian culture on African culture and also on the Asiatic as well. When we discover the deeper and more ancient practice of the postures system in Ancient Egypt that was called "Hatha Yoga" in India, we are able to find a new and expanded understanding of the practice that constitutes a discipline of spiritual practice that informs and revitalizes the Indian practices as well as all spiritual disciplines. **$19.99** ISBN 1-884564-60-7

39. The Black Ancient Egyptians

This present volume, The Black Ancient Egyptians: The Black African Ancestry of the Ancient Egyptians, formed one subject in the larger work: The African Origins of Civilization, Religion, Yoga Mysticism and Ethics Philosophy. It was felt that this subject needed to be discussed because even in the early 21st century, the idea persists that the Ancient Egyptians were peoples originally from Asia Minor who came into North-East Africa. Yet there is ample evidence from ancient writings and perhaps more importantly, iconographical evidences from the Ancient Egyptians themselves that proves otherwise. This handy volume has been designed to be accessible to young adults and all others who would like to have an easy reference with documentation on this important subject. This is an important subject because the frame of reference with which we look at a culture depends strongly on our conceptions about its origins. in this case, if we look at the Ancient Egyptians as Asiatic peoples we would treat them and their culture in one way. If we see them as Africans we not only see them in a different light but we also must ascribe Africa with a glorious legacy that matches any other culture in human history. We would also look at the culture and philosophies of the Ancient Egyptians as having African insights instead of Asiatic ones. Those insights inform our knowledge bout other African traditions and we can also begin to understand in a deeper way the effect of Ancient Egyptian culture on African culture and also on the Asiatic as well. ISBN 1-884564-21-6 $19.99

40. The Limits of Faith: The Failure of Faith-based Religions and the Solution to the Meaning of Life

Is faith belief in something without proof? And if so is there never to be any proof or discovery? If so what is the need of intellect? If faith is trust in something that is real is that reality historical, literal or metaphorical or philosophical? If knowledge is an essential element in faith why should there by so much emphasis on believing and not on understanding in the modern practice of religion? This volume is a compilation of essays related to the nature of religious faith in the context of its inception in human history as well as its meaning for religious practice and relations between religions in modern times. Faith has come to be regarded as a virtuous goal in life. However, many people have asked how can it be that an endeavor that is supposed to be dedicated to spiritual upliftment has led to more conflict in human history than any other social factor? ISBN 1884564631 SOFT COVER - $19.99, ISBN 1884564623 HARD COVER - $28.95

41. Redemption of The Criminal Heart Through Kemetic Spirituality and Maat Philosophy

Special book dedicated to inmates, their families and members of the Law Enforcement community. ISBN: 1-884564-70-4

$5.00

42. COMPARATIVE MYTHOLOGY

What are Myth and Culture and what is their importance for understanding the development of societies, human evolution and the search for meaning? What is the purpose of culture and how do cultures evolve? What are the elements of a culture and how can those elements be broken down and the constituent parts of a culture understood and compared? How do cultures interact? How does enculturation occur and how do people interact with other cultures? How do the processes of acculturation and cooptation occur and what does this mean for the development of a society? How can the study of myths and the elements of culture help in understanding the meaning of life and the means to promote understanding and peace in the world of human activity? This volume is the exposition of a method for studying and comparing cultures, myths and other social aspects of a society. It is an expansion on the Cultural Category Factor Correlation method for studying and comparing myths, cultures, religions and other aspects of human culture. It was originally introduced in the year 2002. This volume contains an expanded treatment as well as several refinements along with examples of the application of the method. the apparent. I hope you enjoy these art renditions as serene reflections of the mysteries of life. ISBN: 1-884564-72-0

Book price $21.95

43. CONVERSATION WITH GOD: Revelations of the Important Questions of Life

$24.99 U.S.

This volume contains a grouping of some of the questions that have been submitted to Sebai Dr. Muata Ashby. They are efforts by many aspirants to better understand and practice the teachings of mystical spirituality. It is said that when sages are asked spiritual questions they are relaying the wisdom of God, the Goddess, the Higher Self, etc. There is a very special quality about the Q & A process that does not occur during a regular lecture session. Certain points come out that would not come out otherwise due to the nature of the process which ideally occurs after a lecture. Having been to a certain degree enlightened by a lecture certain new questions arise and the answers to these have the effect of elevating the teaching of the lecture to even higher levels. Therefore, enjoy these exchanges and may they lead you to enlightenment, peace and prosperity. Available Late Summer 2007 ISBN: 1-884564-68-2

44. MYSTIC ART PAINTINGS

(with Full Color images) This book contains a collection of the small number of paintings that I have created over the years. Some were used as early book covers and others were done simply to express certain spiritual feelings; some were created for no purpose except to express the joy of color and the feeling of relaxed freedom. All are to elicit mystical awakening in the viewer. Writing a book on philosophy is like sculpture, the more the work is rewritten the reflections and ideas become honed and take form and become clearer and imbued with intellectual beauty. Mystic music is like meditation, a world of its own that exists about 1 inch above ground wherein the musician does not touch the ground. Mystic Graphic Art is meditation in form, color, image and reflected image which opens the door to the reality behind the apparent. I hope you enjoy these art renditions and my reflections on them as serene reflections of the mysteries of life, as visual renditions of the philosophy I have written about over the years.   ISBN   1-884564-69-0 $19.95

45. ANCIENT EGYPTIAN HIEROGLYPHS FOR BEGINNERS

This brief guide was prepared for those inquiring about how to enter into Hieroglyphic studies on their own at home or in study groups. First of all you should know that there are a few institutions around the world which teach how to read the Hieroglyphic text but due to the nature of the study there are perhaps only a handful of people who can read fluently. It is possible for anyone with average intelligence to achieve a high level of proficiency in reading inscriptions on temples and artifacts; however, reading extensive texts is another issue entirely. However, this introduction will give you entry into those texts if assisted by dictionaries and other aids. Most Egyptologists have a basic knowledge and keep dictionaries and notes handy when it comes to dealing with more difficult texts. Medtu Neter or the Ancient Egyptian hieroglyphic language has been considered as a "Dead Language." However, dead languages have always been studied by individuals who for the most part have taught themselves through various means. This book will discuss those means and how to use them most efficiently. ISBN 1884564429 **$28.95**

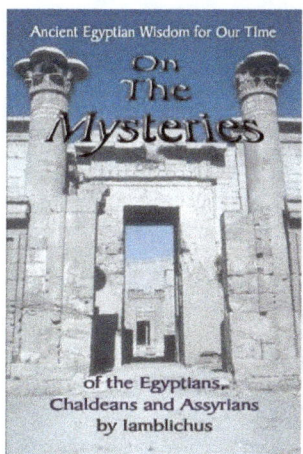

46. ON THE MYSTERIES: Wisdom of An Ancient Egyptian Sage -with Foreword by Muata Ashby

This volume, On the Mysteries, by Iamblichus (Abamun) is a unique form or scripture out of the Ancient Egyptian religious tradition. It is written in a form that is not usual or which is not usually found in the remnants of Ancient Egyptian scriptures. It is in the form of teacher and disciple, much like the Eastern scriptures such as Bhagavad Gita or the Upanishads. This form of writing may not have been necessary in Ancient times, because the format of teaching in Egypt was different prior to the conquest period by the Persians, Assyrians, Greeks and later the Romans. The question and answer format can be found but such extensive discourses and corrections of misunderstandings within the context of a teacher - disciple relationship is not usual. It therefore provides extensive insights into the times when it was written and the state of practice of Ancient Egyptian and other mystery religions. This has important implications for our times because we are today, as in the Greco-Roman period, also besieged with varied religions and new age philosophies as well as social strife and war. How can we understand our times and also make sense of the forest of spiritual traditions? How can we cut through the cacophony of religious fanaticism, and ignorance as well as misconceptions about the mysteries on the other in order to discover the true purpose of religion and the secret teachings that open up the mysteries of life and the way to enlightenment and immortality? This book, which comes to us from so long ago, offers us transcendental wisdom that applied to the world two thousand years ago as well as our world today. ISBN 1-884564-64-X $25.95

47. The Ancient Egyptian Wisdom Texts -Compiled by Muata Ashby

The Ancient Egyptian Wisdom Texts are a genre of writings from the ancient culture that have survived to the present and provide a vibrant record of the practice of spiritual evolution otherwise known as religion or yoga philosophy in Ancient Egypt. The principle focus of the Wisdom Texts is the cultivation of understanding, peace, harmony, selfless service, self-control, Inner fulfillment and spiritual realization. When these factors are cultivated in human life, the virtuous qualities in a human being begin to manifest and sinfulness, ignorance and negativity diminish until a person is able to enter into higher consciousness, the coveted goal of all civilizations. It is this virtuous mode of life which opens the door to self-discovery and spiritual enlightenment. Therefore, the

Wisdom Texts are important scriptures on the subject of human nature, spiritual psychology and mystical philosophy. The teachings presented in the Wisdom Texts form the foundation of religion as well as the guidelines for conducting the affairs of every area of social interaction including commerce, education, the army, marriage, and especially the legal system. These texts were sources for the famous 42 Precepts of Maat of the Pert-m-Heru (Book of the Dead), essential regulations of good conduct to develop virtue and purity in order to attain higher consciousness and immortality after death. ISBN1-884564-65-8 $18.95

48. THE KEMETIC TREE OF LIFE

THE KEMETIC TREE OF LIFE: Newly Revealed Ancient Egyptian Cosmology and Metaphysics for Higher Consciousness The Tree of Life is a roadmap of a journey which explains how Creation came into being and how it will end. It also explains what Creation is composed of and also what human beings are and what they are composed of. It also explains the process of Creation, how Creation develops, as well as who created Creation and where that entity may be found. It also explains how a human being may discover that entity and in so doing also discover the secrets of Creation, the meaning of life and the means to break free from the pathetic condition of human limitation and mortality in order to discover the higher realms of being by discovering the principles, the levels of existence that are beyond the simple physical and material aspects of life. This book contains color plates   **ISBN: 1-884564-74-7**

$27.95 U.S.

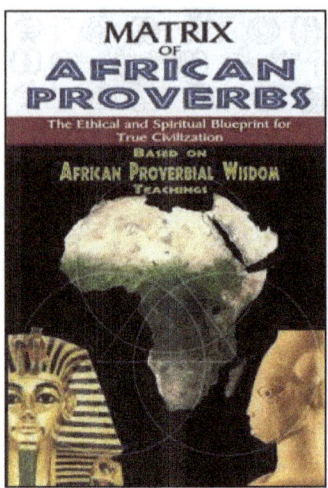

49-MATRIX OF AFRICAN PROVERBS: The Ethical and Spiritual Blueprint

This volume sets forth the fundamental principles of African ethics and their practical applications for use by individuals and organizations seeking to model their ethical policies using the Traditional African values and concepts of ethical human behavior for the proper sustenance and management of society. Furthermore, this book will provide guidance as to how the Traditional African Ethics may be viewed and applied, taking into consideration the technological and social advancements in the present. This volume also presents the principles of ethical culture, and references for each to specific injunctions from Traditional African Proverbial Wisdom Teachings. These teachings are compiled from varied Precolonial African societies including Yoruba, Ashanti, Kemet, Malawi, Nigeria, Ethiopia, Galla, Ghana and many more. ISBN 1-884564-77-1

50- **Growing Beyond Hate: Keys to Freedom from Discord, Racism, Sexism, Political Conflict, Class Warfare, Violence, and How to Achieve Peace and Enlightenment**---INTRODUCTION: WHY DO WE HATE? Hatred is one of the fundamental motivating aspects of human life; the other is desire. Desire can be of a worldly nature or of a spiritual, elevating nature. Worldly desire and hatred are like two sides of the same coin in that human life is usually swaying from one to the other; but the question is why? And is there a way to satisfy the desiring or hating mind in such a way as to find peace in life? Why do human beings go to war? Why do human beings perpetrate violence against one another? And is there a way not just to understand the phenomena but to resolve the issues that plague humanity and could lead to a more harmonious society? Hatred is perhaps the greatest scourge of humanity in that it leads to misunderstanding, conflict and untold miseries of life and clashes between individuals, societies and nations. Therefore, the riddle of Hatred, that is, understanding the sources of it and how to confront, reduce and even eradicate it so as to bring forth the fulfillment in life and peace for society, should be a top priority for social scientists, spiritualists and philosophers. This book is written from the perspective of spiritual philosophy based on the mystical wisdom and sema or yoga philosophy of the Ancient Egyptians. This philosophy, originated and based in the wisdom of Shetaut Neter, the Egyptian Mysteries, and Maat, ethical way of life in society and in spirit, contains Sema-Yogic wisdom and understanding of life's predicaments that can allow a human being of any ethnic group to understand and overcome the causes of hatred, racism, sexism, violence and disharmony in life, that plague human society. ISBN: 1-884564-81-X

52. Guide to Creating a Kemetic Marriage Contract

This marital contract guide reflects actual Ancient Egyptian Principles for Kemetic Marriage as they are to be applied for our times. The marital contract allows people to have a framework with which to face the challenges of marital relations instead of relying on hopes or romantic dreams that everything will workout somehow; in other words, love is not all you need. The latter is not an evolved, mature way of handling one of the most important aspects of human life. Therefore, it behooves anyone who wishes to enter into a marriage to explore the issues, express their needs and seek to avoid costly mistakes, and resolve conflicts in the normal course of life or make sure that their rights and dignity will be protected if any eventuality should occur. Marital relations in Ancient Egypt were not like those in other countries of the time and not like those of present day countries. The extreme longevity of Ancient Egyptian society, founded in Maat philosophy, allowed the social development of marriage to evolve and progress to a high level of order and balance. Maat represents truth, righteous, justice and harmony in life. This meant that the marital partner's rights were to be protected with equal standing before the law. So there was no disparity between rights of men or rights of women. Therefore, anyone who wants to enter into a marriage based on Kemetic principles must first and foremost adhere to this standard…equality in the rights of men and women. This guide demonstrates procedures for following the Ancient Egyptian practice of formalizing marriage with a contract that spells out the important concerns of each partner in the marital relationship, based on Maatian principles [of righteous, truth, harmony and justice] so that the rights and needs of each partner may be protected within the marriage. It also allows the partners to think about issues that arise out of the marital relations so that they may have a foundation to fall back on in the event that those or other unforeseen issues arise and cause conflict in the relationship. By having a document of expressed concerns, needs and steps to be taken to address them, it is less likely that issues which affect the relationship in a negative way will arise, and when they do, they will be better handled, in a more balanced, just and amicable way.

EBOOK ISBN 978-1-937016-59-3, HARDCOPY BOOK ISBN: 1-884564-82-8

53-Ancient Egyptian Mysteries of The Kybalion: A Hermetic Mystic Psychology Primer Paperback – November 28, 2014

This Volume is a landmark study by a renounced mystic philosopher, Sebai Dr. Muata Ashby. It is study not just to philosophize but to be practiced for the purpose of attaining enlightenment. The book is divided into three sections. Part 1 INTRODUCTION presents a brief history of Hermeticism, its origins in the Ancient Egyptian Mysteries (Neterianism) the Kybalion and the origins of the personality known as Hermes Trismegistus. Part 2 presents the essential teachings of the Kybalion text, a set of MAXIMS, without interpretation. Part 3 presents glosses (commentary and explanation) on the essential teachings of the Kybalion based on the philosophy of the Ancient Egyptian Mysteries as determined by Sebai Dr. Muata Ashby based on studies and translations of original Ancient Egyptian Hieroglyphic texts; the source from which the Kybalion teaching is derived. The Glosses are an edited and expanded version of Lessons given by Sebai Dr. Muata Ashby in the form of lectures on the teachings of the Kybalion.

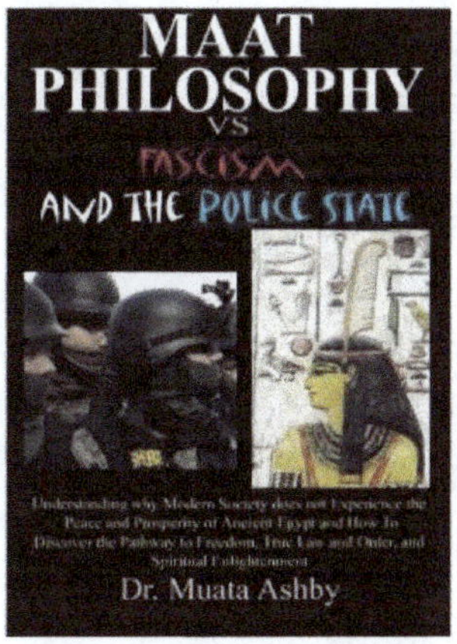

54-Maat Philosophy Versus Fascism and the Police State: Understanding why Modern Society does not Experience the Peace and Prosperity of Ancient Egypt ... Law and Order, and Spiritual Enlightenment Paperback – January 1, 2014

Understanding why Modern Society does not Experience the Peace and Prosperity of Ancient Egypt and How To Discover the Pathway to Freedom, True Law and Order, and Spiritual Enlightenment. Understanding the Corporate State and How Maatian Philosophy can Leads to Freedom, Prosperity and Enlightenment

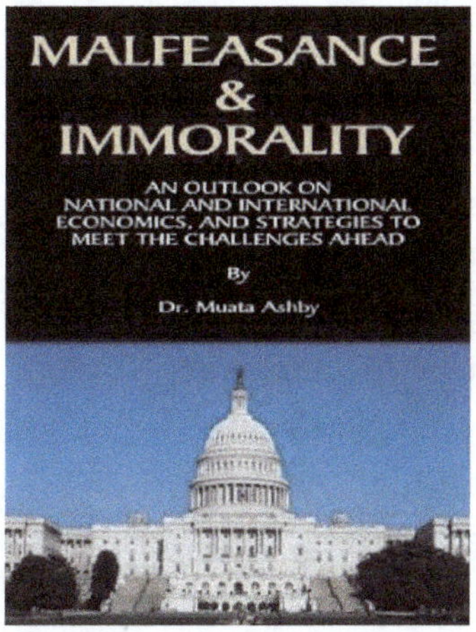

55- MALFEASANCE & IMMORALITY: An Analysis of the World Economic Crash of 2008, the Corrupt Political and Financial Institutions that Caused it and Strategies to Survive the Future Collapse of the Economy

The following is a first ever publication, by the Sema Institute, of a �White Paper�. The term is defined as: A white paper is an authoritative report or guide that often addresses issues and how to solve them. White papers are used to educate readers and help people make decisions. They are often used in politics and business. This paper serves as an update to the book Dollar Crisis: The Collapse of Society and Redemption Through Ancient Egyptian Fiscal & Monetary Policy (2008). That book was a continuation and expansion of issues presented in the book The Collapse of Civilization and the Death of American Empire (2006). Those books contained a detailed analysis of economic and political as well as social issues and how Maat Philosophy could offer insights into the nature of the problem, its sources and possible solutions as well as a means to develop an economic system (Fiscal and Monetary policies) that can work for all members of society. This paper contains an analysis of economic events and possible future outcomes based on those events as well as ideas individuals or groups may use in order to develop plans of action to deal with the possible detrimental events that may occur in the near and intermediate future. It serves as an update to the previous publications. This paper is divided into two parts. The first section is a summary which contains the conclusions of each section of Part 2. This was done so that the reader may have a quick and easy understanding of what is happening with the economy and finally, the actions that should be considered to meet the challenges ahead

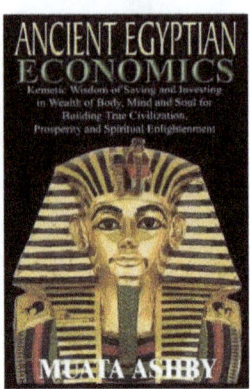

56- ANCIENT EGYPTIAN ECONOMICS

Ancient Egyptian Economics: Kemetic Wisdom of Saving and Investing in Wealth of Body, Mind and Soul for Building True Civilization, Prosperity and Spiritual Enlightenment------ Question: Why has the subject of finances and economics become important, I thought the spiritual teachings and Ancient Egyptian Philosophy and money were separate? Answer: Finances and money are an integral part of Ancient Egyptian culture as an instrument for promoting Maat ethics in the form of the well-being of the 'hekat'. The hekat are the people and the "Heka" is the Pharaoh. The Pharaoh was like a shepherd leading a flock and moneys were controlled righteously to promote the welfare of the people. In that tradition we have applied the philosophy of maatian economics to promote the well-being of those who are following this path as well as those who may read the books so they may avoid financial trouble as much as possible and have better capacity to practice the teachings. In order to have a successful life, human beings need a certain amount of money and wealth, but money and wealth are not the goal. They are a foundation that enables the true goal of life, enlightenment, to be realized. Therefore, we are only fulfilling the duty of transmitting wisdom about wealth to promote Maat, righteousness, truth and well-being, for all. This volume explores the mysteries of wealth based on the teachings of the sages of Ancient Egypt and the means to promote prosperity that allows a person to create the conditions for discovering inner peace and spiritual enlightenment. HTP-Peace

57- NETERIAN AWAKENING Journal of Neterian Culture Vol 1-12 In one Volume

This is a single file containing 12 volumes of The Neterian Awakening Journal. The Neterian Awakening Journal was a publication where the culture and community of Shetaut Neter spirituality was explored. In it Sebai Dr. Muata Ashby and Dr. Dja Ashby along with members of the Temple of Shetaut Neter presented articles, festival reviews, Questions and Answer columns and many other important aspects of Neterian culture and spirituality beyond those presented in other volumes of the book series that are useful in understanding the practice of Neterian Spirituality and the path to achieving a �Neterian Spiritual Awakening.� Part of its mission was: To promote the study of Shetaut Neter (Neterianism, Neterian Religion) as a spiritual path. Instruct the serious followers of Shetaut Neter spirituality who would like to receive literature in between the publication of major books that will fill the needs of their daily spiritual practice. Neterian Awakening Journal explores the varied aspects of Shetaut Neter spirituality not covered in the books. NAJ provides a forum for the development of a Neterian Community of those who wish to follow the Neterian Spiritual Path of African Religious Culture

58- Little Book of Neter: Introduction to Shetaut Neter Spirituality and Religion Paperback – June 7, 2007

The Little Book of Neter is a summary of the most important teachings of Shetaut Neter for all aspirants to have for easy reference and distribution. It is designed to be portable and low cost so that all can have the main teachings of Shetaut Neter at easy access for personal use and also for sharing with others the basic tenets of Neterian spirituality.

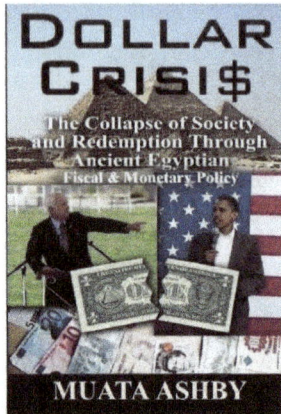

59- Dollar Crisis: The Collapse of Society and Redemption Through Ancient Egyptian Monetary Policy by Muata Ashby (2008-07-24)

This book is about the problems of the US economy and the imminent collapse of the U.S. Dollar and its dire consequences for the US economy and the world. It is also about the corruption in government, economics and social order that led to this point. Also it is about survival, how to make it through this perhaps most trying period in the history of the United States. Also it is about the ancient wisdom of life that allowed an ancient civilization to grow beyond the destructive corruptions of ignorance and power so that the people of today may gain insight into the nature of their condition, how they got there and what needs to be done in order to salvage what is left and rebuild a society that is sustainable, beneficial and an example for all humanity.

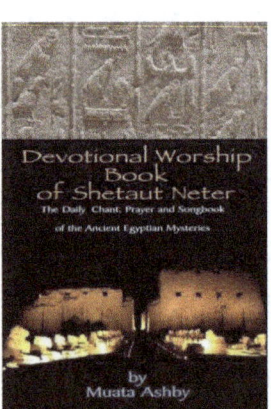

60- Devotional Worship Book of Shetaut Neter: Medu Neter song, chant and hymn book for daily practice [Paperback] [2007] (Author) Muata Ashby Paperback – 2007

Ushet Hekau Shedi Sema Taui Uashu or Ushet means "to worship the Divine," "to propitiate the Divine." Ushet is of two types, external and internal. When you go to pilgrimage centers, temples, spiritual gatherings, etc., you are practicing external worship or spiritual practice. When you go into your private meditation room on your own and your utter words of power, prayers and meditation you are practicing internal worship or spiritual practice. Ushet needs to be understood as a process of not only an outer show of spiritual practice, but it is also a process of developing love for the Divine. Therefore, Ushet really signifies a development in Devotion towards the Divine. This practice is also known as sma uash or Yoga of Devotion. Ushet is the process of discovering the Divine and allowing your heart to flow towards the Divine. This program of life allows a spiritual aspirant to develop inner peace, contentment and universal love, and these qualities lead to spiritual enlightenment or union with the Divine. It is recommended that you see the book "The Path of Divine Love" by Dr. Muata Ashby. This volume will give details into this form of Sema or Yoga.

61- Initiation Into Egyptian Yoga and Neterian Religion Workbook for Beginning and Advancing Aspirants

What is Initiation? The great personalities of the past known to the world as Isis, Hathor, Jesus, Buddha and many other great Sages and Saints were initiated into their spiritual path but how did initiation help them and what were they specifically initiated into? This volume is a template for such lofty studies, a guidebook and blueprint for aspirants who want to understand what the path is all about, its requirements and goals, as they work with a qualified spiritual guide as they tread the path of Kemetic Spirituality and Yoga disciplines. This workbook helps by presenting the fundamental teachings of Egyptian Yoga and Neterian Spirituality with questions and exercises to help the aspirant gain a foundation for more advanced studies and practices

HIEROGLYPH TRANSLATION SERIES BY
Dr. Muata Ashby

Egyptian Book of the Dead Hieroglyph Translations Using the Trilinear Method: Understanding th Mystic Path to Enlightenment...

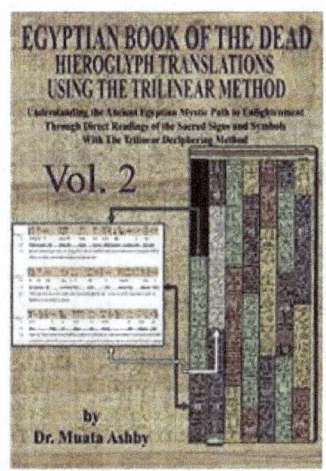

Egyptian Book of the Dead Hieroglyph Translations Using The Trilinear Method Vol. 2: Understanding the Mystic Path to...
by Muata Ashby

EGYPTIAN BOOK OF THE DEAD HIEROGLYPH TRANSLATIONS USING THE TRILINEAR METHOD Volume 3: Understanding the Mystic Path to...
by Muata Ashby

EGYPTIAN BOOK OF THE DEAD HIEROGLYPH TRANSLATIONS USING THE TRILINEAR METHOD Volume 4: Understanding the Mystic Path to...

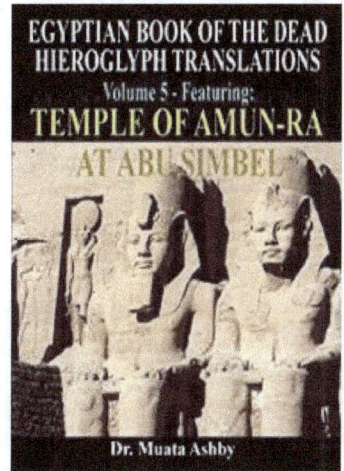

EGYPTIAN BOOK OF THE DEAD HIEROGLYPH TRANSLATIONS USING THE TRILINEAR METHOD Volume 5: Featuring Temple of Amun-Ra at Ab...
by Muata Ashby

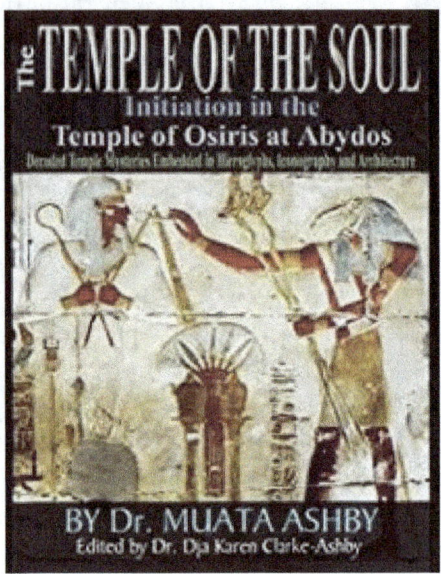

Temple of the Soul Initiation Philosophy in the Temple of Osiris at Abydos: Decoded Temple Mysteries Translations of Temple Inscriptions...
by Muata Ashby

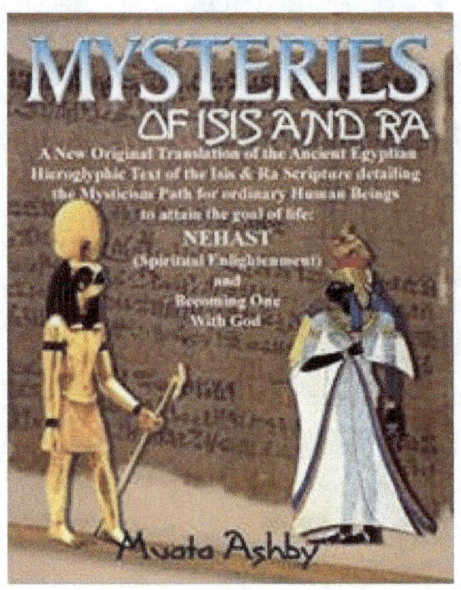

Mysteries of Isis and Ra: A New Original Translation Hieroglyphic Scripture of t
by Muata Ashby

www.ingramcontent.com/pod-product-compliance
Lightning Source LLC
Chambersburg PA
CBHW081149290426
44108CB00018B/2489